An introduction

TAWHĪD

AND

SUNNAH

according to the understanding of the Salaf of the Ummah

Written by Abū Hājar

AL-AQEEDAH

1443h / 2022 www.Al-Aqeedah.com

ISBN: 9798449578297

3rd Edition.

Written by:

Abū Hājar

Published by:

Al-Aqeedah in association with Dar Al-Hady Al-Auwal

Contact:

contact@al-aqeedah.com

alhadyalauwal@gmail.com

Contents

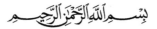

In the Name of Allāh, the Most Beneficent, the Most Merciful

And may the peace and abundant blessings of Allāh be upon Muhammad, his Family, his Companions and those who follow them in goodness until the Day of Judgment

And thereafter:

The correct intention

The Prophet (sall Allāhu 'alayhi wa sallam) said:

إِنَّمَا الْأَعْمَالُ بِالنِّيَّاتِ وَإِنَّمَا لِكُلِّ امْرِئٍ مَا نَوَى فَمَنْ كَانَتْ هِجْرَتُهُ إِلَى اللهِ وَرَسُولِهِ فَهِجْرَتُهُ إِلَى اللهِ وَرَسُولِهِ
وَمَنْ كَانَتْ هِجْرَتُهُ لِدُنْيَا يُصِيبُهَا أَوِ امْرَأَةٍ يَنْكِحُهَا فَهِجْرَتُهُ إِلَى مَا هَاجَرَ إِلَيْهِ

"Verily the deeds are (judged) according to their intentions, and verily for every person there is (the reward of) what he has intented. So whoever performed hijrah to Allāh and His Messenger, then his hijrah is for Allāh and His Messenger. And whoever performed hijrah to some dunyā in order to achieve it, or for a woman in order to marry her, then his hijrah is for that which he performed hijrah for." (Sahīh Al-Bukhārī and Sahīh Muslim)

Verily, the intention of a person can change his deeds from being something that benefits him, to being something which leads him into destruction. Just as the Prophet (sall Allāhu 'alayhi wa sallam) informed about this in a *hadīth* about the events on the Day of Judgment:

وَرَجُلٌ تَعَلَّمَ الْعِلْمَ، وَعَلَّمَهُ وَقَرَأَ الْقُرْآنَ، فَأُتِيَ بِهِ فَعَرَّفَهُ نِعَمَهُ فَعَرَفَهَا، قَالَ: فَما عَمِلْتَ فِيها؟ قَالَ: تَعَلَّمْتُ الْعِلْمَ، وَعَلَّمْتُهُ وَقَرَأْتُ فِيكَ الْقُرْآنَ، قَالَ: كَذَبْتَ، وَلَكِنَّكَ تَعَلَّمْتَ الْعِلْمَ لِيُقَالَ: عالِمٌ، وَقَرَأْتَ الْقُرْآنَ لِيُقَالَ: هُوَ قارِئٌ، فَقَدْ قِيلَ، ثُمَّ أُمِرَ بِهِ فَسُحِبَ عَلَى وجْهِهِ حَتَّى أُلْقِيَ فِي النَّارِ

"And a man, who learned the knowledge, taught it (to others) and recited the Qurān. Then he will be brought forth and He makes him aware of His blessings, and he acknowledges them. He will say: 'What did you do with it?' He will say: 'I learned the knowledge and taught it, and for You I recited the Qurān.' He will say: 'You have lied. Rather, you learned the knowledge so it would be said: He is a scholar. And you recited the Qurān so it would be said: He is a reciter. And it has verily been said.' Then orders are given regarding him, and he is dragged on his face until he is thrown in Hellfire." (Sahīh Muslim)

So the reader is advised to invoke the Name of Allāh and to correct his intention before beginning to read this book, and before every deed he performs. The successful is the one who changes his intention to be solely for Allāh. So whatever he does is only to achieve the Satisfaction of Allāh and to protect himself from the Wrath of Allāh. As for the one who seeks knowledge only to discuss, only to find mistakes or to elevate himself to a higher level by lowering others and pointing out their mistakes, then his intention will surely render his deeds void, and there will be no benefit in them.

Allāh – the Exalted – said:

$$ ﴿ وَقَدِمْنَا إِلَى مَا عَمِلُوا مِنْ عَمَلٍ فَجَعَلْنَاهُ هَبَاءً مَنْثُورًا ﴾ $$

"And We will come to what they performed of (good) deeds, and then We will turn it into scattered dust." (Al-Furqān 25:23)

Ibn Abī Hātim narrated in his *tafsīr* of the verse:

حَدَّثَنَا أَبِي، ثَنَا هِشَامُ بْنُ عُبَيْدِ اللَّهِ الرَّازِيُّ، قَالَ: سَمِعْتُ ابْنَ الْمُبَارَكِ ، يَقُولُ فِي قَوْلِهِ: " وَقَدِمْنَا إِلَى مَا عَمِلُوا مِنْ عَمَلٍ فَجَعَلْنَاهُ هَبَاءً مَنْثُورًا قَالَ: كُلُّ عَمَلٍ صَالِحٍ لَا يُرَادُ بِهِ وَجْهُ اللَّهِ

My father narrated to me (and said): Hishām ibn 'Ubayd-Allāh Ar-Rāzī narrated to us and said: I heard Ibn Al-Mubārak say regarding His Words: **"And We will come to what they performed of (good) deeds, and then We will turn it into scattered dust."** He said: *"(This is) every good deed by which the Face of Allāh is not sought."* (Tafsīr Ibn Abī Hātim – Sūrah Al-Furqān)

Introduction

These are simple words describing the fundaments upon which the religion of Islām is built. Allāh – the Exalted – has chosen Islām as the religion for His slaves, and He does not accept anything but it. So whoever wants to meet Allāh in a state which will guarantee him entrance into Paradise, then he must base his religion in this life upon that which has been revealed by Allāh to His Messenger (*sallAllāhu 'alayhi wa sallam*), and he must not die except upon this.

The Messenger of Allāh (*sallAllāhu 'alayhi wa sallam*) is Muhammad ibn 'Abdullāh Al-Qurashī (*sallAllāhu 'alayhi wa sallam*) who was born in Makkah. He received the revelation from Allāh – the Exalted – through the angel Jibrīl (*'alayhi as-salām*) at the age of forty. Ten years after the first revelation the Messenger of Allah (*sallAllāhu 'alayhi wa sallam*) was taken on a night journey in which the five daily prayers was revealed to him. After this he (*sallAllāhu 'alayhi wa sallam*) remained in Makkah for another three years after which he emigrated to Madīnah. Here he continued to invite towards his Lord until Allāh – the Exalted – took his soul at the age of sixty-three, where he (*sallAllāhu 'alayhi wa sallam*) had fulfilled his mission. He was buried in Madīnah where his grave is still present. May the peace and abundant blessings of Allāh be upon the final Prophet and Messenger from Allāh. Āmīn.

Allāh – the Exalted – has made the religion which He is pleased with very easy, and He – the Exalted – does not want any difficulty for mankind. Allāh – the Exalted – says:

﴿ هُوَ اجْتَبَاكُمْ وَمَا جَعَلَ عَلَيْكُمْ فِي الدِّينِ مِنْ حَرَجٍ مِلَّةَ أَبِيكُمْ إِبْرَاهِيمَ ﴾

"He chose you, and He did not make any difficulty for you in the religion; (which is) the *millah* of Ibrāhīm your father."
(Al-Hajj 22:78)

So let not anyone think for a second, that Allāh has made the correct path difficult to spot among the different types of misguidances, or that Allāh has allowed that a person follows a way or a path, and

8

then "hopes" that this is the right path which Allāh is pleased with. Rather Allāh revealed the Book with clarification and He sent a Messenger to be a bearer of glad tidings for those who follow the revelation and a warner for those who deviate from it. He did this in order for a person to be upon *yaqīn* (full certainty) in his religion and so his heart may feel the tranquility of being upon the truth and long for the meeting with its Lord. Allāh – the Exalted – said:

﴿ لَا إِكْرَاهَ فِي الدِّينِ قَدْ تَبَيَّنَ الرُّشْدُ مِنَ الْغَيِّ ﴾

"There is no compulsion in the religion. Verily have the Straight Path become clear from the wrong path." (Al-Baqarah 2:256)

And He – the Exalted – said:

﴿ رُسُلًا مُبَشِّرِينَ وَمُنْذِرِينَ لِئَلَّا يَكُونَ لِلنَّاسِ عَلَى اللَّهِ حُجَّةٌ بَعْدَ الرُّسُلِ وَكَانَ اللَّهُ عَزِيزًا حَكِيمًا ﴾

"Messengers as bearer of glad tidings and warners. In order that mankind will have no argument against Allāh after the messengers. And Allāh is ever Almighty and All-Wise." (An-Nisā 4:165)

And He – the Exalted – said:

﴿ يُدَبِّرُ الْأَمْرَ يُفَصِّلُ الْآيَاتِ لَعَلَّكُمْ بِلِقَاءِ رَبِّكُمْ تُوقِنُونَ ﴾

"He arranges the affairs (and) **explains the *āyāt*** (evidences, verses, signs) **in details, in order for you to have full certainty in the meeting with your Lord."** (Ar-Ra'd 13:2)

And He – the Exalted – said:

﴿ إِنَّمَا الْمُؤْمِنُونَ الَّذِينَ آمَنُوا بِاللَّهِ وَرَسُولِهِ ثُمَّ لَمْ يَرْتَابُوا ﴾

"Verily the believers are those who believe in Allāh, and thereafter do not doubt." (Al-Hujurāt 49:15)

And the Messenger of Allāh (*sallAllāhu 'alayhi wa sallam*) said:

قَدْ تَرَكْتُكُمْ عَلَى الْبَيْضَاءِ لَيْلُهَا كَنَهَارِهَا لاَ يَزِيغُ عَنْهَا بَعْدِي إلاَّ هَالِكٌ

"I have verily left you upon a clear path. Its night is like its day. No-one deviates from it after me, except that he will be destroyed." (Sunan Ibn Mājah – *sahīh*)

And that which the Messenger (*sallAllāhu 'alayhi wa sallam*) has left for us, is the Qurān the Word of Allāh, which was sent by Allāh through Jibrīl (*'alayhi as-salām*) to Muhammad (*sallAllāhu 'alayhi wa sallam*), and the *Sunnah* which is everything which the Prophet (*sallAllāhu 'alayhi wa sallam*) has said, done, showed to us and confirmed.

So the intended with this text is to clarify the fundamental principles based upon which this religion is built in an easy, simple and categorized way, so the Muslim may know how to seek his religion, from whom and from where he should accept and from whom and from where he should reject, and for him to have a template with which he can verify whether or not that which he believes in is correct and thereby achieve full certainty in his religion. As for each individual issue mentioned, then this text only suffices as a short introduction.

All success is from Allāh, while all mistakes are from the author.

The sources of the religion

Al-Islām is built upon two primary sources[1], and that is the Qurān and the *Sunnah*. Everything which does not have its foundation in any of these two, then it is misguidance and rejected for the one who believes in it. This is proven by the words of the Messenger of Allāh (*sallAllāhu 'alayhi wa sallam*):

مَنْ أَحْدَثَ فِي أَمْرِنَا هذا مَا لَيْسَ مِنْهُ فَهُو رَدٌّ

"Whoever introduces something in this affair of ours which is not from it, then it will be rejected." (Sahīh Al-Bukhārī and Sahīh Muslim)

And in another version:

مَنْ عَمِلَ عَمَلاً لَيْسَ عَلَيْهِ أَمْرُنَا فَهوَ رَدٌّ

"Whoever performs a deed which we have not commanded then it will be rejected." (Sahīh Muslim)

But can anyone understand the Qurān and the *Sunnah* as he wishes or desires? The answer is no.

Allāh – the Exalted – chose to reveal His religion upon a people who – by the permission of Allāh – were capable of comprehending it, following it and protecting it. Allāh – the Exalted – testified to the righteousness of those generations several places in His Book. From this testimony are His – the Exalted – words:

---

[1] Among the legislative sources of Islām are also the *ijmā'* (agreement of the Muslims) and the *qiyās* (analogy based on other evidences from the Qurān and *Sunnah*). The statements and the beliefs of the *Sahābah* (*radiAllāhu 'anhum*) are furthermore considered to be a part of the *Sunnah* itself, since it is not claimed that they would speak about the religion from themselves, rather they would only speak based on what they knew from the Messenger of Allāh (*sallAllāhu 'alayhi wa sallam*). Wherever the *Sahābah* (*radiAllāhu 'anhum*) disagreed, then this is an evidence for the permissibility of disagreeing in such an issue.

﴿ وَمَنْ يُشَاقِقِ الرَّسُولَ مِنْ بَعْدِ مَا تَبَيَّنَ لَهُ الْهُدَى وَيَتَّبِعْ غَيْرَ سَبِيلِ الْمُؤْمِنِينَ نُوَلِّهِ مَا تَوَلَّى وَنُصْلِهِ جَهَنَّمَ وَسَاءَتْ مَصِيرًا ﴾

"And whoever contradicts (or opposes) the Messenger after the right path has been shown clearly to him, and follows other than the believers' way. We shall keep him on the path he has chosen, and burn him in Hell - what an evil destination." (An-Nisā 4:115)

And His – the Exalted – words:

﴿ وَالسَّابِقُونَ الْأَوَّلُونَ مِنَ الْمُهَاجِرِينَ وَالْأَنْصَارِ وَالَّذِينَ اتَّبَعُوهُمْ بِإِحْسَانٍ رَضِيَ اللَّهُ عَنْهُمْ وَرَضُوا عَنْهُ وَأَعَدَّ لَهُمْ جَنَّاتٍ تَجْرِي تَحْتَهَا الْأَنْهَارُ خَالِدِينَ فِيهَا أَبَدًا ذَلِكَ الْفَوْزُ الْعَظِيمُ ﴾

"And the first forerunners (in īmān) among the Muhājirīn and the Ansār and those who followed them in goodness. Allāh is pleased with them and they are pleased with Him, and He has prepared for them gardens beneath which rivers flow, wherein they will abide forever. That is the great attainment."
(At-Tawbah 9:100)

And the Messenger of Allāh (sallAllāhu 'alayhi wa sallam) said:

خَيْرُ النَّاسِ قَرْنِي ثُمَّ الَّذِينَ يَلُونَهُمْ ثُمَّ الَّذِينَ يَلُونَهُمْ

"The best people are those of my generation, then those who come after them, then those who come after them." (Sahīh Al-Bukhārī and Sahīh Muslim)

The generation of the Messenger of Allāh (sallAllāhu 'alayhi wa sallam) is the *Sahābah* (radiAllāhu 'anhum) who lived with and saw the Messenger of Allāh (sallAllāhu 'alayhi wa sallam). They understood the Qurān and the *Sunnah* best, because they lived during its revelation, they experienced the scenarios which it spoke of and they are those who were closest to the Messenger of Allāh (sallAllāhu 'alayhi wa sallam), asking him questions, hearing his speech and seeing his deeds.

The generation after them is the *tābi'ūn* (the followers) who are those who learned from the *Sahābah* (*radiAllāhu 'anhum*). Thus their status in the religion is based upon them learning from the *Sahābah* who learned from the Messenger of Allāh (*sallAllāhu 'alayhi wa sallam*).

The generations after them is the *tābi' at-tābi'īn* (the followers of the followers) who are those who learned from the followers of the *Sahābah* (*radiAllāhu 'anhum*). Thus their status in the religion is based upon them learning from the *tābi'ūn*, who learned from the *Sahābah* who learned from the Messenger of Allāh (*sallAllāhu 'alayhi wa sallam*).

These are the three generations whom the Messenger of Allāh (*sallAllāhu 'alayhi wa sallam*) has described as the best of generations from this Ummah, and they are our **Salaf** (predecessors). So whoever wants to follow that which Allāh is pleased with and love, he must follow these three generations in their religion, whose sources are directly from the Qurān and *Sunnah*. Because there will never be any people after them who are better.

Anas Ibn Mālik (*radiAllāhu 'anhu*) said:

اصْبِرُوا، فإنَّه لا يَأْتِي عَلَيْكُم زَمَانٌ إِلَّا الذي بَعْدَهُ شَرٌّ منه، حتَّى تَلْقَوْا رَبَّكُمْ سَمِعْتُهُ مِن نَبِيِّكُمْ صَلَّى اللهُ عليه وسلَّمَ

"Have patience. Because verily there will not come a time upon you, except that (the time) after it is worse than it. Until you meet you Lord. I heard that from your Prophet (sallAllāhu 'alayhi wa sallam)." (Sahīh Al-Bukhārī)

And 'Abdullāh ibn Mas'ūd (*radiAllāhu 'anhu*) said:

لَيْسَ عَامٌ إِلاَّ وَالَّذِي بَعْدَهُ شَرٌّ مِنْهُ؛ لا أَقُولُ: عَامٌ أَمْطَرُ مِنْ عَامٍ, وَلا عَامٌ أَخْصَبُ مِنْ عَامٍ, وَلا أَمِيرٌ خَيْرٌ مِنْ أَمِيرٍ, لَكِنْ ذَهَابُ عُلَمَائِكُمْ وَخِيَارِكُمْ, ثُمَّ يَحْدُثُ أَقْوَامٌ يَقِيسُونَ الأُمُورَ بِآرَائِهِمْ؛ فَيُهْدَمُ الإِسْلامُ وَيُثْلَمُ

"There is no year except that the year after it is worse than it. I am not speaking about one year which has more rain than another, nor a year which is more fertile than another, nor a leader which is better than another leader. Rather (I am speaking about) the disappearance of your scholars and the best people among you, and then a people will emerge who measure the affairs according to their own opinion (and not the Qurān and Sunnah), and then Islām will be destroyed and broken." (Al-Bida' by Ibn Al-Waddāh)

So the people of truth are those who say:

"We follow and believe in the Qurān and the Sunnah, according to the understanding of the Salaf."

And this is not merely a statement with them.

Rather there is not a verse in the Book of Allāh, or a *hadīth* from the Messenger of Allāh (*sallAllāhu alayhi wa sallam*), or any belief which is held in the religion, except that they investigate and ask:

Is this how the *Salaf* have understood and acted upon this verse?

Is this how the *Salaf* have understood and acted upon this *hadīth*?

Is this how the *Salaf* have believed in this issue?

With this they uphold the boundaries of Islām by not letting any form of misguidance nor innovation enter upon them in their religion. And with this they are truthful in their claim of following the Qurān and *Sunnah* in accordance with the understanding of the *Salaf*. And with this they can profess to be followers of and believers in Tawhīd and *Sunnah* in reality, and not just as an empty claim with no substance to it.

Abū Bakr Al-Ājurrī (d. 320h) gathered the meaning of what have been mentioned in this section when he mentioned:

14

وَأَخْبَرَنَا ابْنُ عَبْدِ الْحَمِيدِ أَيْضًا قَالَ نا زُهَيْرُ بْنُ مُحَمَّدٍ قَالَ : أَخْبَرَنَا سُلَيْمَانُ بْنُ حَرْبٍ قَالَ : حَدَّثَنَا حَمَّادُ بْنُ زَيْدٍ ، عَنْ عَاصِمٍ الْأَحْوَلِ قَالَ : قَالَ أَبُو الْعَالِيَةِ : تَعَلَّمُوا الْإِسْلَامَ ، فَإِذَا تَعَلَّمْتُمُوهُ فَلَا تَرْغَبُوا عَنْهُ ، وَعَلَيْكُمْ بِالصِّرَاطِ الْمُسْتَقِيمِ فَإِنَّهُ الْإِسْلَامُ ، وَلَا تُحَرِّفُوا الصِّرَاطَ يَمِينًا وَلَا شِمَالًا ، وَعَلَيْكُمْ بِسُنَّةِ نَبِيِّكُمْ صَلَّى اللَّهُ عَلَيْهِ وَسَلَّمَ وَالَّذِي عَلَيْهَا أَصْحَابُهُ ، فَإِنَّا قَدْ قَرَأْنَا الْقُرْآنَ مِنْ قَبْلِ أَنْ يَفْعَلُوا الَّذِي فَعَلُوهُ خَمْسَ عَشْرَةَ سَنَةً ، وَإِيَّاكُمْ وَهَذِهِ الْأَهْوَاءَ الَّتِي تُلْقِي بَيْنَ النَّاسِ الْعَدَاوَةَ وَالْبَغْضَاءَ قَالَ : فَحَدَّثْتُ بِهِ الْحَسَنَ فَقَالَ : صَدَقَ وَنَصَحَ ، وَحَدَّثْتُ بِهِ حَفْصَةَ بِنْتَ سِيرِينَ ، فَقَالَتْ : يَا بُنَيَّ أَحَدَّثْتَ بِهَذَا مُحَمَّدًا ؟ قُلْتُ : لَا ، قَالَتْ : فَحَدِّثْهُ إِذَنْ قَالَ مُحَمَّدُ بْنُ الْحُسَيْنِ : عَلَامَةُ مَنْ أَرَادَ اللَّهُ بِهِ خَيْرًا : سُلُوكُ هَذَا الطَّرِيقِ , كِتَابُ اللَّهِ ، وَسُنَنُ رَسُولِ اللَّهِ صَلَّى اللَّهُ عَلَيْهِ وَسَلَّمَ ، وَسُنَنُ أَصْحَابِهِ رَضِيَ اللَّهُ عَنْهُمْ وَمَنْ تَبِعَهُمْ بِإِحْسَانٍ ، وَمَا كَانَ عَلَيْهِ أَئِمَّةُ الْمُسْلِمِينَ فِي كُلِّ بَلَدٍ إِلَى آخِرِ مَا كَانَ مِنَ الْعُلَمَاءِ مِثْلَ الْأَوْزَاعِيِّ وَسُفْيَانَ الثَّوْرِيِّ وَمَالِكِ بْنِ أَنَسٍ ، وَالشَّافِعِيِّ ، وَأَحْمَدَ بْنِ حَنْبَلٍ ، وَالْقَاسِمِ بْنِ سَلَّامٍ ، وَمَنْ كَانَ عَلَى مِثْلِ طَرِيقَتِهِمْ ، وَمُجَانَبَةُ كُلِّ مَذْهَبٍ يَذُمُّهُ هَؤُلَاءِ الْعُلَمَاءُ

"And Ibn 'Abdul-Hamīd also narrated to us and said: Zuhayr ibn Muhammad narrated to us and said: Sulaymān ibn Harb narrated to us and said: Hammād ibn Zayd narrated to us, from 'Āsim Al-Ahwal who said: Abū Al-'Āliyah said: 'Learn Al-Islām, and then when you have learned it then don't turn away from it. And it is upon you to follow the Straight Path, and verily is it Al-Islām. And do not deviate from it right or left. And it is upon you to follow the Sunnah of your Prophet (sallAllāhu 'alayhi wa sallam) and that which his Companions are upon. Because verily did we read the Qurān fifteen years before they did what they did. And be aware of these desires (i.e. innovations) which cause enmity and hatred among the people.' He said: 'So I narrated it (i.e. these words) to Al-Hasan, so he said: 'He has spoken the truth and given a good advice.' And I narrated it to Hafsah bint Sīrīn, so she said: 'O my son, have you narrated this to Muhammad (ibn Sīrīn)?' So I said: 'No.' So she said: 'Then narrate it to him.'" And Muhammad ibn Al-Hasan said: 'The sign of the one whom Allāh wants good for is: Traversing this Path: The Book of Allāh, the Sunan of the Messenger of Allāh (sallAllāhu 'alayhi wa sallam), the Sunan (i.e. narrations) from his Companions (radiAllāhu 'anhu) and those who followed them in goodness, and that which the aimmah (leaders) of the Muslims in all countries were upon, until the end of what there was of scholars. Such as Al-Awzā'ī, Sufyān Ath-Thawrī,

Mālik ibn Anas, Ash-Shāfi'ī, Ahmad ibn Hanbal, Al-Qāsim ibn Salām, and whoever were upon the same path as them. And avoiding every madhhab (way, path, opinion) which these scholars have criticized.'" (Ash-Sharī'ah by Al-Ājurrī 1/301)

And Abū 'Amr Al-Awzā'ī (d. 157h) said:

وأنا أوصيك بواحدة، فإنها تجلو الشك عنك، وتصيب بالاعتصام بها سبيل الرشد إن شاء الله – تعالى – -: تنظر إلى ما كان عليه أصحاب رسول الله – صلى الله عليه وسلم – من هذا الأمر، فإن كانوا اختلفوا فيه، فخذ بما وافقك من أقاويلهم، فإنك حينئذ منه في سعة وإن كانوا اجتمعوا منه على أمر واحد لم يشذ عنه منهم أحد، فأين المذهب عنهم، فإن الهلكة في خلافهم، وإنهم لم يجتمعوا على شيء قط فكان الهدى في غيره، وقد أثنى الله – عز وجل – على أهل القدوة بهم فقال: (وَالَّذِينَ اتَّبَعُوهُم بِإِحْسَانٍ) [التوبة: 100] واحذر كل متأول للقرآن على خلاف ما كانوا عليه

"And I advise you to one thing, which verily will remove the doubt from you, and by holding on to it you will achieve the Straight Path, if Allāh – the Exalted – wills: You look into what the Companions of the Messenger of Allāh (sallAllāhu 'alayhi wa sallam) were upon in this issue. Then if they differed in it, then take whatever agrees with you from their sayings. In that case you will be at ease in the issue. And if they agreed in the issue upon one opinion, and no-one among them deviated from it, then to where is the madhhab that opposes them? Because verily the destruction lies is disagreeing with them. Because they have verily never agreed upon one issue, and then the guidance (i.e. truth) has been in something else than it. And verily did Allāh – 'azza wa jalla – praise those who followed their example, when He said: **"And those who followed them in goodness."** *(At-Tawbah 9:100). And be aware of everyone who interprets the Qurān to something else than what they were upon."* (Al-Ibānah Al-Kubrā by Ibn Battah 2/254)

And Al-Awzā'ī (d. 157h) also said:

عليك بآثار من سلف وإن رفضك الناس، وإيّاك وآراء الرجال وإن زخرفوها لك بالقول

"It is obligatory upon you (to follow) the āthār (narrations) of those who came before, even if the people would reject you. And be aware of the

16

opinions of men, even if they beautify their words for you." (Ash-Sharī'ah by Al-Ājurrī)

And Abū Sa'īd Ad-Dārimī (d. 280h) said:

الله تعالى أثنى على التابعين في كتابه فقال: {والسابقون الأولون من المهاجرين والأنصار والذين اتبعوهم بإحسان رضي الله عنهم} فشهد باتباع الصحابة واستيجاب الرضوان من الله تعالى باتباعهم أصحاب محمد ﷺ. واجتمعت الكلمة من جميع المسلمين أن سموهم التابعين ولم يزالوا يأثرون عنهم بالأسانيد كما يأثرون عن الصحابة ويحتجون بهم في أمر دينهم ويرون آراءهم ألزم من آراء من بعدهم للاسم الذي استحقوا من الله تعالى ومن جماعة المسلمين الذين سموهم تابعي أصحاب محمد ﷺ

"Allāh – the Exalted – praised the tābi'ūn in His Book, when He said: **"And the first forerunners (in īmān) among the Muhājirīn and the Ansār and those who followed them in goodness. Allāh is pleased with them."** *So He testified to their following of the Sahābah, and them deserving the Pleasure of Allāh – the Exalted – due to their following of the Companions of Muhammad (sallAllāhu 'alayhi wa sallam). And the word is united among all the Muslims that they were called 'At-Tābi'ūn' and they continue to narrate from them with the chains of narration, just as they narrated from the Sahābah. And they use them as an argument in the affairs of their religion, and they consider their opinion more binding than the opinion of those who came after them, due to the name which they deserved from Allāh – the Exalted – and from the Jamā'ah of the Muslims, who called them the followers of the Companions of Muhammad (sallAllāhu 'alayhi wa sallam)."* (An-Naqd by Ad-Dārimī)

And Abū Al-Qāsim Al-Lālakāī (d. 418h) said:

أستدلُّ على صحة مذاهب أهل السنة بما ورد في كتاب الله تعالى فيها، وبما روي عن رسول الله ﷺ، فإن وجدت فيها جميعا ذكرتُها، وإن وجدت في أحدهما دون الآخر ذكرته، وإن لم أجد فيها إلا عن الصحابة رضي الله عنهم والذين أمر الله ورسوله أن يقتدى بهم، ويهتدى بأقوالهم، ويستضاء بأنوارهم لمشاهدتهم الوحي والتنزيل، ومعرفتهم معاني التأويل؛ احتججت بها، فإن لم يكن فيها أثر عن صحابي فعن التابعين لهم بإحسان الذين في قولهم الشفاء والهدى، والتدين بقولهم القربة إلى الله والزلفى، فإذا رأيناهم قد أجمعوا على شيء عولنا عليه، ومن أنكروا عليه، أو ردوا عليه بدعته أو كفروه حكمنا به

17

واعتقدناه. ولم يزل من لدن رسول الله إلى يومنا هذا قوم يحفظون هذه الطريقة، ويتدينون بها، وإنما هلك من حاد عن هذه الطريقة لجهله طرق الاتباع.

"I use as evidence for the madhāhib (pl. madhhab) of Ahlus-Sunnah that which is mentioned in the Book of Allāh – the Exalted – regarding it, and that which is narrated from the Messenger of Allāh (sallAllāhu 'alayhi wa sallam). So if I find something in both of them, then I mention it all. And if I find something in only one of them without the other, then I mention that. And if I don't find anything regarding it except from the Sahābah (radiAllāhu 'anhum); those whom Allāh and His Messenger has ordered to take as an example, and to follow their words, and to seek light from their lights, due to them testifying the revelation and their knowledge regarding the meaning of the interpretations, then I use that as evidence. But if there is no narration regarding it from a companion, then from those who followed them in goodness; those in whose words there is a cure and guidance. And worshipping Allāh with their opinion is nearness to Allāh and closeness (to Him). So if we see that they agreed upon something then we rely on it. And whoever's opinion they criticized, or they refuted his bid'ah (innovation) or they declared takfir upon him, then we will judge with that and believe in it. And there continue to be, from the Messenger of Allāh (sallAllāhu 'alayhi wa sallam) until this day of ours, a people who protect this way and take it as their religion. And verily is the person destroyed who turns away from this path, due to his ignorance regarding the path of following (the narratins)." (Usūl I'tiqād Ahlus-Sunnah by Al-Lālakāī 1/27)

So these are the words from Allāh the Exalted, His Messenger (sallAllāhu 'alayhi wa sallam), the Sahābah (radiAllāhu 'anhum) and the scholars of Islām which all point to, that the religion is what has come in the Qurān and the *Sunnah*, according to the understanding of the *Salaf*. And that is a path of submitting to and following the evidences and narrations.

May Allāh make us from them. *Āmīn.*

The testimonies of Islām (At-Tawhīd and *Ar-Risālah*)

The Muslim enters into the religion with the two testimonies. If he meets Allāh based upon their true meanings and having fulfilled their requirements, then Allāh has promised to enter him into Paradise. These two testimonies are: *Lā ilāha illa Allāh* (there is no-one worthy of worship besides Allāh), ***Muhammadun RasulAllāh*** (Muhammad is the Messenger of Allāh).

Lā ilāha illa Allāh being the Tawhīd (Oneness) of Allāh which every prophet and messenger – from Nūh (*'alayhi as-salām*) to Muhammad (*sallAllāhu 'alayhi wa sallam*) – has been sent inviting towards, while *Muhammadun RasūlAllāh* is the *Risālah* (Message) which is the legislation and knowledge which is specific to Muhammad (*sallAllāhu 'alayhi wa sallam*).

There is nothing that the Muslim does in his religion except that it has a relation to these two testimonies. And this is due to the fact that every act of worship – both in deeds and beliefs – has **two conditions for it to accepted by Allāh**:

1. That it is performed with *ikhlās* which is sincerity in intention, meaning that it is solely performed for Allāh without including any form of major or minor *shirk*, which is associating partners with Allāh in worship or in intention.
2. That it is performed according to the **Sunnah** of the Messenger of Allāh (*sallAllāhu 'alayhi wa sallam*), meaning that it is performed without any form of innovation.

And the evidences for these two conditions have already been mentioned in what has gone forth.

Thus, whoever bears witness to *Lā ilāha illa Allāh, **Muhammadun RasūlAllāh***, has born witness to the fact, that he only worships one *ilāh* (deity, god) – both in beliefs and in deeds – and that he only worships Allāh the same way that His Messenger (*sallAllāhu 'alayhi wa sallam*) has shown us, both in beliefs and in deeds. Therefore a person cannot be a Muslim who is free from *shirk* (i.e. associating partners with Allāh in worship) and *bida'* (innovation), without knowing the true meaning of these two testimonies, believing in their meanings, acting upon them and avoiding whatever negates them.

And one of these testimonies do not benefit without the other. Whoever worships Allāh alone, but does not believe in the Messenger of Allāh (*sallAllāhu 'alayhi wa sallam*) nor follow his path, then he is not a Muslim. And whoever believes in the Messenger of Allāh (*sallAllāhu 'alayhi wa sallam*) but does not worship Allāh alone – by associating partners with Him in worship – then he is not a Muslim. Furthermore the two testimonies are undeniably related to each other, which mean that nullifying one of them automatically means nullifying the other, which will become evident in this book.

The first testimony: *Lā ilāha illa Allāh*

Every type of worship in Islām has its pillars and its conditions which must be fulfilled in order for it to be accepted. For the prayer to be accepted its conditions must be fulfilled such as being sane, being of age, being in a state of ritual purity, having covered the *'awrah* etc. And when the conditions are fulfilled it will be accepted from the slave when he performs the pillars of the prayer, such as the first *takbīrah* (the saying of *'Allāhu akbar'* at the beginning of the prayer), the Fātihah (the first *sūrah* of the Qurān, which must be recited in each unit of the prayer), the *rukū'* (the bowing), the *sujūd* (the prostration) etc.

Likewise it is with the biggest and most noble of worships; the testimony of *Lā ilāha illa Allāh*. The conditions for *Lā ilāha illa Allāh* are seven:

1. *Ikhlās;* that it is said <u>sincerely</u> for Allāh alone. This negates *shirk* (associating partners with Allāh in worship) and *riyā* (showing off or performing deeds to achieve praise).
2. *Sidq;* that it is said <u>truthfully</u> while meaning it. This negates *nifāq* (showing or saying something outwardly while hiding the opposite inside).
3. *Qabūl;* that a person <u>accepts</u> the meaning of it and what it requires of deeds and beliefs. This negates **rejection**.
4. *'Ilm;* that it is said while having <u>knowledge</u> about what it means, necessitates and what negates it. This negates **ignorance.**
5. *Inqiyād;* that it is said while <u>submitting to and acting upon</u> its meaning and requirements. This negates **leaving.**
6. *Mahabbah;* that a person <u>loves</u> its meaning. This negates **hatred.**
7. *Yaqīn;* that it is said with <u>certain faith</u> in its meaning. This negates **doubt.**

It was said to Wahb ibn Munabbih (d. 114h):

أَلَيْسَ لَا إِلَهَ إِلَّا اللَّهُ مِفْتَاحُ الْجَنَّةِ؟ قَالَ: "بَلَى، وَلَكِنْ مَا مِنْ مِفْتَاحٍ إِلَّا وَلَهُ أَسْنَانٌ، فَإِنْ جِئْتَ بِمِفْتَاحٍ لَهُ
أَسْنَانٌ فُتِحَ لَكَ، وَإِلَّا لَمْ يُفْتَحْ لَكَ

"Is Lā ilāha illa Allāh not the key to Paradise? So he (i.e. Wahb) said: 'Yes certainly. But there is no key except that it has teeth. So if you come with the key and it has teeth then (the door) will be opened for you. And if not, then it will not be opened for you." (Al-Bukhārī)

When these conditions are fulfilled by the slave then his performance of and belief in the pillars of *Lā ilāha illa Allāh* will be accepted. But as for the one who says *Lā ilāha illa Allāh*, but he does not do this sincerely for Allāh, rather he does it for other reasons, or he says it while not meaning it, or he does not accept or submit to its meaning, or he is ignorant about what it means and necessitates, or he hates it or doubts whether it is the truth or not, then the testimony of this person will not benefit him on the Day of Judgment, even though he was considered a Muslim in *dunyā* and treated accordingly due to not openly showing any nullifiers of Islām or that he negated any of these conditions.

As for the pillars of *Lā ilāha illa Allāh*, then the testimony of *Lā ilāha illa Allāh* is made up by two pillars:

The first is: **Lā ilāha**. Translated this means: 'There is no *ilāh* (worshipped)', and what is intended is: 'There is no-one who with right is worshipped'. And this is the part of the testimony which negates divinity (or worthiness of worship) for everything. And it is also called *al-kufr bit-tāghūt*, which means the rejection of *tāghūt* (something which is worshipped besides Allāh).

The second is: **Illa Allāh**. Translated this means: 'Besides Allāh.' And this is the part of the testimony which affirms the divinity (or worthiness of worship) for Allāh alone. And it is also called *al-imānu billāh* (the belief in Allāh).

And among the evidences for these two pillars are the words of Allāh the Exalted:

$$﴿ فَمَنْ يَكْفُرْ بِالطَّاغُوتِ وَيُؤْمِنْ بِاللَّهِ فَقَدِ اسْتَمْسَكَ بِالْعُرْوَةِ الْوُثْقَى لَا انْفِصَامَ لَهَا وَاللَّهُ سَمِيعٌ عَلِيمٌ ﴾$$

"Whoever disbelieves in (or rejects) *tāghūt* and believes in Allāh, then he has grasped the most trustworthy handhold that will never break. And Allāh is All-Hearer, All-Knower."
(Al-Baqarah 2:256)

And His – the Exalted – words:

$$﴿ وَلَقَدْ بَعَثْنَا فِي كُلِّ أُمَّةٍ رَسُولًا أَنِ اعْبُدُوا اللَّهَ وَاجْتَنِبُوا الطَّاغُوتَ ﴾$$

"And verily, We have sent among every *Ummah* (nation) a Messenger (proclaiming): 'Worship Allāh (Alone), and avoid (or keep away from) *tāghūt* (everything worshipped besides Allāh).'"
(An-Nahl 16:36)

And His – the Exalted – words:

$$﴿ وَالَّذِينَ اجْتَنَبُوا الطَّاغُوتَ أَنْ يَعْبُدُوهَا وَأَنَابُوا إِلَى اللَّهِ لَهُمُ الْبُشْرَى فَبَشِّرْ عِبَادِ ﴾$$

"And those who avoid *tāghūt* by not worshipping it, and turn in repentance to Allāh, for them are the glad tidings. So give the glad tidings to My slaves." (Az-Zumar 39:17)

What easily can be understood from these verses – and that which is already known by mankind through the *fitrah* (natural disposition) – is that Allāh demands from His creation that they worship Him alone, and do not associate any partners with Him the Exalted.

'Abdullāh ibn 'Amr (*radiAllāhu 'anhu*) narrated that the Prophet (*sallAllāhu 'alayhi wa sallam*) said:

$$مَن لقِيَ اللهَ لا يشركُ به شيئًا؛ لم تضُرَّهُ معه خطيئةٌ، ومَن مات وهو يشركُ به؛ لم ينفَعْهُ معه حسنةٌ.$$

"Whoever meets Allāh without having associated partners with Him (in worship), then with that (being fulfilled) no mistake (or sin) will harm him. And whoever dies while he has associating

something with Him (in worship), then no good deed will benefit along with that." (Narrated by Imām Ahmad – Its *isnād* is correct according to the conditions of Al-Bukhārī and Muslim)

Mu'ādh ibn Jabal (*radiAllāhu 'anhu*) said:

فقلتُ : يا رسولَ اللهِ أخبرني بعملٍ يُدخِلُني الجنَّةَ ويباعِدُني من النَّارِ ، قالَ : لقد سألتَني عَن عظيمٍ ، وإنَّهُ ليسيرٌ على من يسَّرَهُ اللهُ عليهِ ، تعبدُ اللهَ ولا تشركُ بِهِ شيئًا ، وتُقيمُ الصَّلاةَ ، وتُؤتِي الزَّكاةَ ، وتصومُ رمضانَ ، وتحُجُّ البيتَ

"I said: 'O Messenger of Allāh, tell me of an act which will take me into Paradise and will keep me away from Hell fire.' He said: 'You have asked me about a major matter, yet it is easy for him for whom Allāh Almighty makes it easy. You should worship Allāh, and not associate anything with Him (in worship), you should perform the prayers, you should pay the zakāt, you should fast in Ramadān, and you should make the pilgrimage to the House.'" (Sunan At-Tirmidhī – *sahīh*)

Ibn Abī Shaybah narrated that 'Umar ibn Al-Khattāb (*radiAllāhu 'anhu*) used to say when he would touch (or kiss) the black stone:

آمنْتُ بِاللهِ وَكَفَرْتُ بِالطَّاغُوتِ

"I have believed in Allāh and rejected tāghūt." (Al-Musannaf by Ibn Abī Shaybah)

Ibn Abī Shaybah also narrated that 'Alī ibn Al-Husayn Zayn Al-'Ābidīn used to say to son (while teaching him):

قُلْ آمنْتُ بِاللهِ وَكَفَرْتُ بِالطَّاغُوتِ

"Say: 'I have believed in Allāh and rejected tāghūt.'" (Al-Musannaf by Ibn Abī Shaybah)

And Ibn Jarīr At-Tabarī (d. 310h) said in his *tafsīr* of the following verse:

24

﴿ وَإِلَٰهُكُمْ إِلَٰهٌ وَاحِدٌ لَا إِلَٰهَ إِلَّا هُوَ الرَّحْمَٰنُ الرَّحِيمُ ﴾

"And your *ilāh* is One *Ilāh*. *Lā ilāha illa Huwa* (there is no-one worthy of worship besides Him). **The Most Merciful, the Most Beneficent."** (Al-Baqarah 2:163)

وأما قوله: " لا إله إلا هو "، فإنه خبرٌ منه تعالى ذكره أنه لا رب للعالمين غيرُه, ولا يستوجبُ على العبادِ العبادةَ سواه, وأنّ كلّ ما سواه فهُم خَلقه, والواجبُ على جميعهم طاعته والانقيادُ لأمره، وتركُ عبادة ما سواه من الأنداد والآلهة، وهجْر الأوثان والأصنام. لأنّ جميع ذلك خلقُه، وعلى جميعهم الدينونة له بالوحدانية والألوهة, ولا تَنبغي الألوهة إلا له,

"Regarding His words: There is no-one worthy of worship besides Him, then this is an information from Him – uplifted is His mention – that there is no Lord of the Worlds besides Him. Nor does anything besides Him deserve the worship of the slaves. And that everything which exists besides Him, then He has created it. And that which is obligatory for all of them is obeying Him and submitting to His order, and leaving the worship of what is beside Him of rivals and false gods, and leaving the idols and statues. This is because He has created all of this. And (obligatory) upon all of them is dedicating the religion for Him through the wahdāniyyah (oneness) and the ulūhiyyah (worship), and the worship is not suitable for anyone but Him." (Tafsīr At-Tabarī)

The Qurān, the *Sunnah*, the words of the *Sahābah* and those who followed them, are filled with this meaning; that *Lā ilāha illa Allāh* means the worthiness of worship for Allāh alone. So no-one can claim ignorance in this issue, rather the one who is ignorant or misguided in this issue due to following something else than these sources, then he has only himself to blame, and on the Day of Judgment he will not be excused for committing *shirk* with Allāh.

Abū Muhammad Al-Barbahārī (d. 329h) said:

واعلم رحمك الله أن الدين إنما جاء من قبل الله تبارك وتعالى لم يوضع على عقول الرجال وآرائهم وعلمه
عند الله وعند رسوله فلا تتبع شيئا بهواك فتمرق من الدين فتخرج من الإسلام فإنه لا حجة لك فقد
بين رسول الله ﷺ لأمته السنة وأوضحها لأصحابه وهم الجماعة وهم السواد الأعظم والسواد الأعظم
الحق وأهله فمن خالف أصحاب رسول الله ﷺ في شيء من أمر الدين فقد كفر .

"And know – may Allāh have mercy upon you – that the religion is what has come from Allāh – tabāraka wa ta'ālā – and it was not put upon the intellects of men and their opinions. And its (i.e. the religion) knowledge is with Allāh and with His Messenger, so do not follow anything with you desires so you will pass through the religion and leave Islām, because there is no excuse for you. Verily did the Messenger of Allāh (sallAllāhu alayhi wa sallam) clarify the Sunnah for his Ummah and he made it clear for his Companions, and they are the Jamā'ah, and they are As-Sawād Al-A'dham, and As-Sawād Al-A'dham is the truth and its people. So whoever opposes the companions of the Messenger of Allāh (sallAllāhu alayhi wa sallam) in anything from issues of the religion then he has committed kufr." (Sharh As-Sunnah by Al-Barbahārī)

The best of all good deeds is Tawhīd (worshipping Allāh alone) while the worst of all evil deeds is *shirk* (worshipping others than Allāh).

The first pillar: *Al-Kufr bit-Tāghūt* (the rejection of *tāghūt*)

First of all *tāghūt* means someone who has transgressed his, hers or its boundaries. In the Islamic context *tāghūt* means something which has transgressed its boundaries by being worshipped, obeyed or followed besides Allāh. This does not apply for the one who is <u>not</u> pleased with being worshipped and disassociates himself from this worship.

Ibn Wahb (d. 197h) said:

قال لي مالك: الطاغوت: ما يعبدون من دون الله

"Mālik (i.e. Imām Mālik) said to me: 'At-Tāghūt is what they worship besides Allāh." (Tafsīr Ibn Abī Hātim)

The head of all *tawāghīt* (pl. *tāghūt*) is Iblīs who is the Shaytān (devil). He refused to obey Allāh in prostrating to Ādam when Allāh created him with His two Hands. Thus he was expelled from Paradise, rejected, humiliated and cursed, and he swore to mislead as many from the children of Ādam as possible by making them commit *shirk*, *kufr* and sins. Many will follow his encouragements to evil, and on the Day of Resurrection he will disassociate himself from those whom he misled and he will not be able to help them with anything.

Allāh – the Exalted – said:

﴿ إِذْ قَالَ رَبُّكَ لِلْمَلَائِكَةِ إِنِّي خَالِقٌ بَشَرًا مِنْ طِينٍ ٧١ فَإِذَا سَوَّيْتُهُ وَنَفَخْتُ فِيهِ مِنْ رُوحِي فَقَعُوا لَهُ سَاجِدِينَ ٧٢ فَسَجَدَ الْمَلَائِكَةُ كُلُّهُمْ أَجْمَعُونَ ٧٣ إِلَّا إِبْلِيسَ اسْتَكْبَرَ وَكَانَ مِنَ الْكَافِرِينَ ٧٤ قَالَ يَا إِبْلِيسُ مَا مَنَعَكَ أَنْ تَسْجُدَ لِمَا خَلَقْتُ بِيَدَيَّ أَسْتَكْبَرْتَ أَمْ كُنْتَ مِنَ الْعَالِينَ ٧٥ قَالَ أَنَا خَيْرٌ مِنْهُ خَلَقْتَنِي مِنْ نَارٍ وَخَلَقْتَهُ مِنْ طِينٍ ٧٦ قَالَ فَاخْرُجْ مِنْهَا فَإِنَّكَ رَجِيمٌ ٧٧ وَإِنَّ عَلَيْكَ لَعْنَتِي إِلَى يَوْمِ الدِّينِ ٧٨ قَالَ رَبِّ فَأَنْظِرْنِي إِلَى يَوْمِ يُبْعَثُونَ ٧٩ قَالَ فَإِنَّكَ مِنَ الْمُنْظَرِينَ ٨٠ إِلَى يَوْمِ الْوَقْتِ الْمَعْلُومِ ٨١ قَالَ فَبِعِزَّتِكَ لَأُغْوِيَنَّهُمْ أَجْمَعِينَ ٨٢ إِلَّا عِبَادَكَ مِنْهُمُ الْمُخْلَصِينَ ﴾

27

"When your Lord said to the angels: 'I will verily create a person from clay. So when I have made him and breated into him (his) soul I have created, then fall down in prostration to him. So the angels prostrated all of them. Except Iblīs he was arrogant and was among the disbelievers. He (i.e. Allāh) said: 'O Iblīs, what prevented you from prostrating to what I have created with My two Hands? Did you become too arrogant (to prostrate) or were you (already) among the haughty?' He said: 'I am better than him, You have created me from fire and You created him from clay.' He said: 'Then go out from it (i.e. Paradise), because you are verily expelled. And verily is My curse upon you until the Day of Judgment.' He said: 'My Lord, then give me respite until the Day they are resurrected.' He said: 'Then you are verily among those given respite. Until the Day of an appointed time.' He said: 'By Your Might, I will verily lead them all astray. Except your slaves among them who have been given sincerity** (in the worship of You).**" (Sād 38:71-83)

And He – the Exalted – said:

﴿ وَقَالَ الشَّيْطَانُ لَمَّا قُضِيَ الْأَمْرُ إِنَّ اللَّهَ وَعَدَكُمْ وَعْدَ الْحَقِّ وَوَعَدْتُكُمْ فَأَخْلَفْتُكُمْ وَمَا كَانَ لِيَ عَلَيْكُمْ مِنْ سُلْطَانٍ إِلَّا أَنْ دَعَوْتُكُمْ فَاسْتَجَبْتُمْ لِي فَلَا تَلُومُونِي وَلُومُوا أَنْفُسَكُمْ مَا أَنَا بِمُصْرِخِكُمْ وَمَا أَنْتُمْ بِمُصْرِخِيَّ إِنِّي كَفَرْتُ بِمَا أَشْرَكْتُمُونِ مِنْ قَبْلُ إِنَّ الظَّالِمِينَ لَهُمْ عَذَابٌ أَلِيمٌ ﴾

"And the *Shaytān* said when the affairs have been decided (on the Day of Resurrection): 'Verily Allāh promised you a promise of truth, and I also promised you but I broke my promise to you. And I did not have any authority over you except that I invited you** (to evil) **and then you answered me** (voluntarily). **So do not blame me, and blame yourselves. I cannot help you, nor can you help me. I verily reject when you associated me as a partner** (with Allāh in worship) **before. Verily the unjust will have a painful punishment.'"** (Ibrāhīm 14:22)

And He – the Exalted – said:

﴿ كَمَثَلِ الشَّيْطَانِ إِذْ قَالَ لِلْإِنْسَانِ اكْفُرْ فَلَمَّا كَفَرَ قَالَ إِنِّي بَرِيءٌ مِنْكَ إِنِّي أَخَافُ اللَّهَ رَبَّ الْعَالَمِينَ ﴾

"As the example of the *Shaytān* when he says to the human:
'Commit *kufr*.' Then when he commits *kufr* he says: 'I am verily
free from you, I verily fear Allāh the Lord of all the worlds."
(Al-Hashr 59:16)

Some examples of *tāghūt* which are found today are the following:

* The one who is worshipped besides Allāh or is satisfied with
being worshipped with any type of worship. Allāh – the Exalted –
said:

﴿ أَلَمْ أَعْهَدْ إِلَيْكُمْ يَا بَنِي آدَمَ أَنْ لَا تَعْبُدُوا الشَّيْطَانَ إِنَّهُ لَكُمْ عَدُوٌّ مُبِينٌ ﴾

"Have I not enjoined upon you, O son of Ādam, that you should
not worship the *Shaytān*? He is verily a clear enemy for you."
(Yāsīn 36:60)

And He – the Exalted – said:

﴿ وَمَنْ يَقُلْ مِنْهُمْ إِنِّي إِلَهٌ مِنْ دُونِهِ فَذَلِكَ نَجْزِيهِ جَهَنَّمَ كَذَلِكَ نَجْزِي الظَّالِمِينَ ﴾

"And whoever among them says: 'I am verily an *ilāh* (deity)
besides Him', such a person We will recompense with Hellfire.
Such do we recompense the unjust." (Al-Anbiyā 21:29)

And He – the Exalted – said:

﴿ وَلَقَدْ بَعَثْنَا فِي كُلِّ أُمَّةٍ رَسُولًا أَنِ اعْبُدُوا اللَّهَ وَاجْتَنِبُوا الطَّاغُوتَ ﴾

"And verily, We have sent among every *Ummah* (nation) a
Messenger (proclaiming): 'Worship Allāh (Alone), and avoid (or
keep away from) *tāghūt* (everything worshipped besides Allāh).'"
(An-Nahl 16:36)

* The one who changes the *hukm* (judgment) of Allāh, such as the
one who gives a *fatwā* (verdict) or passes a law stating that *zinā*

(fornication) is allowed, or he says that the one who commits *shirk* is a Muslim. Allāh – the Exalted – said:

﴿ أَلَمْ تَرَ إِلَى الَّذِينَ يَزْعُمُونَ أَنَّهُمْ آمَنُوا بِمَا أُنْزِلَ إِلَيْكَ وَمَا أُنْزِلَ مِنْ قَبْلِكَ يُرِيدُونَ أَنْ يَتَحَاكَمُوا إِلَى الطَّاغُوتِ وَقَدْ أُمِرُوا أَنْ يَكْفُرُوا بِهِ وَيُرِيدُ الشَّيْطَانُ أَنْ يُضِلَّهُمْ ضَلَالًا بَعِيدًا ﴾

"Have you not seen those who claim to believe in what was revealed to you and what was revealed to those who came before you, they wish to seek judgment with the *tāghūt*, and they were verily ordered to reject them. And the *Shaytān* wishes to misguide them into a great misguidance." (An-Nisā 4:60)

* The one who judges or rules between people with manmade laws that contradict the *Sharī'ah* and have its basis in other legislations than the *Sharī'ah*. Such as presidents, parliamentarians, political leaders and everyone who takes part in legislative bodies whose foundation is other than the *Sharī'ah*, such as democracy, secularism, communism etc. Allāh – the Exalted – said:

﴿ وَمَنْ لَمْ يَحْكُمْ بِمَا أَنْزَلَ اللَّهُ فَأُولَٰئِكَ هُمُ الْكَافِرُونَ ﴾

"And whoever does not judge with what Allāh has revealed, then these are the disbelievers." (Al-Māidah 5:44)

* The one who claims to know the unseen, so people come and ask him about that.

Allāh – the Exalted – said:

﴿ قُلْ لَا يَعْلَمُ مَنْ فِي السَّمَاوَاتِ وَالْأَرْضِ الْغَيْبَ إِلَّا اللَّهُ ﴾

"Say: 'Those who are in the heavens and the earth do not know the unseen, except Allāh." (An-Naml 27:65)

* The one whom people believe can benefit and harm like Allāh can benefit and harm, so they ask him for benefit and seek refuge with

him from harm, and he does not reject this, or the dead people in the graves and tombs whom are sought and invoked in these issues.

Allāh – the Exalted – said:

﴿ يَدْعُو مِنْ دُونِ اللَّهِ مَا لَا يَضُرُّهُ وَمَا لَا يَنْفَعُهُ ذَلِكَ هُوَ الضَّلَالُ الْبَعِيدُ ﴾

"He invokes besides Allāh, that which does not harm him and that which does not benefit him. That is the far away misguidance." (Al-Hajj 22:12)

* Nationalism, when people love and hate, and ally and show enmity based upon nationality and not for the sake of Allāh, then nationality has become a *tāghūt* for them which they worship. And this is when a person prefers the disbelieving people of his own nationality over the Muslims, and helps them against them and claims that they are better than the Muslims due to their nationality.

Allāh – the Exalted – said:

﴿ يَا أَيُّهَا الَّذِينَ آمَنُوا لَا تَتَّخِذُوا الْيَهُودَ وَالنَّصَارَى أَوْلِيَاءَ بَعْضُهُمْ أَوْلِيَاءُ بَعْضٍ وَمَنْ يَتَوَلَّهُمْ مِنْكُمْ فَإِنَّهُ مِنْهُمْ إِنَّ اللَّهَ لَا يَهْدِي الْقَوْمَ الظَّالِمِينَ ﴾

"O you who believe, do not take the Jews and the Christians as allies, they are verily the allies of one another. And whoever of you takes them as allies, then he is verily one of them. Verily Allāh does not guide an unjust people." (Al-Māidah 5:51)

* Whims and desires. Many ignorant people say: *"I feel that if I do this and that then I am a good person and Allāh will not punish me."* This, while he is performing things that nullify his Islām. With this he has made his own whims and desires his *ilāh*, due to believing in it rather than believing in the Islāmic texts. He also becomes a *kāfir* and a worshipper of his own desires, if he commits sins due to the belief that the *Sharī'ah* is not binding upon him, or he changes the judgments according to his desires.

Allāh – the Exalted – said:

31

$$ ﴿ أَرَأَيْتَ مَنِ اتَّخَذَ إِلَهَهُ هَوَاهُ ﴾ $$

**"Have you seen the one who takes his desires as his *ilāh*
(worshipped one)?" (Al-Furqān 25:43)**

The detailed meaning of ***al-kufr bit-tāghūt*** can be found in the
following verses:

$$ ﴿ قَدْ كَانَتْ لَكُمْ أُسْوَةٌ حَسَنَةٌ فِي إِبْرَاهِيمَ وَالَّذِينَ مَعَهُ إِذْ قَالُوا لِقَوْمِهِمْ إِنَّا بُرَآءُ مِنْكُمْ وَمِمَّا
تَعْبُدُونَ مِنْ دُونِ اللَّهِ كَفَرْنَا بِكُمْ وَبَدَا بَيْنَنَا وَبَيْنَكُمُ الْعَدَاوَةُ وَالْبَغْضَاءُ أَبَدًا حَتَّى تُؤْمِنُوا
بِاللَّهِ وَحْدَهُ ﴾ $$

**"Indeed there has been an excellent example for you in Ibrāhīm
and those with him, when they said to their people: 'Verily, we
are free from you and whatever you worship besides Allāh, we
have rejected you, and there has started between us and you,
hostility and hatred for ever, until you believe in Allāh Alone.'"**
(Al-Mumtahanah 60:4)

And His – the Exalted – words:

$$ ﴿ ذَلِكَ بِأَنَّ اللَّهَ هُوَ الْحَقُّ وَأَنَّ مَا يَدْعُونَ مِنْ دُونِهِ هُوَ الْبَاطِلُ وَأَنَّ اللَّهَ هُوَ الْعَلِيُّ الْكَبِيرُ ﴾ $$

**"That is because Allāh He is the Truth, and that which they
invoke besides Him is the falsehood. And that Allāh He is Most
High, the Great." (Al-Hajj 22:62)**

And His – the Exalted – words:

$$ ﴿ وَيَعْبُدُونَ مِنْ دُونِ اللَّهِ مَا لَا يَنْفَعُهُمْ وَلَا يَضُرُّهُمْ وَكَانَ الْكَافِرُ عَلَى رَبِّهِ ظَهِيرًا ﴾ $$

**"And they worship besides Allāh that which do not benefit them
nor harm them. And the disbeliever is ever a helper (of the
Shaytān) against his Lord." (Al-Furqān 25:55)**

And that which is required in order to fulfill ***al-kufr bit-tāghūt*** (the
rejection of *tāghūt*) in belief, words and deeds is:

- Leaving the worship of the *tāghūt*.
- The rejection of the divinity for *tāghūt*, because they are falsehood.
- The rejection of the worship performed to *tāghūt* by believing it is invalid and void and that the *tāghūt* does not bring about benefit or harm.
- The rejection of those who worship *tāghūt* by knowing they are not Muslims.
- Hating these people and what they worship.
- Having enmity towards them.

And as for saying to a *mushrik* (one who commits *shirk*) to his face that he is a *mushrik* or a *kāfir*, or showing him enmity and hatred openly in speech and deeds, then this is dependent upon the principle of *masālih* (benefits) and *mafāsid* (harms) according to the rules of the *Sharī'ah*.

That which is enough for a person to be a Muwahhid (one who only worships Allāh) is, that he leaves the worship of *tāghūt*, he rejects divinity for them, he knows that the *tāghūt* neither brings benefit nor harm through the worship of them[2], and that he knows and believes that whoever worships something else than Allāh, then he is a *mushrik* and not a Muslim, and that he hates the *mushrikūn* (those who commit *shirk*).

Whoever does not fulfill this pillar as it has been described he has not rejected *tāghūt*, and by that he is a *mushrik* and not a Muslim.

And the best way of learning *al-kufr bit-tāghūt* is acquiring knowledge about Allāh, the belief in Him, the worship of Him, His Names and His Attributes and then not dedicating any of this to others than Him the Most High.

---

[2] Naturally the one who worships the *tāghūt* and dies upon this, will suffer the great harm of entering and remaning in Hellfire forever. What is meant here is that the worshipped *tāghūt* cannot cause harm to the slave in this life, just as he cannot benefit him. Rather all harm and benefit is a decree from Allāh.

Declaring *takfīr* upon the *mushrik*

Allāh has created mankind upon *fitrah* (natural disposition) through which they know their Lord and His Tawhīd[3]. Allāh – the Exalted – said:

﴿ وَإِذْ أَخَذَ رَبُّكَ مِنْ بَنِي آدَمَ مِنْ ظُهُورِهِمْ ذُرِّيَّتَهُمْ وَأَشْهَدَهُمْ عَلَى أَنْفُسِهِمْ أَلَسْتُ بِرَبِّكُمْ قَالُوا بَلَى شَهِدْنَا أَنْ تَقُولُوا يَوْمَ الْقِيَامَةِ إِنَّا كُنَّا عَنْ هَذَا غَافِلِينَ ٧ أَوْ تَقُولُوا إِنَّمَا أَشْرَكَ آبَاؤُنَا مِنْ قَبْلُ وَكُنَّا ذُرِّيَّةً مِنْ بَعْدِهِمْ أَفَتُهْلِكُنَا بِمَا فَعَلَ الْمُبْطِلُونَ ﴾

"And (remember) when your Lord brought forth from the Children of Ādam, from their loins, their seed (or from Ādam's loin his offspring) **and made them testify as to themselves** (saying): **'Am I not your Lord?' They said: 'Yes, we testify.' In order for you not to say on the Day of Resurrection: 'Verily, we have been unaware of this.' Or that you would say: 'Verily did our forefathers commit *shirk* before, and we were** (merely) **offspring after them. So will you destroy us for something which the doers of falsehood did?"** (Al-A'rāf 7:172-173)

And He – the Exalted – said:

﴿ فَأَقِمْ وَجْهَكَ لِلدِّينِ حَنِيفًا فِطْرَتَ اللَّهِ الَّتِي فَطَرَ النَّاسَ عَلَيْهَا لَا تَبْدِيلَ لِخَلْقِ اللَّهِ ذَلِكَ الدِّينُ الْقَيِّمُ وَلَكِنَّ أَكْثَرَ النَّاسِ لَا يَعْلَمُونَ ﴾

"So direct your face toward the religion, *hanīf* (i.e. free from *shirk*). (This is) the *fitrah* of Allāh upon which He has created all people. No change should there be in the creation of Allāh. That is the correct religion, but most of the people do not know." (Ar-Rūm 30:30)

Through the *fitrah* a person knows the ugliness of *shirk* and that only Allāh is worthy of worship. He furthermore knows that the one who worships other than Allāh is not a Muslim who only

---

[3] This does not apply to the Names and Attributes of Allāh which can only be known through the texts of Qurān and *Sunnah*. This is mentioned in the section of Tawhīd Al-Asmā was-Sifāt.

worships One God. Thus, if you ask a person – who has not been corrupted by the doubts and arguments of *Shayṭān* and his disciple among mankind – if the person worshipping others than Allāh is a monotheist, he will surely say: "No". And whoever is not a monotheist, then he inevitably is a polytheist (i.e. a *mushrik*).

Furthermore, when the first pillar of *Lā ilāha illa Allāh* is leaving the worship of *ṭāghūt* (anything which is worshipped besides Allāh), then the one who commits *shirk* by worshipping the *ṭāghūt*, naturally has not fulfilled this pillar of the testimony and his testimony is invalid, just as if a person would leave out making *sujūd* in his prayer, then his prayer would also be invalid due to not having fulfilled a pillar of the prayer.

Add to this that in the Arabic language the one who performs the deed of *shirk*, by worshipping others than Allāh, he is given the name *mushrik*. And only a person who does not know the rules of the Arabic language refuses to name the person committing *shirk* as a *mushrik*.

And the conclusion is, that the one who refuses to declare *takfīr* upon the *mushrik* (i.e. he refuses to consider the person committing *shirk* as being a non-muslim), he has opposed the *fiṭrah*, the evidences, the language and common sense. Allāh – the Exalted – testified to and explained this fact when He clarified the impossibility of the one worshipping only Allāh being equal to the one worshipping others along with Allāh:

﴿ ضَرَبَ اللَّهُ مَثَلًا رَجُلًا فِيهِ شُرَكَاءُ مُتَشَاكِسُونَ وَرَجُلًا سَلَمًا لِرَجُلٍ هَلْ يَسْتَوِيَانِ مَثَلًا الْحَمْدُ لِلَّهِ بَلْ أَكْثَرُهُمْ لَا يَعْلَمُونَ ﴾

"Allāh gave an example of a (slave) man belonging to many partners disputing with one another, and a (slave) man belonging entirely to one master. Are those two equal in comparison? All praise is due to Allāh. But most of them do not know." (Az-Zumar 39:29)

At-Ṭabarī (d. 310h) said in his *tafsīr* of this verse:

35

يَقُول تَعَالَى ذِكْرُه : مَثَّلَ اللهُ مَثَلًا لِلْكَافِرِ بِاللهِ الَّذِي يَعْبُد آلِهَة شَتَّى , وَيُطِيعُ جَمَاعَة مِنْ الشَّيَاطِين , وَالْمُؤْمِن الَّذِي لَا يَعْبُد إِلَّا اللهَ الْوَاحِد

"He – exalted is His mention – says: Allāh gave an example of the kāfir billāh (disbeliever in Allāh) who worships different deities, and obeys a group of the shayātīn (devils). And (an example) of the believer who do not worship anyone besides Allāh." (Tafsīr At-Tabarī)

And he also mentioned in his *tafsīr* of the verse:

حَدَّثَنَا بِشْر , قَالَ : ثنا يَزِيد , قَالَ : ثنا سَعِيد , عَنْ قَتَادَة , قَوْله : { ضَرَبَ اللهُ مَثَلًا رَجُلًا فِيهِ شُرَكَاء مُتَشَاكِسُونَ } قَالَ : هَذَا الْمُشْرِك تَتَنَازَعُهُ الشَّيَاطِين , لَا يُقِرّ بِهِ بَعْضهُمْ لِبَعْضٍ " وَرَجُلًا سَالِمًا لِرَجُلٍ " قَالَ : هُوَ الْمُؤْمِن أَخْلَصَ الدَّعْوَة وَالْعِبَادَة

"Bishr narrated to us and said: Yazīd narrated to us and said: Sa'īd narrated to us, from Qatādah (regarding) His words: **"Allāh gave an example of a (slave) man belonging to many partners disputing with one another."** *He said: 'This is the mushrik regarding whom the shayātīn (devils) dispute, none of them acknowledges him (as belonging) to anyone among them.* **"And a (slave) man belonging entirely to one master."** *He said: 'This is the believer who sincerily devotes the invocation and worship (to Allāh).'"* (Tafsīr At-Tabarī)

As for telling the *mushrik* to his face that he is not a Muslim, then this is not a must for having fulfilled the *takfīr*, but it is a must that he believes that the one who commits *shirk* is upon *kufr* and not upon Islām. Allāh has clearly described the one who ascribes partners and rivals with Allāh in worship as being upon *kufr*, when He – the Exalted – said:

﴿ وَجَعَلَ لِلَّهِ أَنْدَادًا لِيُضِلَّ عَنْ سَبِيلِهِ قُلْ تَمَتَّعْ بِكُفْرِكَ قَلِيلًا إِنَّكَ مِنْ أَصْحَابِ النَّارِ ﴾

"And he sets up rivals to Allāh, in order to mislead others from His Path. Say: 'Take pleasure in your *kufr* (disbelief) for a while: surely, you are among the dwellers of Hellfire." (Az-Zumar 39:8)

And He – the Exalted – said:

36

﴿ وَمَن يَدْعُ مَعَ اللَّهِ إِلَـٰهًا آخَرَ لَا بُرْهَانَ لَهُ بِهِ فَإِنَّمَا حِسَابُهُ عِندَ رَبِّهِ إِنَّهُ لَا يُفْلِحُ الْكَافِرُونَ ﴾

"And whoever invokes (or worships), besides Allāh, any other ilāh (deity), of whom he has no proof, then his reckoning is only with his Lord. Verily the _kāfirūn_ (the disbelievers) will not be successful." (Al-Muminūn 23:117)

And the Messenger of Allāh (_sallAllāhu 'alayhi wa sallam_) also testified that whoever dies upon _shirk_, he will enter Hellfire. And no-one enters Hellfire forever except a _kāfir_. 'Abdullāh ibn Mas'ūd (_radiAllāhu 'anhu_) said:

قَالَ: النبِيُّ صَلَّى اللهُ عليه وسلَّمَ كَلِمَةً وقُلتُ أُخْرَى، قَالَ النبِيُّ صَلَّى اللهُ عليه وسلَّمَ: مَن مَاتَ وهُوَ يَدْعُو مِن دُونِ اللَّهِ نِدًّا دَخَلَ النَّارَ وقُلتُ أَنَا: مَن مَاتَ وهُوَ لا يَدْعُو لِلَّهِ نِدًّا دَخَلَ الجَنَّةَ.

"The Prophet (sallAllāhu 'alayhi wa sallam) said one thing, and I said another thing. The Prophet (sallAllāhu 'alayhi wa sallam) said: 'Whoever dies, and he is invoking a rival besides Allāh, he will enter Hellfire.' And I said: 'Whoever dies, and he does not invoke a rival with Allāh, he will enter Paradise." (Sahīh Al-Bukhārī)

Add to this that the Prophet (_sallAllāhu 'alayhi wa sallam_) would connect the _hukm_ (judgment) of Islām in _dunyā_ with the fact that a person does not worship anything else but Allāh[4].

The Messenger of Allāh (_sallAllāhu 'alayhi wa sallam_) said:

مَن قَالَ: لا إِلَهَ إِلَّا اللَّهُ، وَكَفَرَ بِما يُعْبَدُ مَن دُونِ اللهِ، حَرُمَ مَالُهُ وَدَمُهُ، وَحِسَابُهُ عَلَى اللَّهِ. وفِي روايَة: مَن وَحَّدَ اللَّهَ... ثُمَّ ذَكَرَ، بِمِثْلِهِ.

"Whoever says: Lā ilāha illa Allāh and rejects everything which is worshipped besides Allāh, his wealth and blood becomes impermissible (to take) and his account is with Allāh." And in

---

[4] This is in what is showed publicly. If he hides his _shirk_ and _kufr_ and shows Islām outwardly, then he is _munāfiq_ and the judgment of Islām is still applied upon him.

37

another version: "Whoever singles out Allāh (in worship)." And then he mentioned the same. (Sahīh Muslim)

So the condition for acquiring the *hukm* (judgment) of Islām in *dunyā* is that he testifies to *Lā ilahā illa Allāh* and that he rejects everything which is worshipped besides Allāh, by not worshipping it. Thus, if he worships something else than Allāh – or shows another *nāqid* (nullifier) among the *nawāqid* of Islām – then the judgment of Islām is removed from him, due to him not having fulfilled the conditions for acquiring this judgment.

So the issue of *takfīr al-mushrik* (declaring *takfīr* upon the one who commits *shirk*) is very easy for the people of truth, since the answer to this issue is clearly stated in the Qurān and the *Sunnah*.

Al-Barbahārī (d. 329h) said:

ولا يخرج أحد من أهل القبلة من الإسلام حتى يرد آية من كتاب الله تعالى أو يرد شيئا من آثار رسول الله ﷺ أو يصلي لغير الله أو يذبح لغير الله وإذا فعل شيئا من ذلك فقد وجب عليك أن تخرجه من الإسلام

"And no-one from the people of the Qiblah (i.e. those who pray) are exited from Islām (i.e. declared takfīr upon) before he rejects a verse from the Book of Allāh – the Exalted – or he rejects something of the narrations of the Messenger of Allāh (sallAllāhu 'alayhi wa sallam), or he prays to other than Allāh, or he slaughters for others than Allāh. But if he does any of these things, then it is obligatory upon you to exit him from Islām." (Sharh As-Sunnah by Al-Barbahārī)

Excuse in ignorance and the one who considers the *mushrik* a Muslim

Allāh did not excuse a person in ignorance, neither did His Messenger (*sallAllāhu 'alayhi wa sallam*) and therefore a Muslim also do not excuse the one who commits *shirk* due to ignorance.

Allāh – the Exalted – said:

﴿ وَإِنْ أَحَدٌ مِنَ الْمُشْرِكِينَ اسْتَجَارَكَ فَأَجِرْهُ حَتَّى يَسْمَعَ كَلَامَ اللَّهِ ثُمَّ أَبْلِغْهُ مَأْمَنَهُ ذَلِكَ بِأَنَّهُمْ قَوْمٌ لَا يَعْلَمُونَ ﴾

"And if anyone of the *mushrikūn* (those who commit *shirk*) seeks your protection then grant him protection, so that he may hear the Word of Allāh (i.e. the Qurān), **and then escort him to where he can be secure, that is because they are men who know not."**
(At-Tawbah 9:6)

And He – the Exalted – said:

﴿ لَمْ يَكُنِ الَّذِينَ كَفَرُوا مِنْ أَهْلِ الْكِتَابِ وَالْمُشْرِكِينَ مُنْفَكِّينَ حَتَّى تَأْتِيَهُمُ الْبَيِّنَةُ ﴾

"Those who disbelieve from among the people of the Scripture (Jews and Christians) **and among the *mushrikūn*, were not going to leave** (their disbelief) **until the clear evidence comes to them."**
(Al-Bayyinah 98:1)

In both of these verses Allāh gives the name *mushrik* to those who ascribe partners and rivals to Him in worship **before** the evidence having reached them, being the Qurān and the Messenger (*sallAllāhu 'alayhi wa sallam*). So if these people were not excused how can anyone claim that a person who claims to be a Muslim, recites the Qurān, mentions the *ahādīth* and lives among the Muslims, is entitled to being excused when Allāh did not excuse those whom the Book and Messenger did not reach yet?

Furthermore the Prophet (*sallAllāhu 'alayhi wa sallam*) said in a *sahīh hadīth* narrated by Abū Hurayrah (*radiAllāhu 'anhu*):

والذي نَفْسُ مُحَمَّدٍ بِيَدِهِ، لا يَسْمَعُ بِي أَحَدٌ مِن هذِهِ الأُمَّةِ يَهُودِيٌّ، ولا نَصْرانِيٌّ، ثُمَّ يَمُوتُ ولَمْ يُؤْمِنْ بِالَّذِي أُرْسِلْتُ بِه، إلَّا كانَ مِن أصْحابِ النَّارِ.

"By the One whose Hand Muhammad's soul is in, no-one from this Ummah, neither a Jew nor a Christian hears about me, and then do not believe in what I have been sent with, except that he is from the people of the fire." (Sahīh Muslim)

So whoever among the Jews, Christians, Majūs, Buddhists, Atheists and all others in this life who heard about the Messenger of Allāh (*sallAllāhu 'alayhi wa sallam*) and then dies upon something else than the Tawhīd of Allāh and the *Risālah* of Muhammad (*sallAllāhu 'alayhi wa sallam*), then he will be in Hellfire. Then how daring and how ignorant is it, to claim that a person who claims to be a Muslim and then breaches his Tawhīd by committing *shirk* is excused while the above mentioned are going to Hellfire?

Add to this that if a person should pray his prayer while being ignorant about the fact that the prayer contains the performance of *sujūd* so he does not perform it, then his prayer is still not valid even if he was ignorant. And likewise is it with Tawhīd. Even if he was ignorant of only one type of *shirk* and he performed it, then he is not excused with his ignorance and his testimony of *Lā ilāha illa Allāh* is not valid until he acquires the required knowledge and corrects his beliefs and disassociates himself from the *shirk* which he performed.

This is because knowledge about Allāh and His Tawhīd is *fard 'ayn* (an obligation upon every single person), and no-one is excused from this obligation if he is of sane mind.

So the one who commits *shirk* and dies upon it without having repented and disassociated himself from it and its people, he will enter Hellfire according to the promise of Allāh – the Exalted – Who does not break His promise.

Allāh – the Exalted said:

40

﴿ إِنَّهُ مَنْ يُشْرِكْ بِاللَّهِ فَقَدْ حَرَّمَ اللَّهُ عَلَيْهِ الْجَنَّةَ وَمَأْوَاهُ النَّارُ وَمَا لِلظَّالِمِينَ مِنْ أَنْصَارٍ ﴾

"Verily whoever commits *shirk* (i.e. associates partners with Allāh in worship), then Allāh has verily made Paradise forbidden for him, and his abode will be the fire. And the unjust will have no helpers." (Al-Maidah 5:72)

And He – the Exalted – said:

﴿ إِنَّ اللَّهَ لَا يَغْفِرُ أَنْ يُشْرَكَ بِهِ وَيَغْفِرُ مَا دُونَ ذَلِكَ لِمَنْ يَشَاءُ وَمَنْ يُشْرِكْ بِاللَّهِ فَقَدْ ضَلَّ ضَلَالًا بَعِيدًا ﴾

"Verily Allāh does not forgive that partners are associated with Him (in worship), and He forgives whatever is besides that for whoever He wills. And whoever commit *shirk* with Allāh, then he has verily gone far astray." (An-Nisa 4:116)

And the Prophet (sallAllāhu 'alayhi wa sallam) said in a *sahīh hadīth* narrated by Abū Hurayrah (radiAllāhu 'anhu):

فَيُنَادِي مُنَادٍ : أَلَا تَتَّبِعُ كُلُّ أُمَّةٍ مَا كَانَت تَعْبُدُ ، فَيَتَّبِعُ الشَّيَاطِينُ ، وَالصَّلِيبُ وَأَوْلِيَاؤُهم إِلَى جَهَنَّمَ ، وَبَقِينَا أَيُّهَا المُؤْمِنُون ، فَيَأْتِينَا رَبُّنَا فَيَقُولُ : عَلَى مَا هَؤُلَاءِ ؟ فَنَقُولُ : نَحْنُ عِبَادُ اللهِ المُؤْمِنُون آمَنَّا بِرَبِّنَا ، وَلَمْ نُشْرِكْ بِهِ شَيْئًا وَهُوَ رَبُّنَا — تَبَارَكَ وَتَعَالَى — وَهُوَ يَأْتِينَا ، وَهُوَ يُثَبِّتُنَا ، وَهَذَا مَقَامُنَا حَتَّى يَأْتِينَا رَبُّنَا ، فَيَقُولُ : أَنَا رَبُّكُم فَانْطَلِقُوا.

"(On Judgment Day) a caller will call: 'Verily every Ummah must follow what it used to worship (in dunyā).' So the shayātīn, the cross and their awliyā are followed to Hellfire. And we will remain, O you believers. Then our Lord will come to us and say: 'Upon what are these?' So we will say: 'We are the slaves of Allāh the believers. We have believed in our Lord and we did not associate anything with Him (in worship), and He is our Lord – tabāraka wa ta'ālā – and He will come to us and He will make us firm, and this is our place until our Lord will come to us.' Then He will say: 'I am your Lord, so go forth.'" (At-Tawhīd by Ibn Khuzaymah – with a firm and correct chain of narration)

So whoever dies upon *shirk* after the Qurān has reached him, he will be in Hellfire. That is regarding his punishment in *al-ākhirah* (the hereafter). But in *dunyā* he is *mushrik* regardless of the Qurān reaching him or not, because he worships others than Allāh and not Allāh alone.

Allāh – the Exalted – said:

﴿ فَرِيقًا هَدَى وَفَرِيقًا حَقَّ عَلَيْهِمُ الضَّلَالَةُ إِنَّهُمُ اتَّخَذُوا الشَّيَاطِينَ أَوْلِيَاءَ مِنْ دُونِ اللَّهِ وَيَحْسَبُونَ أَنَّهُمْ مُهْتَدُونَ ﴾

"A group He guided and for a group the misguidance became a reality. Verily, they took the *shayatīn* (devils) as *awliyā* (helpers, supporters, allied) besides Allāh, while they think that they are rightly guided." (Al-A'rāf 7:30)

At-Tabarī (d. 310h) said in his *tafsīr* of the verse:

يَقُول تَعَالَى ذِكْره : إِنَّ الْفَرِيق الَّذِي حَقَّ عَلَيْهِمْ الضَّلَالَة إِنَّمَا ضَلُّوا عَنْ سَبِيل اللَّه وَجَارُوا عَنْ قَصْد الْمَحَجَّة , بِاتِّخَاذِهِمْ الشَّيَاطِين نُصَرَاء مِنْ دُون اللَّه وَظُهَرَاء , جَهْلًا مِنْهُمْ بِخَطَأٍ مَا هُمْ عَلَيْهِ مِنْ ذَلِكَ ; بَلْ فَعَلُوا ذَلِكَ وَهُمْ يَظُنُّونَ أَنَّهُمْ عَلَى هُدًى وَحَقٍّ , وَأَنَّ الصَّوَاب مَا أَتَوْهُ وَرَكِبُوا . وَهَذَا مِنْ أَبْيَن الدَّلَالَة عَلَى خَطَأ قَوْل مَنْ زَعَمَ أَنَّ اللَّه لَا يُعَذِّب أَحَدًا عَلَى مَعْصِيَة رَكِبَهَا أَوْ ضَلَالَة اِعْتَقَدَهَا إِلَّا أَنْ يَأْتِيهَا بَعْد عِلْم مِنْهُ بِصَوَاب وَجْههَا فَيَرْكَبهَا عِنَادًا مِنْهُ لِرَبِّهِ فِيهَا

"He – Exalted is His mention – says: Verily the group for whom the misguidance became a reality, they verily went astray from the Path of Allāh and deviated from the intended goal, by taking the shayatīn as supporters and helpers besided Allāh, due to <u>ignorance</u> from them regarding the mistake they are upon in this. Rather they did this while they were thinking they are upon guidance and the truth, and that the correct is what they have come with and performed. And this (verse) is among the clearest of evidences for the mistake of the opinion of the one who claims that Allāh will not punish anyone for a sin which he performed or a misguidance which he believed in, except if he performs (or believes in) it after having knowledge about its correct reality and then he performs it out of stubbornness from him towards his Lord." (Tafsīr At-Tabarī)

And the same meaning is found in the following verses:

﴿قُلْ هَلْ نُنَبِّئُكُمْ بِالْأَخْسَرِينَ أَعْمَالًا ۞ الَّذِينَ ضَلَّ سَعْيُهُمْ فِي الْحَيَاةِ الدُّنْيَا وَهُمْ يَحْسَبُونَ أَنَّهُمْ يُحْسِنُونَ صُنْعًا ﴾

"Say: 'Shall we inform you about the biggest losers with regards to their deeds? (They are) those whose efforts in this life were wasted while they were thinking that they were doing good.'"
(Al-Kahf 18:103-104)

At-Tabarī said in his *tafsīr* of this verse:

وَهَذَا مِنْ أَدِلَّةِ الدَّلَائِلِ عَلَى خَطَأِ قَوْلِ مَنْ زَعَمَ أَنَّهُ لَا يَكْفُرُ بِاللَّهِ أَحَدٌ إِلَّا مِنْ حَيْثُ يَقْصِدُ إِلَى الْكُفْرِ بَعْدَ الْعِلْمِ بِوَحْدَانِيَّتِهِ , وَذَلِكَ أَنَّ اللَّهَ تَعَالَى ذِكْرُهُ أَخْبَرَ عَنْ هَؤُلَاءِ الَّذِينَ وَصَفَ صِفَتَهُمْ فِي هَذِهِ الْآيَةِ , أَنَّ سَعْيَهُمُ الَّذِي سَعَوْا فِي الدُّنْيَا ذَهَبَ ضَلَالًا , وَقَدْ كَانُوا يَحْسَبُونَ أَنَّهُمْ مُحْسِنُونَ فِي صُنْعِهِمْ ذَلِكَ , وَأَخْبَرَ عَنْهُمْ أَنَّهُمْ هُمُ الَّذِينَ كَفَرُوا بِآيَاتِ رَبِّهِمْ . وَلَوْ كَانَ الْقَوْلُ كَمَا قَالَ الَّذِي زَعَمُوا أَنَّهُ لَا يَكْفُرُ بِاللَّهِ أَحَدٌ إِلَّا مِنْ حَيْثُ يَعْلَمُ , لَوَجَبَ أَنْ يَكُونَ هَؤُلَاءِ الْقَوْمُ فِي عَمَلِهِمُ الَّذِي أَخْبَرَ اللَّهُ عَنْهُمْ أَنَّهُمْ كَانُوا يَحْسَبُونَ فِيهِ أَنَّهُمْ يُحْسِنُونَ صُنْعَه , كَانُوا مُثَابِينَ مَأْجُورِينَ عَلَيْهَا , وَلَكِنَّ الْقَوْلَ بِخِلَافِ مَا قَالُوا , فَأَخْبَرَ جَلَّ ثَنَاؤُهُ عَنْهُمْ أَنَّهُمْ بِاللَّهِ كَفَرَة , وَأَنَّ أَعْمَالَهُمْ حَابِطَة.

"And this (verse) is among the clearest of evidences for the mistake of the opinion of the one who claims that no-one commits kufr to Allāh, except if he intends to commit kufr after having knowledge about His wahdāniyyah (oneness). And this is because Allāh – Exalted is His mention – informed about these people whom He described in this verse, that their efforts which they did in dunyā went astray, and they were verily thinking that they were doing good in this. And He informed that they are those who committed kufr in the verses of their Lord. And if the (correct) opinion were as the one who claims that no-one commits kufr to Allāh except when he knows (it is kufr), then this necessitates that these people (mentioned in the verse) in their deeds – which He informed that they were thinking that they were doing good in – were rewarded and recompensed for it. But the opinion is opposite of what they say. So He – Exalted is His praise – informed about them that they are disbelievers in Allāh, and that their deeds are in vain." (Tafsīr At-Tabarī)

Thus, the one who excuses the *mushrik* in ignorance – or any other excuse – and declares him a Muslim, he himself is not a Muslim due to the following:

* His testimony of *Lā ilāha illa Allāh* is not valid since the first condition for the validity of the testimony is knowledge. So he must know the meaning of the testimony, what it necessitates and what contradicts it, by which he knows the difference between Tawhīd and *shirk*. Furthermore, the person who does not know that the one who commits *shirk* is not a Muslim, he has in reality not known the meaning of *Lā ilāha illa Allāh*, which is to worship Allāh alone and not ascribing partners to Him in worship. Rather in his understanding of Islām a person can be a Muslim without rejecting *tāghūt*, while Allāh – the Exalted – said:

﴿ وَالَّذِينَ اجْتَنَبُوا الطَّاغُوتَ أَنْ يَعْبُدُوهَا وَأَنَابُوا إِلَى اللَّهِ لَهُمُ الْبُشْرَى ۚ فَبَشِّرْ عِبَادِ ﴾

"And those who avoid *tāghūt* by <u>not</u> worshipping it and turn in repentance to Allah, for them are the glad tidings (of Paradise). **So give the glad tidings to My slaves."** (Az-Zumar 39:17)

* He has not rejected *tāghūt* which is the first pillar that must be fulfilled in order for his testimony of *Lā ilāha illa Allāh* to be valid. And this is because it is included in *al-kufr bit- tāghūt*, to consider the one who worships *tāghūt* as a non-Muslim. And the evidence for this is the words of Allāh the Exalted:

﴿ قُلْ يَا أَيُّهَا الْكَافِرُونَ ، لَا أَعْبُدُ مَا تَعْبُدُونَ ، وَلَا أَنْتُمْ عَابِدُونَ مَا أَعْبُدُ ، وَلَا أَنَا عَابِدٌ مَا عَبَدْتُمْ ، وَلَا أَنْتُمْ عَابِدُونَ مَا أَعْبُدُ ، لَكُمْ دِينُكُمْ وَلِيَ دِينِ ﴾

"Say: 'O you disbelievers. I do not worship what you worship. Nor do you worship what I worship. Nor will I (ever) worship what you worship. Nor will you worship what I worship. For you is your religion, and for me is my religion.'" (Al-Kāfirūn)

The Prophet (*sallAllāhu 'alayhi wa sallam*) said about this *Sūrah*:

فَإِنَّهَا بَرَاءَةٌ مِنَ الشِّرْكِ

"Verily it is the disassociation from shirk." (Sahīh Ibn Hibbān)

And by this we learn, that the disassociation from *shirk* and the rejection of *tāghūt* includes:

1. The disassociation from what is worshipped.

﴿ لَا أَعْبُدُ مَا تَعْبُدُونَ ﴾

"I do not worship what you worship."

2. The disassociation from the worship itself.

﴿ لَكُمْ دِينُكُمْ وَلِيَ دِينِ ﴾

"For you is your religion, and for me is my religion."

And verily is the religion worship.

3. The disassociation from the worshipper.

﴿ قُلْ يَا أَيُّهَا الْكَافِرُونَ ﴾

"Say: 'O you disbelievers.'"

* He has entered into the major *walā* (alliance, loyalty, love) with the *mushrikūn*, by considering them as Muslim, by which the *walā* to them becomes obligatory upon him. Having this form of *walā* is *kufr* which brings a person out of Islām, due to words of Allāh the Exalted:

﴿ وَمَنْ يَتَوَلَّهُمْ مِنْكُمْ فَإِنَّهُ مِنْهُمْ إِنَّ اللَّهَ لَا يَهْدِي الْقَوْمَ الظَّالِمِينَ ﴾

"And whoever of you takes them as allies, then he is verily one of them. Verily Allāh does not guide an unjust people."
(Al-Māidah 5:51)

* He (i.e. the one who considers the *mushrik* a Muslim) has furthermore rejected describing a person with *kufr* whom Allāh has described with *kufr*. And the one who rejects even one verse from the Qurān, he is *kāfir*.

Allāh – the Exalted – said:

﴿ بَلَى قَدْ جَاءَتْكَ آيَاتِي فَكَذَّبْتَ بِهَا وَاسْتَكْبَرْتَ وَكُنْتَ مِنَ الْكَافِرِينَ ﴾

"Yes! Verily, there came to you My *āyāt* (proofs, evidences, verses, lessons, signs) and you denied them, and were proud and were among the disbelievers." (Az-Zumar 39:59)

And He – the Exalted – said:

﴿ وَمَا يَجْحَدُ بِآيَاتِنَا إِلَّا الْكَافِرُونَ ﴾

"And no-one reject Our *āyāt* (proofs, signs, verses, lessons) except the disbelievers." (Al-'Ankabūt 29:47)

So just like declaring *takfīr* upon the *mushrik* is necessary for you in order to have fulfilled your *kufr bit-tāghūt*, then it is naturally also necessary for the next man in order for his *kufr bit-tāghūt* to be valid. So the *hukm* of the one who considers the *mushrik* a Muslim is that he did not fulfill his *kufr bit-tāghūt* and therefore he has not fulfilled *Lā ilāha illa Allāh*, and by that he is not a Muslim.

The *Salaf* would declare *takfīr* upon the one who refrained from declaring *takfīr* upon a person who had uttered words or committed and act of major *shirk* or kufr, stating that whoever does not declare takfīr upon the *kāfir*, he himself is a *kāfir*.

Imām Ahmad (d. 241h) – *rahimahullāh* – said:

فمن قال: مخلوق، فهو كافر بالله العظيم، ومن لم يكفره فهو كافر.

"So whoever says: '(The Quran is) created', then he is a disbeliever in Allāh the All-Mighty, and whoever does not declare takfir upon him, he is (also) a kāfir." (Usūl As-Sunnah by Imām Ahmad – the *riwāyah* of Musaddad)

And in the 'aqīdah of Abū Hātim Ar-Rāzī (d. 277h) and Abū Zur'ah Ar-Rāzī (d. 264h) – rahimahumā Allāh – they said:

ومن زعم أن القرآن مخلوق، فهو كافر بالله العظيم كفراً ينقل عن الملة، ومن شك في كفره ممن يفهم فهو كافر

"And whoever claims that the Qurān is created, he is a disbeliever in Allāh the All-Mighty with a kufr that brings him out of the millah (religion). And whoever doubts in his kufr – among those who understand – he is (also) a kāfir." (Sharh Usūl I'tiqād Ahlus-Sunnah Wal-Jamā'ah by Al-Lālakāī)

And it was narrated it "As-Sunnah from the Masāil of Al-Karmānī" that Abū Bakr ibn 'Ayyāsh (d. 193h) said when he was asked regarding the one who says that the Qurān is created:

كافر، وكل من لم يقل: إنه كافر؛ فهو كافر. ثم قال: أيُشك في اليهودي والنصراني؛ أنهما كافران؟ فمن شك في هؤلاء أنهم كفار؛ فهو كافر، والذي يقول: القرآن مخلوق. مثلهما

"(He is a) kāfir. And whoever does not say that he is a kāfir, then he is (also) a kāfir." Then he said: *"Does one doubt that the Jew and the Christian both are disbelievers? So whoever doubts regarding these that they are kuffār, then he (himself) is a kāfir. And the one who says that the Qurān is created is like them (i.e. the Jew and the Christian)."* (As-Sunnah by Al-Karmānī)

And Sufyān ibn 'Uyaynah (d 198h) said:

الْقُرْآنُ كَلَامُ اللَّهِ عَزَّ وَجَلَّ، مَنْ قَالَ: مَخْلُوقٌ، فَهُوَ كَافِرٌ، وَمَنْ شَكَّ فِي كُفْرِهِ فَهُوَ كَافِرٌ

"The Qurān is the Word of Allāh 'azza wa jalla. Whoever says (that it is) created, he is a kāfir. And whoever doubts regarding his kufr, he is (also) a kāfir.'" (As-Sunnah by 'Abdullāh)

The second pillar: *Al-Imānu billāh* (the belief in Allāh)

Believing in Allāh – in the language – means to acknowledge the presence of a Creator and Sustainer etc. And this is the belief which is mentioned in the following verse:

﴿ وَمَا يُؤْمِنُ أَكْثَرُهُمْ بِاللَّهِ إِلَّا وَهُمْ مُشْرِكُونَ ﴾

"And most of them do not believe in Allāh, except that they are *mushrikūn* (i.e. associating partners with Allāh in worship)."
(Yūsuf 12:106)

But this type of belief is not sufficient for becoming a Muslim, rather a Muslim must believe in Allāh according to the Islāmic Legislation, and not just according to the language. This belief in Allāh is called At-Tawhīd (The Oneness of Allāh). This is the type of belief which is mentioned in the following verse:

﴿ الَّذِينَ آمَنُوا وَلَمْ يَلْبِسُوا إِيمَانَهُمْ بِظُلْمٍ أُولَٰئِكَ لَهُمُ الْأَمْنُ وَهُمْ مُهْتَدُونَ ﴾

"Those who believe and do not mix their belief with injustice (i.e. *shirk*), for those there is safety and they are the rightly guided." (Al-An'ām 6:82)

'Abdullāh ibn Mas'ūd (*radiAllāhu 'anhu*) said:

لَمَّا نَزَلَتْ {الَّذِينَ آمَنُوا وَلَمْ يَلْبِسُوا إِيمَانَهُمْ بِظُلْمٍ } [الأنعام: 82] شَقَّ ذَلِكَ عَلَى المُسْلِمِينَ، فَقَالُوا: يا رَسُولَ اللَّهِ، أَيُّنَا لا يَظْلِمُ نَفْسَهُ؟ قَالَ: لَيسَ ذَلِكَ إِنَّمَا هو الشِّرْكُ أَمَّ تَسْمَعُوا ما قَالَ لُقْمَانُ لِابْنِهِ وهو يَعِظُهُ {يَا بُنَيَّ لا تُشْرِكْ بِاللَّهِ إِنَّ الشِّرْكَ لَظُلْمٌ عَظِيمٌ}

"When the verse: **"Those who believe and do not mix their belief with injustice (i.e. shirk), for those there is safety and they are the rightly guided."** *was revealed this was hard (to hear) for the Muslims. So they said: 'O Messenger of Allāh, who of us does not make injustice to himself (by sinning)?' He said: 'That is not what is meant. Verily it is shirk. Did you not hear what Luqmān said to his son while he was advising*

him: "O my son, do not commit *shirk* to Allāh. Verily *shirk* is a big injustice."" (Saḥīḥ Al-Bukhārī)

In order to make it easier for the people, Tawḥīd has been divided into three categories which are:

1. Tawḥīd *Ar-Rubūbiyyah*, which means the Tawḥīd of Lordship. This type of Tawḥīd includes the slave's belief in the actions of Allāh.

2. Tawḥīd *Al-Ulūhiyyah*, which means the Tawḥīd of Divinity (or Worship). This type of Tawḥīd includes the slave's deeds which he performs to worship Allāh.

3. Tawḥīd *Al-Asmā was-Sifāt*, which means the Tawḥīd of Names and Attributes. This type of Tawḥīd includes the descriptions of Allāhs Names and Attributes which are found in the Qurān and in the *Sunnah.*

Muhammad ibn Nasr Al-Marwazī (d. 294h) said when explaining *īmān*:

فأصله الإقرار بالقلب عن المعرفة، وهو الخضوع لله بالعبودية، والخضوع له بالربوبية، وكذلك خضوع اللسان بالإقرار بالإلهية بالإخلاص له من القلب، واللسان، أنه واحد لا شريك له،

"Then its asl (fundament) is the acknowledgement of the heart regarding the knowledge (about Allāh and His religion). And this is the submission to Allāh in the 'ubūdiyyah (worship), and the submission to Him in the Rubūbiyyah (Lordship). And likewise the submission of the tongue by acknowledging the ilāhiyyah (divinity) by having sincerity for Him in the heart and upon the tongue (regarding) Him being One without any partner." (Ta'dhīm Qadr As-Salāh by Al-Marwazī 2/702)

And Imām Ahmad ibn Hanbāl (d. 241h) said:

نعبد الله بصفاته كما وصف به نفسه قد أجمل الصفة لنفسه ولا نتعدى القرآن والحديث فنقول كما

قال ونصفه كما وصف نفسه ولا نتعدى ذلك نؤمن بالقرآن كله محكمه ومتشابهه ولا نزيل عنه تعالى

ذكره صفة من صفاته

*"We worship Allāh by His Attributes, just as He has described Himself.
He has verily outlined the description of Himself. And we do not
transgress the Qurān and the hadīth, so we say just as they have said, and
we describe Him just as He has described Himself and we do not transgress
(or invalidate) this. We believe in all of the Qurān, both that of it which is
clear and that which is doubious, and we do not remove from Him –
uplifted is His mention – any Attribute from His Attributes."* (Al-Ibānah
Al-Kubrā by Ibn Battah)

And Ibn Battah (d. 387 h) said:

وذلك أنَّ أصل الإيمان بالله الذي يجب على الخلق اعتقاده في إثبات الإيمان به ثلاثة أشياء: أحدها:
أن يعتقد العبد ربانيته ليكون بذلك مباينًا لمذهب أهل التعطيل الذين لا يثبتون صانعًا. والثاني: أن
يعتقد وحدانيته ليكون مباينًا بذلك مذاهب أهل الشرك الذين أقروا بالصانع وأشركوا معه في العبادة
غيره. والثالث: أن يعتقده موصوفًا بالصفات التي لا يجوز إلا أن يكون موصوفًا بها من العلم والقدرة
والحكمة وسائر ما وصف به نفسه في كتابه. إذ قد علمنا أنَّ كثيرًا ممن يقر به ويوحده بالقول المطلق
قد يلحد في صفاته فيكون إلحاده في صفاته قادحًا في توحيده. ولأنَّا نجد الله تعالى قد خاطب عباده
بدعائهم إلى اعتقاد كل واحدة من هذه الثلاث والإيمان بها.

*"And this is because the asl (foundation) of īmān in Allāh – which is
obligatory upon the creation to believe in regarding the establishment of
the belief in Him – are in three things. The first: That the slave believes in
His Lordship in order for him to be free from the madhhab of the people of
ta'tīl (invalidation) who do not establish (or believe in) a creator. The
second: That he believes in His Oneness in order for him to free from the
madhāhib of the people of shirk who acknowledged a Creator but associated
others as partners with Him in worship. The third: That he believes that
He is described with the Attributes which it is not possible except that He
is described with them such as knowledge, capability, wisdom and the rest
of what He has described Himself with in His Book. Since we have verily*

known that many of those who acknowledge Him and unify Him in worship in general words verily deviate in His Attributes, and then his deviation in His Attributes is a breach in his Tawhīd. And because we find that Allāh – the Exalted – verily has addressed His slaves by calling them to believing in every one of these three and the īmān in them." (Al-Ibānah 'an Sharī'ah Al-Firqah An-Nājiyah)

So a person cannot be a Muslim without believing in and performing all three types of Tawhīd without associating partners with Allāh in any of these, or if he believes in them in a way which is contradictory to what is stated in the Qurān and the *Sunnah* according to the understanding of the *Salaf*. And verily did Allāh – the Exalted – gather all three types of Tawhīd in His words:

﴿ رَبُّ السَّمَاوَاتِ وَالْأَرْضِ وَمَا بَيْنَهُمَا فَاعْبُدْهُ وَاصْطَبِرْ لِعِبَادَتِهِ هَلْ تَعْلَمُ لَهُ سَمِيًّا ﴾

"The Lord of the heavens and the earth and whatever is between them, so worship Him and be steadfast in the worship of Him. Do you know anyone equal to Him in name (i.e. someone sharing His Names and Attributes)**?"** (Maryam 19:65)

At-Tabarī (d. 310h) mentioned in his *tafsīr* of the verse:

حَدَّثَنَا بِشْرٌ ، قَالَ : ثَنَا يَزِيدُ ، قَالَ : ثَنَا سَعِيدٌ ، عَنْ قَتَادَةَ ، قَوْلُهُ (هَلْ تَعْلَمُ لَهُ سَمِيًّا) لَا سَمِيَّ لِلَّهِ وَلَا عَدْلَ لَهُ ، كُلُّ خَلْقِهِ يُقِرُّ لَهُ ، وَيَعْتَرِفُ أَنَّهُ خَالِقُهُ ، وَيَعْرِفُ ذَلِكَ ، ثُمَّ يَقْرَأُ هَذِهِ الْآيَةَ (وَلَئِنْ سَأَلْتَهُمْ مَنْ خَلَقَهُمْ لَيَقُولُنَّ اللَّهُ).

"Bishr narrated to us and said: Yazid narrated to us and said: Sa'id narrated to us, from Qatadah (regarding) His words: **"Do you know anyone equal to Him in name?"** *(He said:) 'There is no-one equal to him in name and nor is anyone similar to Him. All of His creation acknowledge Him and recognize that He is his creator and know this.' Then he read this verse:* **"And if you asked them who created them, they will verily say: 'Allah'."** (Az-Zukhruf 43:87)." (Tafsīr At-Tabarī)

The people whom the Messenger of Allāh (*sallAllāhu 'alayhi wa sallam*) were sent amongst (i.e. the *kuffār* of Quraysh), believed in Allāh, but only in some aspects of His *Rubūbiyyah*. So they acknowledged Allāh as their Creator and Sustainer, and they performed several types of worship for Him. But due to them worshipping the statues besides Him, by invoking them and taking them as intermediaries between themselves and Allāh, then Allāh rejected their socalled *īmān* and sent His Prophet (*sallAllāhu 'alayhi wa sallam*) to warn them.

Allāh – the Exalted – said:

﴿ قُلْ لِمَنِ الْأَرْضُ وَمَنْ فِيهَا إِنْ كُنْتُمْ تَعْلَمُونَ ٨٤ سَيَقُولُونَ لِلَّهِ قُلْ أَفَلَا تَذَكَّرُونَ ٨٥ قُلْ مَنْ رَبُّ السَّمَاوَاتِ السَّبْعِ وَرَبُّ الْعَرْشِ الْعَظِيمِ ٨٦ سَيَقُولُونَ لِلَّهِ قُلْ أَفَلَا تَتَّقُونَ ٨٧ قُلْ مَنْ بِيَدِهِ مَلَكُوتُ كُلِّ شَيْءٍ وَهُوَ يُجِيرُ وَلَا يُجَارُ عَلَيْهِ إِنْ كُنْتُمْ تَعْلَمُونَ ٨٨ سَيَقُولُونَ لِلَّهِ قُلْ فَأَنَّى تُسْحَرُونَ ﴾

"Say: 'To whom belongs the earth and whatever is in it, if you (really) know?' Then they will say: 'To Allāh'. Say: 'Will you then not be reminded?' Say: 'Who is the Lord of the seven heavens and the Lord of the Mighty Throne?' They will say: 'Allāh is.' Say: 'Will you then not fear (Allāh)?' Say: 'In whose Hand is the sovereignty over everything, and He protects while nothing protects against Him, if you really know?' They will say: 'Allāh.' Say: 'Then how are you deceived (away from worshipping only Him)?'" (Al-Muminūn 23:84-89)

And He – the Exalted – said:

﴿ وَلَئِنْ سَأَلْتَهُمْ مَنْ نَزَّلَ مِنَ السَّمَاءِ مَاءً فَأَحْيَا بِهِ الْأَرْضَ مِنْ بَعْدِ مَوْتِهَا لَيَقُولُنَّ اللَّهُ قُلِ الْحَمْدُ لِلَّهِ بَلْ أَكْثَرُهُمْ لَا يَعْقِلُونَ ﴾

"And if you would ask them: 'Who sends down water from the sky with which He brings the earth back to life after its death?' Then they would verily say: 'Allāh (does).' Say: 'All praise is due to Allāh, but most of them do not understand."
(Al-'Ankabūt 29:63)

So a person may claim night and day that he is a believer in Allāh, and he may perform lots of worship for Allāh, but if his *īmān* is not according the the Islāmic Legislation so that he has fulfilled the three types of Tawḥīd, then his *īmān* is invalid and Allāh does not accept it.

Tawhīd *Ar-Rubūbiyyah* (Tawhīd of Lordship)

Tawhīd *Ar-Rubūbiyyah* is the belief in Oneness of Allāh in the Creation, the Lordship, the Arrangement, and His Oneness in His Actions. Those who commit *shirk* believe in many aspects of this type of Tawhīd, yet it is not enough to save them from the punishment of Allāh, because they worship others than Allāh. This was the situation of the *kuffār* (disbelievers) of Quraysh[5] which has previously been mentioned. The description of Tawhīd *Ar-Rubūbiyyah* can be found in the following verses.

Allāh – the Exalted – said:

﴿ قُلْ مَنْ يَرْزُقُكُمْ مِنَ السَّمَاءِ وَالْأَرْضِ أَمَّنْ يَمْلِكُ السَّمْعَ وَالْأَبْصَارَ وَمَنْ يُخْرِجُ الْحَيَّ مِنَ الْمَيِّتِ وَيُخْرِجُ الْمَيِّتَ مِنَ الْحَيِّ وَمَنْ يُدَبِّرُ الْأَمْرَ فَسَيَقُولُونَ اللَّهُ فَقُلْ أَفَلَا تَتَّقُونَ ﴾

"Say (O Muhammad): 'Who provides for you from the sky and from the earth? And who owns hearing and sight? And who brings out the living from the dead and brings out the dead from the living? And who disposes the affairs?' They will say: 'Allāh.' Say: 'Will you not then be afraid?'" (Yūnus 10:31)

And He – the Exalted – said:

﴿ اللَّهُ الَّذِي رَفَعَ السَّمَاوَاتِ بِغَيْرِ عَمَدٍ تَرَوْنَهَا ثُمَّ اسْتَوَى عَلَى الْعَرْشِ وَسَخَّرَ الشَّمْسَ وَالْقَمَرَ كُلٌّ يَجْرِي لِأَجَلٍ مُسَمًّى يُدَبِّرُ الْأَمْرَ يُفَصِّلُ الْآيَاتِ لَعَلَّكُمْ بِلِقَاءِ رَبِّكُمْ تُوقِنُونَ ﴾

"Allāh is He Who raised the heavens without any pillars that you can see. Then, He rose above the Throne (in a manner that suits His Majesty). **He has subjected the sun and the moon, each of them running** (its course) **for a term appointed. He regulates all affairs, explaining the *āyāt*** (proofs, evidences, verses, lessons, signs) **in detail, that you may believe with certainty in the meeting with your Lord."** (Ar-Ra'd 13:2)

And He – the Exalted – said:

---

[5] Quraysh is the tribe of the Prophet (*sallAllāhu 'alayhi wa sallam*).

$$\left\{ \text{أَلَا لَهُ الْخَلْقُ وَالْأَمْرُ ۗ تَبَارَكَ اللَّهُ رَبُّ الْعَالَمِينَ} \right\}$$

"Surely, His is the creation and Commandment. Blessed be Allāh, the Lord of *Al-'Ālamīn* (all that exists)." (Al-A'rāf 7:54)

And He – the Exalted – said:

$$\left\{ \text{وَلَئِنْ سَأَلْتَهُمْ مَنْ خَلَقَهُمْ لَيَقُولُنَّ اللَّهُ ۖ فَأَنَّىٰ يُؤْفَكُونَ} \right\}$$

"And if you asked them who created them, they will surely say: 'Allāh'. How then are they turned away (from the worship of Allāh alone)?" (Az-Zukhruf 43:87)

And this type of Tawhīd is the reason that only Allāh deserves to be worshipped and no-one else but Him. He is our Lord and Creator, and therefore He is the one who deserves that we worship Him. Allāh – the Exalted – said:

$$\left\{ \text{يَا أَيُّهَا النَّاسُ اعْبُدُوا رَبَّكُمُ الَّذِي خَلَقَكُمْ وَالَّذِينَ مِنْ قَبْلِكُمْ لَعَلَّكُمْ تَتَّقُونَ} \right\}$$

"O mankind, worship your Lord, Who created you and those who were before you so that you may become God-fearing."
(Al-Baqarah 2:21)

And He – the Exalted – said:

$$\left\{ \text{ذَٰلِكُمُ اللَّهُ رَبُّكُمْ ۖ لَا إِلَٰهَ إِلَّا هُوَ ۖ خَالِقُ كُلِّ شَيْءٍ فَاعْبُدُوهُ ۚ وَهُوَ عَلَىٰ كُلِّ شَيْءٍ وَكِيلٌ} \right\}$$

"That is Allāh your Lord. There is no-one worthy of worship besides Him. The Creator of everything, so worship Him. And He is the Disposer of all things." (Al-An'ām 6:102)

The One who Creates, Provides, Sustains, Benefits, Harms, Upholds, Maintains, Knows, Gives life, Takes life, Legislates, Forgives, Punishes, Decrees, Protects, Cures, Clothes, Feeds, Exposes, Hides, Honors, Humiliates, Destroys, Shows mercy and Answers His slaves, is the One who deserves to be worshipped. And naturally those who cannot do any of these things – and do not own any partnership with Allah nor do they help Him in any it

– are not in any way entitled that even the smallest type of worship should be dedicated towards them. And these things mentioned above are all from the Actions of Allāh, which are specific for Him – the Exalted – and they are the reason that He Alone is deserving of being worshipped and no-one else but Him the Most High. He – the Exalted – said:

﴿ قُلِ ادْعُوا الَّذِينَ زَعَمْتُمْ مِنْ دُونِ اللَّهِ لَا يَمْلِكُونَ مِثْقَالَ ذَرَّةٍ فِي السَّمَاوَاتِ وَلَا فِي الْأَرْضِ وَمَا لَهُمْ فِيهِمَا مِنْ شِرْكٍ وَمَا لَهُ مِنْهُمْ مِنْ ظَهِيرٍ ﴾

"Say invoke those whom you claim (to be gods) besides Allah. They do not own (even) an atom's weight in the heavens, nor on earth. And they do not hold any partnership (with Allah) in any of them, nor does He have from among them any helper."
(Saba 34:22)

Qatādah (d. 118h) said regarding this verse:

مَا لِلَّهِ مِنْ شَرِيكٍ فِي السَّمَاءِ وَلَا فِي الْأَرْضِ (وَمَا لَهُ مِنْهُمْ) مِنَ الَّذِينَ يَدْعُونَ مِنْ دُونِ اللَّهِ (مِنْ ظَهِيرٍ) مِنْ عَوْنٍ بِشَيْءٍ .

"Allāh does not have any partners in the heaven nor on earth. **"And He does not have from among them."** *(Meaning) those whom they invoke besides Allāh* **"any helper"** *who aids in anything."* (Tafsīr At-Tabarī)

56

Shirk in Tawhīd Ar-Rubūbiyyah

Among the types of *shirk* which people commit in this type of Tawhīd are the following:

* Believing that something else created the creation.

* Believing that someone else than Allāh can harm or benefit, such as a person in a grave, a living person (in things which humans are not capable of), the position of the stars on the sky etc.

* Believing that someone else has the right to legislate for people. Legislating is the right of Allāh and it is from His actions. So believing that someone else has this right is ascribing him as a partner or rival with Allāh in this specific action of Allāh.

* Believing that someone besides Allāh can affect the affairs of the heavens and the earth and whatever is in them.

* Believing that someone besides Allāh knows the unseen. Knowing the unseen is a specific characteristic of Allāh and therefore whoever believes someone else knows what only Allāh knows, then he has ascribed a partner or a rival to Allāh in this specific characteristic.

Whoever ascribes anything which is from Tawhīd *Ar-Rubūbiyyah* to others than Allāh then he has committed *shirk* in Tawhīd *Ar-Rubūbiyyah* and by this he leaves the fold of Islām and becomes a *mushrik*.

Tawhīd Al-Ulūhiyyah (Tawhīd of divinity or worship)

Tawhīd Al-Ulūhiyyah is the realization of Lā ilāha illa Allāh. That which all the prophets and messenger was sent to invite towards. And this is dedicating all types of worship solely to Allāh and not to anyone but Him.

As for worship then it is a comprehensive term that includes all inwardly and outwardly sayings and deeds which Allāh is pleased with and which He loves. It is the slave's humbleness and submissiveness towards His Lord, by performing that which He has obliged upon him and avoiding that which He has prohibited for him. The purpose of the creation of mankind and jinn is that they should worship Allāh Alone.

He – the Exalted – said:

﴿ وَمَا خَلَقْتُ الْجِنَّ وَالْإِنْسَ إِلَّا لِيَعْبُدُونِ ﴾

"And I created not the *jinn* and mankind except that they should worship Me (Alone)." (Adh-Dhāriyāt 51:56)

Among the types of worship which must be directed solely to Allāh, are the following:

* *As-Salāh* (the prayer):

﴿ وَأَقِيمُوا الصَّلَاةَ وَآتُوا الزَّكَاةَ ﴾

"And establish the prayer and give the *zakah*." (Al-Baqarah 2:43)

* *Rukū'* (bowing) and *sujūd* (prostrating):

﴿ يَا أَيُّهَا الَّذِينَ آمَنُوا ارْكَعُوا وَاسْجُدُوا ﴾

"O you who believe, perform *ruku'* and *sujud*" (Al-Hajj 22:77)

* *Ad-Du'ā* (the invocation):

﴿ وَقَالَ رَبُّكُمُ ادْعُونِي أَسْتَجِبْ لَكُمْ ﴾

"And your Lord said: 'Invoke Me and I will answer you.'" (Al-
Ghāfir 40:60)

* *Adh-Dhabh* (the slaughtering):

﴿ فَصَلِّ لِرَبِّكَ وَانْحَرْ ﴾

"So pray to your Lord and slaughter (for Him)."
(Al-Kawthar 108:2)

* *Al-Khawf* (the fear) of Allāh:

﴿ إِنَّمَا ذَلِكُمُ الشَّيْطَانُ يُخَوِّفُ أَوْلِيَاءَهُ فَلَا تَخَافُوهُمْ وَخَافُونِ إِنْ كُنْتُمْ مُؤْمِنِينَ ﴾

**"It is only the *Shaytān* that suggests to you the fear of his allies,
so fear them not, but fear Me, if you are** (true) **believers."**
(Ālu 'Imrān 3:175)

* *At-Tawakkul* (putting your trust in Allāh):

﴿ وَعَلَى اللَّهِ فَتَوَكَّلُوا إِنْ كُنْتُمْ مُؤْمِنِينَ ﴾

"And put your trust in Allāh if you are (true) **believers"**
(Al-Māidah 5:23)

So *tawakkul* is a type of worship, and it is the heart putting its trust
in Allāh and relying upon Him, regarding the achievement of what
is good and the removal of what is bad.

* *Al-Istighfār* (asking for forgiveness):

﴿ وَاسْتَغْفِرُوا رَبَّكُمْ ثُمَّ تُوبُوا إِلَيْهِ إِنَّ رَبِّي رَحِيمٌ وَدُودٌ ﴾

**"And ask your Lord for forgiveness and turn unto Him in
repentance. Verily, my Lord is Most Merciful, Most Loving."**
(Hūd 11:90)

* *Al-Inābah* (turning in repentance):

﴿ وَأَنِيبُوا إِلَى رَبِّكُمْ وَأَسْلِمُوا لَهُ مِنْ قَبْلِ أَنْ يَأْتِيَكُمُ الْعَذَابُ ثُمَّ لَا تُنْصَرُونَ ﴾

"And turn in repentance to your Lord and submit yourselves to Him, before the torment comes upon you, then you will not be helped." (Az-Zumar 39:54)

* *Al-Isti'ādhah* (seeking refuge):

﴿ قُلْ أَعُوذُ بِرَبِّ الْفَلَقِ ﴾

"Say: 'I seek refuge with the Lord of the daybreak.'" (Al-Falaq 113:1)

* *Al-Jihād* (striving) with life and wealth:

﴿ انْفِرُوا خِفَافًا وَثِقَالًا وَجَاهِدُوا بِأَمْوَالِكُمْ وَأَنْفُسِكُمْ فِي سَبِيلِ اللَّهِ ﴾

"March forth, whether you are light (being healthy, young and wealthy) or heavy (being ill, old and poor), and strive with your wealth and your lives in the Cause of Allāh." (At-Tawbah 9:41)

* *Al-Hukm* (the judgment) between people with what Allāh has revealed:

﴿ وَأَنِ احْكُمْ بَيْنَهُمْ بِمَا أَنْزَلَ اللَّهُ وَلَا تَتَّبِعْ أَهْوَاءَهُمْ وَاحْذَرْهُمْ أَنْ يَفْتِنُوكَ عَنْ بَعْضِ مَا أَنْزَلَ اللَّهُ إِلَيْكَ ﴾

"And so judge (you O Muhammad) between them by what Allāh has revealed and follow not their vain desires, but beware of them lest they turn you away from some of that which Allāh has revealed to you." (Al-Māidah 5:49)

And He – the Exalted – said:

﴿ إِنَّا أَنْزَلْنَا إِلَيْكَ الْكِتَابَ بِالْحَقِّ لِتَحْكُمَ بَيْنَ النَّاسِ بِمَا أَرَاكَ اللَّهُ ﴾

"Surely, We have sent down to you the Book in truth that you may judge between men by that which Allāh has shown you." (An-Nisā 4:105)

* *At-Tahākum* (seeking judgment) from Allāh and His Messenger:

﴿ فَإِنْ تَنَازَعْتُمْ فِي شَيْءٍ فَرُدُّوهُ إِلَى اللَّهِ وَالرَّسُولِ إِنْ كُنْتُمْ تُؤْمِنُونَ بِاللَّهِ وَالْيَوْمِ الْآخِرِ ﴾

"And if you differ in anything amongst yourselves, then refer it to Allāh and His Messenger, if you believe in Allāh and in the Last Day." (An-Nisā 4:59)

And He – the Exalted – said:

﴿ وَمَا اخْتَلَفْتُمْ فِيهِ مِنْ شَيْءٍ فَحُكْمُهُ إِلَى اللَّهِ ﴾

"And in whatsoever you differ, the *hukm* (judgment) thereof is with Allāh." (Ash-Shūrā 42:10)

And He – the Exalted – said:

﴿ فَلَا وَرَبِّكَ لَا يُؤْمِنُونَ حَتَّى يُحَكِّمُوكَ فِيمَا شَجَرَ بَيْنَهُمْ ثُمَّ لَا يَجِدُوا فِي أَنْفُسِهِمْ حَرَجًا مِمَّا قَضَيْتَ وَيُسَلِّمُوا تَسْلِيمًا ﴾

"But no, by your Lord, they can have no faith, until they make you (O Muhammad) judge in all disputes between them, and find in themselves no resistance against your decisions, and accept (them) with full submission." (An-Nisā 4:65)

* *At-Tā'ah* (obedience) to Allāh in what He has allowed and forbidden:

﴿ فَكُلُوا مِمَّا ذُكِرَ اسْمُ اللَّهِ عَلَيْهِ إِنْ كُنْتُمْ بِآيَاتِهِ مُؤْمِنِينَ ﴾

"So eat from that which the Name of Allāh has been mentioned upon, if you (truly) believe in His verses." (Al-An'ām 6:118)

And He – the Exalted – said:

﴿ إِنَّمَا حَرَّمَ عَلَيْكُمُ الْمَيْتَةَ وَالدَّمَ وَلَحْمَ الْخِنْزِيرِ وَمَا أُهِلَّ بِهِ لِغَيْرِ اللَّهِ ﴾

"Verily, He has only forbidden the *maytah* (dead animals) for you, the blood, the flesh of swine, and that which is slaughtered as a sacrifice for others than Allāh." (Al-Baqarah 2:173)

So it is obedience – and thereby an act of worship – to consider what Allāh has made allowed as being allowed, and what Allāh has made forbidden as being forbidden.

* And from the types of worship are also: Loving for the sake of Allāh and hating for the sake of Allāh, giving for the sake of Allāh and withholding for the sake of Allāh, allying for the sake of Allāh and having enmity for the sake of Allāh, *Ar-Raghbah* (the wishing or longing), *Ar-Rahbah* (awe), *Al-Istighāthah* (asking for help), *Ash-Shukr* (gratitude), *Tilawatul-Qurān* (reciting the Qur'an), *Dhikr Allāh* (remembrance of Allāh) and *As-Siyām* (the fast) and other than this.

Shirk in Tawhīd Al-Ulūhiyyah

Shirk in Tawhīd Al-Ulūhiyyah is dedicating any of the above mentioned types of worship, or others types, to someone else than Allāh. Among the types of shirk which are widespread today are:

* Making du'ā to dead people in the graves, the angels or others. And the conditions for a du'ā (invocation, question, request) not being shirk, is that the one who is asked is (1) alive, (2) capable of what he is asked and (3) present at the time. If one of these three conditions are not present then the du'ā is shirk and takes the person out of Islām. What is requested does not determine whether or not is it shirk, since the dead is not able to do anything anyway.

* Seeking refuge or protection with others than Allāh.

* Slaughtering for others than Allāh.

* Voting in democratic elections and thereby giving the right to legislate to others than Allāh.

* Seeking judgment in disputes with the courts that judges with manmade law.

* Believing something forbidden is allowed, or that something allowed is forbidden, based upon desires, traditions, others legislations than the Sharī'ah or the sayings of men. This is shirk in obedience.

* Striving in the cause of tāghūt, such as being a policeman or soldier for tāghūt.

* Aiding the kuffār against the Muslims with wealth, advice or weapons.

So whoever ascribes anything which is classified as worship in the Islāmic legislation to others than Allāh then he has committed shirk in Tawhīd Al-Ulūhiyyah and by this he leaves the fold of Islām and becomes a mushrik.

Tawhid *Al-Asmā was-Sifāt* (Tawhīd of Names and Attributes)

Tawhid *Al-Asmā was-Sifāt* is the belief in the descriptions of Allāh which has come in the Qurān and the *ahādīth* from the Messenger of Allāh (*sallAllāhu 'alayhi wa sallam*) and the sayings of the *Sahābah* (*radiAllāhu 'anhum*) and those who narrated from them, without denying it, without distorting its meanings, without comparing Allāh with the creation and without describing how.

Rather, a person must believe in what has been described in the way it has been described, and accept the narrations as they have been narrated in order to avoid falling in *shirk* or *bida'* (innovation) in this type of Tawhīd.

The basis for this, are the words of Allāh – the Exalted – who said:

﴿ لَيْسَ كَمِثْلِهِ شَىْءٌ وَهُوَ السَّمِيعُ الْبَصِيرُ ﴾

"There is nothing like Him, and He is the All-Hearer, the All-Seer." (Ash-Shūrā 42:11)

So whatever Allāh or His Messenger (*sallAllāhu 'alayhi wa sallam*) and the *Sahābah* (*radiAllāhu 'anhum*) has informed us about, regarding the description of Allāh, then Allāh is alone in this description and He is not equal to His creation in any of it, even though some words might be used for both Allāh and the slave, such as a *Karīm* (Generous) Lord and a *karīm* (generous) man. Because the generousity of the man is limitied to what Allāh has given him and dependent upon the decree of Allāh, while the Geneorusity of Allāh is unlimited, unrestrained and He spends out of His bounty on whom He wants however He wants.

Allāh – the Exalted – said:

﴿ وَلِلَّهِ الْأَسْمَاءُ الْحُسْنَى فَادْعُوهُ بِهَا وَذَرُوا الَّذِينَ يُلْحِدُونَ فِي أَسْمَائِهِ سَيُجْزَوْنَ مَا كَانُوا يَعْمَلُونَ ﴾

"And the Most Beautiful Names belong to Allāh, so call on Him by them, and leave those who deny (or utter impious speech against) **His Names. They will be recompensed for what they used to do."** (Al-A'rāf 7:180)

And He – the Exalted – said:

﴿ قُلِ ادْعُوا اللَّهَ أَوِ ادْعُوا الرَّحْمَنَ أَيًّا مَا تَدْعُوا فَلَهُ الْأَسْمَاءُ الْحُسْنَى ﴾

"Say (O Muhammad): **'Invoke Allāh or invoke *Ar-Rahmān*** (the Most Benificent). **No matter by which Name you invoke Him, then to Him belong the Best Names.'"** (Al-Isrā 17:110)

And He – the Exalted – said:

﴿ هُوَ اللَّهُ الْخَالِقُ الْبَارِئُ الْمُصَوِّرُ لَهُ الْأَسْمَاءُ الْحُسْنَى يُسَبِّحُ لَهُ مَا فِي السَّمَاوَاتِ وَالْأَرْضِ وَهُوَ الْعَزِيزُ الْحَكِيمُ ﴾

"He is Allāh, the Creator, the Inventor of all things, the Bestower of forms. To Him belong the Best Names. All that is in the heavens and the earth glorify Him. And He is the All-Mighty, the All-Wise." (Al-Hashr 59:24)

And He – the Exalted – said:

﴿ قُلْ هُوَ اللَّهُ أَحَدٌ ، اللَّهُ الصَّمَدُ ، لَمْ يَلِدْ وَلَمْ يُولَدْ ، وَلَمْ يَكُنْ لَهُ كُفُوًا أَحَدٌ ﴾

"Say (O Muhammad): **'He is Allāh, (the) One. Allāh is *As-Samad*** (The Self-Sufficient Master, Whom all creatures need, while He needs no-one). **He begets not, nor was He begotten. And there is no equal to Him.'"** (Al-Ikhlās 112)

Some of Allāhs Names and Attributes are known from the *fitrah*, such as Allāh being the Creator who is Capable of everything, the Disposer of affairs, the Legislator, that Allāh Sees and Hears, that Allāh Speaks whenever He wishes, that Allāh has Knowledge about everything, that Allāh has Life, that Allāh is in 'Uluw (i.e. above the heavens separated from His creation) and similar to these things which describe Allāh with attributes of perfection and negate any flaws, mistakes or deficiency for Him the Exalted. Whoever rejects any of these or claims to ignorant about them, he is kāfir.

Then there are other things about Allāh which only can be known through a text from either the Qurān or Sunnah or the sayings of the Sahābah. These are things such as Allāh descending to the lowest heaven every night, Allāh sits, Allāh laughs, Allāh has a flank and a chest, Allāh becomes amazed etc. These are things which can only be known through the texts and therefore whoever is ignorant about these does not become a kāfir until the evidence is established upon him. Many of these issues the scholars spoke of in their explanation and clarification of the <u>Sunnah,</u> which is mentioned in this book under the second testimony of **Muhammadun Rasūl-Allāh**, due to them being mentioned in the Sunnah of the Prophet (sallAllāhu 'alayhi wa sallam) or in the words of the Sahābah (radiAllāhu 'anhum).

And regarding the Tawhīd of Al-Asmā was-Sifāt there are some points which must be understood in order for the slave to fulfill this type of Tawhīd in its desired form and which prove the correct understanding and implementation of this type of Tawhīd.

1) The Tawhīd of Al-Asmā was-Sifāt and establishing the Attributes is from the muhkamāt (clear issues) and not from the mutashābihāt (unclear or doubious issues), and it is from the issues of ijmā' (scholarly agreement) and not from the issues of ikhtilāf (disagreement).

Allāh – the Exalted – said:

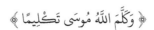

﴿ وَكَلَّمَ اللَّهُ مُوسَى تَكْلِيمًا ﴾

"And Allāh spoke to Musa directly." (An-Nisā 4:164)

In this verse the Attribute of speaking (*kallama*) is confirmed with the root of the verb (i.e. *taklīman*), and in the Arabic language that which is confirmed with the root is impossible to interpret to something else than the apparent meaning of the word. And this is a well-known fact even among the leaders of misguidance which they themselves affirm when they speak about the Arabic language.

Based upon this it is not allowed to interpret the Names and Attributes of Allāh to something else than their apparent meanings since they have been mentioned in a clear and clarified way in the Book of Allāh and the *Sunnah* of His Messenger (*sallAllāhu 'alayhi wa sallam*). Furthermore, there does not exist even one word from the *Salaf* in which they allow interpreting the Names and Attributes to something else than their apparent meanings, or to claim that they are metaphorical and should not be understood according to their apparent meanings. So this also proves that this issue is an issue of *ijmā'* in which there is no disagreement at all.

Ibn Battah (d. 387h) said:

فإن أهل الإثبات من أهل السنة يجمعون على الإقرار بالتوحيد وبالرسالة بأن الإيمان قول وعمل ونية ، وبأن القرآن كلام الله غير مخلوق ، ومجمعون على أن ما شاء الله كان ، وما لم يشأ لا يكون ، وعلى أن الله خالق الخير والشر ومقدرهما ، وعلى أن الله يرى يوم القيامة ، وعلى أن الجنة والنار مخلوقتان باقيتان ببقاء الله ، وأن الله على عرشه بائن من خلقه ، وعلمه محيط بالأشياء ، وأن الله قديم لا بداية له ولا نهاية ولا غاية ، بصفاته التامة لم يزل عالما ، ناطقا ، سميعا ، بصيرا ، حيا ، حليما ، قد علم ما يكون قبل أن يكون ، وأنه قدر المقادير قبل خلق الأشياء ، ومجمعون على إمامة أبي بكر ، وعمر ، وعثمان ، وعلي عليهم السلام ، وعلى تقديم الشيخين وعلى أن العشرة في الجنة جزما وحتما لا شك فيه ، ومجمعون على الترحم على جميع أصحاب رسول الله صلى الله عليه وسلم ، والاستغفار لهم ، ولأزواجه ، وأولاده ، وأهل بيته ، والكف عن ذكرهم إلا بخير ، والإمساك وترك النظر فيما شجر بينهم ، فهذا وأشباهه مما يطول شرحه لم يزل الناس مذ بعث الله نبيه صلى الله عليه وسلم إلى وقتنا هذا مجمعون عليه في شرق الأرض وغربها وبرها وبحرها وسهلها وجبلها يرويه العلماء رواة الآثار ، وأصحاب الأخبار ، ويعرفه الأدباء والعقلاء ، ويجمع على الإقرار به الرجال والنسوان والشيب والشبان والأحداث

، والصبيان في الحاضرة والبادية ، والعرب ، والعجم ، لا يخالف ذلك ولا ينكره ، ولا يشذ عن الإجماع
مع الناس فيه إلا رجل خبيث زائغ مبتدع محقور مهجور مدحور ، يهجره العلماء ، ويقطعه العقلاء ،
إن مرض لم يعودوه ، وإن مات لم يشهدوه.

"Verily the people of establishing (the Attributes) from the people of Sunnah are in agreement upon the acknowledgement of Tawhīd and the Risālah (Message); that the īmān is in speech, deeds and intention and that the Qurān is the Word of Allāh and not created. And they agree upon that whatever Allāh wants will be and whatever He does not want will never be, that Allāh has created both the good and evil and predestined it, that Allāh is seen on the Day of Resurrection, that Paradise and Hellfire are two creations which will remain by Allāh letting them remain, that Allāh is upon His Throne separated from His creation and His knowledge encompasses everything, that Allāh is Eternal and has no beginning, no end and (His capabilities, Deeds and Attributes have) no boundaries. With His perfect Attributes He has always been knowledgable, speaking, hearing, seeing, alive and forbearing. He knows what will be before it is, and (they agreed) that He predestined the destinies before everything was created. And they are in agreement regarding the leadership (after the death of the Prophet (sallAllāhu 'alayhi wa sallam)) of Abū Bakr, 'Umar, 'Uthmān and 'Alī (alayhim as-salām), and upon the preference of the two Shaykh (Abū Bakr and 'Umar) and that the ten are in Paradise will full certainty and no doubt regarding it. And they are in agreement regarding the tarahhum (asking for mercy) upon all the Companions of the Messenger of Allāh (sallAllāhu 'alayhi wa sallam) and asking for forgiveness for them, his wives, his children and the people of his household, and not mentioning any of these except with good while refraining from and not looking into the disputes between them. So this (i.e. what has been mentioned) and what is similar to it is from that which has a long explanation and the people since Allāh sent His Prophet (sallAllāhu 'alayhi wa sallam) until this time of ours are in agreement regarding this, in the east of the earth and in the west of it, in its seas and on its land, on its flat parts and in its mountains. The scholars and narrators of the āthār (narrations) narrate it and (so do) the people of information, the people of manners and intelligence know it, and men,

*women, old, young, children, the young people from both the city and the
desert, the Arabs and the non-Arabs all agree on this. No-one disagrees
with this, rejects it or deviates from the agreement of the people regarding
this except a dirty, deviant, innovative, hated, forsaken, repelled man
whom the scholars disassociate from and the intelligent cut off. If he is
sick they do not visit him and if he dies they do not witness his burial."*
(Al-Ibānah 'an Sharī'ah Al-Firqah An-Nājiyah)

So here it is clearly seen that the issues of the Names and Attributes
of Allāh are considered included in the issues of agreement among
both the scholars and also the regular of the Muslims.

**2) The way of *Ahlus-Sunnah* is establishing the mentioned
Attribute in the Book and the *Sunnah* according to its real
meaning, without *tahrīf* (distortion), *ta'tīl* (invalidation), *takyīf*
(explaining) and *tamthīl* (comparing).**

Allah – the Exalted – said:

$$ \lbrace \text{لَيْسَ كَمِثْلِهِ شَيْءٌ وَهُوَ السَّمِيعُ الْبَصِيرُ} \rbrace $$

**"There is nothing like Him, and He is the All-Hearer, the All-
Seer." (Ash-Shūrā 42:11)**

In this verse the negation of the four forbidden things can be found.
Because His words: **"There is nothing like Him"**, negates *takyīf*
and *tamthīl* which is that the slave explains the condition of the
Attribute of Allāh or that he compares the Attribute by saying 'A
Hand just like a hand', or 'Sight just like a sight'. And His words:
"And He is the All-Hearer, the All-Seer" negates *tahrīf* and *ta'tīl*,
which is that the slave claims that the Sight of Allāh means His
knowledge or that he completely rejects that Allah can see.

Ibn Mājishun (d. 146h) said:

اعلم – رحمك الله – أن العصمة في الدين أن تنتهي في الدين حيث انتهى بك ولا تجاوز ما قد حد

لك فإن من قوام الدين معرفة المعروف وإنكار المنكر فما بسطت عليه المعرفة وسكنت إليه الأفئدة

وذكر أصله في الكتاب والسنة وتوارثت علمه الأمة : فلا تخافن في ذكره وصفته من ربك ما وصف من نفسه عيا ؛ ولا تتكلفن بما وصف لك من ذلك قدرا. وما أنكرته نفسك ولم تجد ذكره في كتاب ربك ولا في حديث عن نبيك – من ذكر صفة ربك – فلا تكلفن علمه بعقلك ؛ ولا تصفه بلسانك ؛ واصمت عنه كما صمت الرب عنه من نفسه فإن تكلفك معرفة ما لم يصف من نفسه من نفسه مثل إنكار ما وصف منها ؛ فكما أعظمت ما جحده الجاحدون مما وصف من نفسه : فكذلك أعظم تكلف ما وصف الواصفون مما لم يصف منها.

"Know – may Allāh have mercy upon you – that the protection in the religion is stopping in religion where it stops with you and not to transgress that which has been limited for you. Because it is verily from the foundation of the religion to know the good and reject the evil. So whatever has been explained to you of knowledge and the hearts find tranquility in it – while its foundation have been mentioned in the Book and the Sunnah and the Ummah has inherited its knowledge – then do not fear any blame for mentioning it and its description from your Lord of what He has described Himself with. And do not feel burdened by what He has described to you of that. And whatever your soul rejects and you do not find the mention of it in the Book of your Lord nor in the hadīth from your Prophet (sallAllāhu 'alayhi wa sallam) – of the mention of the description of your Lord – then do not burden your mind with the knowledge of it, and do not describe it with your tongue. Remain silent about it just like the Lord has remained silent about it regarding Himself. For verily burdening yourself with the knowledge of what He has not described Himself with is just like rejecting that which He has described. So just like you consider it a big thing what the rejectors have rejected of what He has described Himself with, then likewise consider it a big thing to burden ones self with what the describers have described of that which He has not described himself with." (Al-Ibānah Al-Kubrā by Ibn Battah)

And Ibn Battah (d. 287h) said:

اعْلَمُوا رَحِمَكُمُ اللَّهُ أَنَّ مِنْ صِفَاتِ الْمُؤْمِنِينَ مِنْ أَهْلِ الْحَقِّ تَصْدِيقَ الْآثَارِ الصَّحِيحَةِ، وَتَلَقِّيَهَا بِالْقَبُولِ، وَتَرْكَ الِاعْتِرَاضِ عَلَيْهَا بِالْقِيَاسِ وَمُوَاضَعَةِ الْقَوْلِ بِالْآرَاءِ وَالْأَهْوَاءِ، فَإِنَّ الْإِيمَانَ تَصْدِيقٌ، وَالْمُؤْمِنُ هُوَ

الْمُصَدِّقُ، قَالَ اللَّهُ عَزَّ وَجَلَّ {فَلَا وَرَبِّكَ لَا يُؤْمِنُونَ حَتَّى يُحَكِّمُوكَ فِيمَا شَجَرَ بَيْنَهُمْ ثُمَّ لَا يَجِدُوا فِي
أَنْفُسِهِمْ حَرَجًا مِّمَّا قَضَيْتَ وَيُسَلِّمُوا تَسْلِيمًا} [النساء: 65] ، فَمِنْ عَلَامَاتِ الْمُؤْمِنِينَ أَنْ يَصِفُوا اللَّهَ
بِمَا وَصَفَ بِهِ نَفْسَهُ، وَبِمَا وَصَفَهُ بِهِ رَسُولُهُ صَلَّى اللَّهُ عَلَيْهِ وَسَلَّمَ مِمَّا نَقَلَتْهُ الْعُلَمَاءُ، وَرَوَاهُ الثِّقَاتُ مِنْ أَهْلِ
النَّقْلِ، الَّذِينَ هُمُ الْحُجَّةُ فِيمَا رَوَوْهُ مِنَ الْحَلَالِ وَالْحَرَامِ وَالسُّنَنِ وَالْآثَارِ، وَلَا يُقَالُ فِيمَا صَحَّ عَنْ رَسُولِ
اللَّهِ صَلَّى اللَّهُ عَلَيْهِ وَسَلَّمَ: كَيْفَ؟ وَلَا لِمَ؟ بَلْ يَتَّبِعُونَ وَلَا يَبْتَدِعُونَ، وَيُسَلِّمُونَ، وَلَا يُعَارِضُونَ، وَيَتَيَقَّنُونَ
وَلَا يَشْكُونَ وَلَا يَرْتَابُونَ

"Know – may Allah have mercy upon you – that from the characteristics of the believers among the people of the truth is to believe in the correct narrations, receiving them with acceptance and to refrain from opposing them with qiyās (analogy) and forming a view based upon opinions and desires. For verily is belief to accept and the believer is the one who accepts. Allah – 'azza wa jalla – said: **"But no, by your Lord, they can have no Faith, until they make you** (O Muhammad) **judge in all disputes between them, and find in themselves no resistance against your decisions, and accept** (them) **with full submission."** (An-Nisā 4:65) *So from the signs of the believers is that they describe Allah with what He has described Himself with and with what His Messenger (sallAllāhu 'alayhi wa sallam) has described Him with from that which the scholars have conveyed, and what the trustworthy people of narration have narrated; those who are the hujjah (argument) in what they narrated of halal, haram, the sunan and the athar. And regarding that which has been correctly narrated from the Messenger of Allah (sallAllāhu 'alayhi wa sallam) it is not said 'how?' nor 'why?', rather they follow and do not innovate, and they submit themselves and do not oppose, and they believe with certainty and they do not doubt nor are they skeptical."* (Al-Ibānah Al-Kubrā by Ibn Battah)

When it came to the Names and Attributes of Allāh the *Salaf* would say: 'Let the narration pass (i.e. accept it) just as it has been narrated' – as it will be mentioned later – and thus they became safe in their religion.

3) The Prophet (sallAllāhu alayhi wa sallam) and the Salaf would point towards the attribute as an affirmation of the real meaning of the Attribute while negating that it should be metaphorical. And this prohibits that the Attribute can be interpreted according to ijtihād, opinion and analogy or claiming that they are metaphorical.

This means that the Prophet (sallAllāhu 'alayhi wa sallam) would point at the time of speaking at – for example – his ear or his eye, or indicate with his hand or finger dependant upon which Attribute he (sallAllāhu 'alayhi wa sallam) was describing, not by way of tamthīl (comparing) rather by way of affirming the Attribute and verifying it. And this occurs many places in the ahādīth and narrations.

Abū Dāwūd (d. 275h) narrated:

حَدَّثَنَا عَلِيُّ بْنُ نَصْرٍ وَمُحَمَّدُ بْنُ يُونُسَ النَّسَائِيُّ الْمَعْنَى قَالَا حَدَّثَنَا عَبْدُ اللهِ بْنُ يَزِيدَ الْمُقْرِئُ حَدَّثَنَا حَرْمَلَةُ يَعْنِي ابْنَ عِمْرَانَ حَدَّثَنِي أَبُو يُونُسَ سُلَيْمُ بْنُ جُبَيْرٍ مَوْلَى أَبِي هُرَيْرَةَ قَالَ سَمِعْتُ أَبَا هُرَيْرَةَ يَقْرَأُ هَذِهِ الْآيَةَ إِنَّ اللَّهَ يَأْمُرُكُمْ أَنْ تُؤَدُّوا الْأَمَانَاتِ إِلَى أَهْلِهَا إِلَى قَوْلِهِ تَعَالَى سَمِيعًا بَصِيرًا قَالَ رَأَيْتُ رَسُولَ اللهِ صَلَّى اللهُ عَلَيْهِ وَسَلَّمَ يَضَعُ إِبْهَامَهُ عَلَى أُذُنِهِ وَالَّتِي تَلِيهَا عَلَى عَيْنِهِ قَالَ أَبُو هُرَيْرَةَ رَأَيْتُ رَسُولَ اللَّهِ صَلَّى اللهُ عَلَيْهِ وَسَلَّمَ يَقْرَؤُهَا وَيَضَعُ إِصْبَعَيْهِ قَالَ ابْنُ يُونُسَ قَالَ الْمُقْرِئُ يَعْنِي إِنَّ اللَّهَ سَمِيعٌ بَصِيرٌ يَعْنِي أَنَّ لِلَّهِ سَمْعًا وَبَصَرًا قَالَ أَبُو دَاوُد وَهَذَا رَدٌّ عَلَى الْجَهْمِيَّةِ

"'Alī ibn Nasr and Muhammad ibn Yūnus An-Nasāī Al-Ma'nā narrated to us and said: 'Abdullāh ibn Yazīd Al-Muqrī narrated to us (and said): Harmalah (i.e. ibn 'Imrān) narrated to us (and said): Abū Yūnus Sulaym ibn Jubayr the mawlā of Abū Hurayrah narrated to me and said: I heard Abū Hurayrah recite this verse: **"Verily Allāh commands you to return trusts to their rightful owners."** *Until His words:* **"All-Hearing, All-Seeing."** *(An-Nisā 4:58) He (Abū Hurayrah) said: 'I saw the Messenger of Allāh (sallAllāhu 'alayhi wa sallam) put his thumb upon his ear and the (finger) that follows it upon his eye.' Abū Hurayrah said: 'I saw the Messenger of Allāh (sallAllāhu 'alayhi wa sallam) recite it and put his two fingers.' Ibn Yūnus said: Al-Muqrī said: 'Verily Allāh is All-Hearing and All-Seeing means, that Allah has hearing and sight.' Abū*

72

Dāwūd said: 'And this is a refutation of the Jahmiyyah.'" (Sunan Abū Dāwūd)

Ibn Mājah (d. 273h) narrated:

حَدَّثَنَا هِشَامُ بْنُ عَمَّارٍ وَمُحَمَّدُ بْنُ الصَّبَّاحِ قَالَا حَدَّثَنَا عَبْدُ الْعَزِيزِ بْنُ أَبِي حَازِمٍ حَدَّثَنِي أَبِي عَنْ عُبَيْدِ
اللَّهِ بْنِ مِقْسَمٍ عَنْ عَبْدِ اللَّهِ بْنِ عُمَرَ قَالَ سَمِعْتُ رَسُولَ اللَّهِ صَلَّى اللَّهُ عَلَيْهِ وَسَلَّمَ وَهُوَ عَلَى الْمِنْبَرِ يَقُولُ
يَأْخُذُ الْجَبَّارُ سَمَاوَاتِهِ وَأَرَضِيهِ بِيَدِهِ وَقَبَضَ يَدَهُ فَجَعَلَ يَقْبِضُهَا وَيَبْسُطُهَا ثُمَّ يَقُولُ أَنَا الْمَلِكُ
أَيْنَ الْجَبَّارُونَ أَيْنَ الْمُتَكَبِّرُونَ قَالَ وَيَتَمَايَلُ رَسُولُ اللَّهِ صَلَّى اللَّهُ عَلَيْهِ وَسَلَّمَ عَنْ يَمِينِهِ وَعَنْ شِمَالِهِ حَتَّى
نَظَرْتُ إِلَى الْمِنْبَرِ يَتَحَرَّكُ مِنْ أَسْفَلِ شَيْءٍ مِنْهُ حَتَّى إِنِّي لَأَقُولُ أَسَاقِطٌ هُوَ بِرَسُولِ اللَّهِ صَلَّى اللَّهُ عَلَيْهِ
وَسَلَّمَ

"Hishām ibn 'Ammār and Muhammad ibn As-Sabbāh narrated to us and said: 'Abdul-'Azīz ibn Abī Hāzim narrated to us (and said): My father narrated to me, from 'Ubayd-Allāh ibn Miqsam, from 'Abdullāh ibn 'Umar who said: I heard the Messenger of Allah (sallAllāhu 'alayhi wa sallam) say while he was standing upon the pulpit: **'Al-Jabbār will take His heavens and His earths in His Hand** – *and he grasped with his hand and began to grasp and unfold it –* **and then He will say: I am Al-Jabbār, I am the King. Where are the oppressors, where are the arrogant?'** *He said: And the Messenger of Allāh (sallAllāhu 'alayhi wa sallam) was swaying from his right to his left until I saw the pulpit moving from below it until I said (to myself): Is it going to fall with the Messenger of Allāh (sallAllāhu 'alayhi wa sallam)?'"* (Sunan Ibn Mājah)

Imām Ahmad (d. 241h) said:

حَدَّثَنَا مُعَاذُ بْنُ مُعَاذٍ، نا حَمَّادُ بْنُ سَلَمَةَ، نا ثَابِتٌ الْبُنَانِيُّ، عَنْ أَنَسِ بْنِ مَالِكٍ رَضِيَ اللَّهُ عَنْهُ، عَنِ النَّبِيِّ
صَلَّى اللَّهُ عَلَيْهِ وَسَلَّمَ: " فِي قَوْلِهِ عَزَّ وَجَلَّ {فَلَمَّا تَجَلَّى رَبُّهُ لِلْجَبَلِ جَعَلَهُ دَكًّا} [الأعراف: 143] قَالَ:
قَالَ: «هَكَذَا، يَعْنِي أَخْرَجَ طَرَفَ الْخِنْصَرِ» قَالَ أَبِي: أَرَنَاهُ مُعَاذٌ فَقَالَ لَهُ حُمَيْدٌ الطَّوِيلُ: مَا تُرِيدُ إِلَى هَذَا
يَا أَبَا مُحَمَّدٍ؟ قَالَ: فَضَرَبَ صَدْرَهُ ضَرْبَةً شَدِيدَةً، وَقَالَ: مَنْ أَنْتَ يَا حُمَيْدُ وَمَا أَنْتَ يَا حُمَيْدُ؟ حَدَّثَنِي بِهِ
أَنَسُ بْنُ مَالِكٍ عَنِ النَّبِيِّ صَلَّى اللَّهُ عَلَيْهِ وَسَلَّمَ، تَقُولُ أَنْتَ مَا تُرِيدُ إِلَيْهِ؟

"Mu'ādh ibn Mu'ādh narrated to us, from Hammād ibn Salamah, from Thābit Al-Bunānī, from Anas ibn Mālik (radiAllāhu 'anhu) from the Prophet (sallAllāhu alayhi wa sallam) regarding His – 'azza wa jalla – words: **"So when his Lord appeared to the mountain He made it collapse to dust."** *(Al-A'rāf 7:143) He said: He (sallAllāhu alayhi wa sallam) said:* **"Like this (i.e. he exposed the tip of the little finger)."** *My father said: "Mu'ādh showed us how (with his little finger), so Humayd At-Tāwil said to him: 'Why are you doing like that, O Abū Muhammad?' He said: So he struck his chest with a hard strike and said: 'Who are you O Humayd and what are you O Humayd? Anas ibn Mālik narrated it to me from the Prophet (sallAllāhu alayhi wa sallam) and you are saying: Why are you doing that?"* (Musnad Imām Ahmad)

Abdullāh ibn Ahmad (d. 290h) said:

سَمِعْتُ أَبِي رَحِمَهُ اللَّهُ، ثنا يَحْيَى بْنُ سَعِيدٍ، بِحَدِيثِ سُفْيَانَ عَنِ الْأَعْمَشِ، عَنْ مَنْصُورٍ، عَنْ إِبْرَاهِيمَ، عَنْ عُبَيْدَةَ، عَنْ عَبْدِ اللَّهِ، عَنِ النَّبِيِّ صَلَّى اللهُ عَلَيْهِ وَسَلَّمَ: «أَنَّ اللَّهَ يُمْسِكُ السَّمَاوَاتِ عَلَى أُصْبُعٍ» قَالَ أَبِي رَحِمَهُ اللَّهُ: جَعَلَ يَحْيَى يُشِيرُ بِأَصَابِعِهِ وَأَرَانِي أَبِي كَيْفَ جَعَلَ يُشِيرُ بِأُصْبُعِهِ يَضَعُ أُصْبُعًا أُصْبُعًا حَتَّى أَتَى عَلَى آخِرِهَا

"I heard my father – rahimahullāh – (who said): Yahyā ibn Sa'īd narrated to us the hadīth of Sufyān, from Al-A'mash, from Mansūr, from Ibrāhīm, from 'Ubaydah, from 'Abdullāh, from the Prophet (sallAllāhu alayhi wa sallam): **"That Allāh will hold the heavens upon one Finger."** *My father – rahimahullāh – said: 'Yahyā began to show with his fingers.' And my father showed me how he began to show with his fingers putting one finger upon another finger until he came to the last of them."* (Kitāb As-Sunnah by 'Abdullāh)

So all these narrations show how the *Salaf* would affirm the real meaning of the Attribute which necessitates the impossibility of interpreting the Attributes according to something else than their actual meanings or explaining their condition without a proof.

Ad-Dārimī (d. 280h) said:

أما ما ذكرت من اجتهاد الرأي في تكييف صفات الرب؛ فإنا لا نجيز اجتهاد الرأي في كثير من الفرائض، والأحكام التي نراها بأعيننا، وتسمع في آذاننا؛ فكيف في صفات الله التي لم ترها العيون، وقصرت عنها الظنون

"Regarding what you have mentioned of ijtihād regarding the condition of the Attributes of the Lord, then we verily do not allow ijtihād of opinion in many issues of the farāid (obligatory acts of worship) and the judgments which we see with our eyes and hear with our ears. Then how (should we allow it) regarding the Attributes of the Lord which the eyes have not seen and the assumptions have been cut off from?" (An-Naqd by Ad-Dārimī)

And Ibn Mandah (d. 395h) said:

وكذلك نقول في ما تقدم من هذه الأخبار في الصفات في كتابنا هذا نرويها من غير تمثيل ولا تشبيه ولا تكييف ولا قياس ولا تأويل على ما نقلها السلف الصادق عن الصحابة الطاهرة عن المصطفى صلى الله عليه وسلم ونجهل من تكلم فيها إلا ببيان عن الرسول صلى الله عليه وسلم أو خبر صحابي حضر التنزيل

"And likewise we say regarding what has gone forth of these narrations regarding the Attributes in this book of ours; (that) we narrate them without tamthīl (giving examples), tashbīh (comparing), takyīf (explaining), qiyās (analogy) and tawīl (interpretation), according to what the truthful Salaf conveyed from the pure Sahābah from Al-Mustafā (sallAllāhu 'alayhi wa sallam). And we declare as ignorant whoever speaks about them except with a clear proof from the Messenger (sallAllāhu 'alayhi wa sallam) or a narration from a Sahābī who was present at (the time of) the revelation." (Kitāb At-Tawhīd by Ibn Mandah)

Shirk in Tawhīd *Al-Asmā was-Sifāt*

Shirk in Tawhid *Al-Asmā was-Sifāt* is making someone equal to Allāh – the Exalted – in anything from His Names and Attributes, or to describe Allāh with any of the attributes of the creation. So whoever describes someone from the creation with any of Allāh Names and Attributes while believing that this created being or thing, holds the meaning of the attribute which is specific for Allāh, then he is *mushrik* in *Al-Asmā was-Sifāt*. Such as the one who describes a person as being hearing while believing he can hear everything just like Allāh hears everything, or that he can hear from a distance or under circumstances in which a normal human-being cannot hear.

Some of the types of *shirk* that people perform, in this type of Tawhīd are the following:

* Deriving names for false deities from the Names of Allāh such as Al-Lāt from Al-Ilāh, and Al'Uzzā from Al-'Azīz.

* The belief of some **Sūfiyyah** and **Rawāfid** that theirs *shuyūkh* and *awliyā* can hear their *du'ā* (invocation) no matter where they are.

* The belief of the **Mushabbihah** who compare the Creator with the creation. An example of this is:

Allāh – the Exalted – said:

﴿ بَلْ يَدَاهُ مَبْسُوطَتَانِ يُنْفِقُ كَيْفَ يَشَاءُ ﴾

"Rather His two Hands are wide outstretched. He spends however He wills." (Al-Māidah 5:64)

Then the **Mushabbih** says: "The Hands of Allāh are like the hands of the creation", and thereby they make Allāh equal to the creation in this Attribute of Allāh.

* The *manhaj* of the **Jahmiyyah** who rejected the Names and attributes of Allāh and distorted their meanings and thereby

76

described Him – the Exalted – with deficiency and nothingness, while claiming to flee from comparing the Creator with the created. Included here are every sect who might go under a different name, but rejects and distorts the meanings of the Names and Attributes of Allāh.

Hammād ibn Zayd (d. 179h) said:

مَثَلُ الْجَهْمِيَّةِ مَثَلُ رَجُلٍ قِيلَ لَهُ: أَفِي دَارِكَ نَخْلَةٌ؟ قَالَ: نَعَمْ. قِيلَ: فَلَهَا خُوصٌ؟ قَالَ: لَا. قِيلَ: فَلَهَا سَعَفٌ. قَالَ: لَا. قِيلَ: فَلَهَا كَرَبٌ؟ قَالَ: لَا. قِيلَ: فَلَهَا جِذْعٌ؟ قَالَ: لَا. قِيلَ: فَلَهَا أَصْلٌ؟ قَالَ: لَا. قِيلَ: فَلَا نَخْلَةَ فِي دَارِكَ. هَؤُلَاءِ الْجَهْمِيَّةُ، قِيلَ لَهُمْ: لَكُمْ رَبٌّ؟ قَالُوا: نَعَمْ. قِيلَ: يَتَكَلَّمُ؟ قَالُوا: لَا. قِيلَ: فَلَهُ يَدٌ؟ قَالُوا: لَا. قِيلَ: فَلَهُ قَدَمٌ؟ قَالُوا: لَا. قِيلَ: فَلَهُ إِصْبَعٌ؟ قَالُوا: لَا. قِيلَ: فَيَرْضَى وَيَغْضَبُ؟ قَالُوا: لَا. قِيلَ: فَلَا رَبَّ لَكُمْ

"The example of the Jahmiyyah is like a man to whom it was said: 'Is there a palm tree in your residence?' He said: 'Yes.' It was said: 'Does it have leaves?' He said: 'No.' It was said: 'Does it then have fronds?' He said: 'No.' It was said: 'Does it then have a stem?' He said: 'No.' It was said: 'Does it then have a trunk?' He said: 'No.' It was said: 'Does it then have a root?' He said: 'No.' It was said: 'Then there is no palm tree in your residence.' It was said to these Jahmiyyah: 'Do you have a lord?' They said: 'Yes.' It was said: 'Does he speak?' They said: 'No.' It was said: 'Does he have a hand?' They said: 'No.' It was said: 'Does he then have a foot?' They said: 'No.' Does he then have a finger?' They said: 'No.' It was said: 'Does he become pleased or angry?' They said: 'No.' It was said: 'Then you do not have a lord.'" (Sharh Madhāhib Ahlus-Sunnah by Ibn Shāhin)

Al-Bukhārī (d. 256h) said:

وَقَالَ بَعْضُ أَهْلِ الْعِلْمِ : " إِنَّ الْجَهْمِيَّةَ هُمُ الْمُشَبِّهَةُ ، لِأَنَّهُمْ شَبَّهُوا رَبَّهُمْ بِالصَّنَمِ ، وَالْأَصَمِّ ، وَالْأَبْكَمِ الَّذِي لَا يَسْمَعُ ، وَلَا يُبْصِرُ ، وَلَا يَتَكَلَّمُ ، وَلَا يَخْلُقُ

"And some from the people of knowledge said: 'Verily the Jahmiyyah they are (in reality) the Mushabbihah[6]. Because they compared their Lord with

---

[6] Those who compares the Creator with the creation.

the statues, the deaf and the mute which cannot hear, cannot see and cannot speak and cannot create." (Khalq Af'āl Al-'Ibād p. 111)

And Ad-Dārimī (d. 280h) said regarding the Jahmiyyah:

ونكفرهم أيضا بالمشهور مِنْ كفرهم، أَنَّهُم لا يُثْبِتُونَ لله تبارك وتعالى وجهًا ولا سمعًا ولا بصرًا ولا عِلْمًا ولا كلامًا ولا صِفَةً، إلا بِتَأْوِيلِ ضُلَّالٍ افْتَضَحُوا وتَبَيَّنَتْ عَوَرَاتُهُم، يقولون: سمعُهُ، وبَصَرُهُ، وعِلْمُهُ، وكَلَامُهُ؛ بمعنًى واحدٍ، وهو بنفسه في كل مكان، وفي كل بيت مغلق، وصُنْدُوقٍ مُقْفَل، قد أحاطتْ به -في دعواهُم- حِيطَاتُها وَأَغْلَاقُهَا وأَقْفَالُها، فإلَى اللهِ نَبْرَأُ من إلهٍ هذِه صِفَتُهُ، وهَذَا أيضًا مَذْهَبٌ واضِحٌ في إِكْفَارِهِم.

"And we also declare takfīr upon them due to what is well-known of their kufr; that they do not establish (i.e. believe in) for Allāh – the Exalted – a Face, Hearing, Seeing, Knowledge, Speech nor (any) attribute, except with the interpretation of misguided people who have been exposed and their mistakes have become clear. They say: 'His Hearing, Seeing, Knowledge and Speech are with the same meaning. And He Himself is everywhere, in every closed house and every locked box.' Verily did – according to their claim – its walls, its bars and its locks surround Him. So to Allāh we declare ourselves free from an ilāh who has this description. And this is also a clear reason for declaring takfīr upon them." (Ar-Rad 'alā Al-Jahmiyyah by Ad-Dārimī p.182)

Ad-Dārimī (d. 280h) also said when speaking about Bishr Al-Marīsī who was one of the leaders of the Jahmiyyah:

والعجب من المريسي صاحب هذا المذهب أنه يدعي توحيد الله بمثل هذا المذهب وما أشبهه وقد عطل جميع صفات الواحد الأحد في قياس مذهبه أن واجده الذي يوحنه إله مجدع منقوص مشوه مشيج مقصوص لا تتم وحدانيته إلا بمخلوق ولا يستغني عن مخلوق من الكلام والعلم والاسم ، ويلك إنما الموحد الصادق في توحيده الذي يوحد الله بكماله وبجميع صفاته في علمه وكلامه وقبضه وبسطه وهبوطه وارتفاعه الغني عن جميع خلقه بجميع صفاته من النفس والوجه والسمع والبصر واليدين والعلم والكلام والقدرة والمشيئة والسلطان القابض الباسط المعز المذل القيوم الحي الفعال لما يشاء هذا

إلى التوحيد أقرب من هذا الذي يوحد إلها مجدعا منقوصا مقصوصا لو كان عبدا على هذه الصفة لم

يكن يساوي تمرتين فكيف يكون مثله إلها للعالمين تعالى الله عن هذه الصفة

"And the strange thing from Al-Marisi – the owner of this madhhab – is that he claims (to believe in) the Tawhid of Allah with this madhhab and what is similar to it, while he verily invalidated all the Attributes of Al-Wahid Al-Ahad. So he claimed according to the measurements of his madhhab that the one whom he worships as an ilah is limbless, imperfect, disfigured and incomplete and that his Oneness is not fulfilled except through a created being, nor is he free of needing created things such as speech, knowledge and name. Woe to you, verily the truthful muwahhid in his Tawhid is the one who unifies Allah in His Perfection and in all of His Attributes, in His knowledge, His speech, His grasp, His outstretch (of Hands), His descent, His ascension; the One who is in no need of His creation in all of His Attributes among the Being, the Face, the Hearing, the Seeing, the two Hands, the Knowledge, the Speech, the Capability, the Mashiah, the Authority, the Withholder, the Extender, the Bestower of honor, the Humiliator, the Living, the Subsisting and the One who does whatever He wants. This person is closer to Tawhid than this person who unifies a limbless, imperfect and incomplete god; if he were a slave with this description then he would not have been worth two dates. So how can someone similar to it be the god of all the worlds? Exalted is Allah far above this description." (Naqd Ad-Dārimī)

Other nullifiers which have not been mentioned

There are a few nullifier of Islām which has not yet been mentioned. These are:

* *Al-Istihzā* (mocking) and *As-Sabb* (cursing). This includes mocking, belittling or cursing at anything from the religion of Islām.

Allāh – the Exalted – said:

﴿ وَلَئِن سَأَلْتَهُمْ لَيَقُولُنَّ إِنَّمَا كُنَّا نَخُوضُ وَنَلْعَبُ قُلْ أَبِاللَّهِ وَآيَاتِهِ وَرَسُولِهِ كُنتُمْ تَسْتَهْزِئُونَ ٦٥ لَا تَعْتَذِرُوا قَدْ كَفَرْتُم بَعْدَ إِيمَانِكُمْ ﴾

"And if you asked them, they will verily say: 'We were only conversing and playing.' Say: 'Is it Allāh, His verses and His Messenger that you were mocking? Do not come with excuses, you have verily committed *kufr* after your *īmān*." (At-Tawbah 9:65-66)

And He – the Exalted said:

﴿ وَإِذَا عَلِمَ مِنْ آيَاتِنَا شَيْئًا اتَّخَذَهَا هُزُوًا أُولَٰئِكَ لَهُمْ عَذَابٌ مُهِينٌ ﴾

"And when he knows something of Our verses he makes fun of it. For those there is a humiliating punishment." (Al-Jāthiyah 45:9)

Ishāq ibn Rāhūyah (d. 238h) said:

أجمع المسلمون على أن من سبَّ الله، أو سبَّ رسولَه – صلى الله عليه وسلم – أو دفع شيئاً مما أنزل الله عزَّ وجلَّ، أو قتل نبيًّا من أنبياء الله، أنَّه كافر بذلك وإنْ كان مُقِرًّا بكلِّ ما أنزل الله.

"The Muslims have agreed upon that the one who curses at Allāh, or curses at His Messenger (sallAllāhu 'alayhi wa sallam), or denies anything from what Allāh – 'azza wa jalla – has revealed, or kills a prophet among the prophets of Allāh, that he is kāfir by doing that, even if he

acknowledges everything which Allāh has revealed." (At-Tamhīd by Ibn 'Abdul-Barr)

* *As-Sihr* (black magic), which is the agreement between a magician and a *shaytān* (a devil among the *jinn*), that the magician will perform some acts of worship for the *shaytān* who in return will help him or obey him in what he demands from him.

Allāh – the Exalted – said:

﴿ وَاتَّبَعُوا مَا تَتْلُو الشَّيَاطِينُ عَلَى مُلْكِ سُلَيْمَانَ وَمَا كَفَرَ سُلَيْمَانُ وَلَكِنَّ الشَّيَاطِينَ
كَفَرُوا يُعَلِّمُونَ النَّاسَ السِّحْرَ وَمَا أُنْزِلَ عَلَى الْمَلَكَيْنِ بِبَابِلَ هَارُوتَ وَمَارُوتَ ﴾

"And they followed what the *shayātīn* recited in the reign of Sulaymān. And Sulaymān did not disbelieve, rather the *shayātīn* disbelieved. They taught the people magic and what was revealed to the two angels in Babel, Hārūt and Mārūt."
(Al-Baqarah 2:102)

And the Prophet (*sallAllāhu 'alayhi wa sallam*) said:

ليس منا من تطيَّر أو تُطيِّر له، أو تَكَهَّن أو تُكُهِّن له، أو سَحَر أو سُحِر له، ومن أتى كاهنًا فصدقه
بما يقول، فقد كفر بما أنزل على محمد صلى الله عليه وسلم

"He is not from us the one who gives omens or has omens done for him, or he foretells or someone foretells for him, or he performs magic or magic is performed for him. And whoever goes to a foreteller and believes in what he says, then he has committed kufr in what was revealed to Muhammad (sallAllāhu 'alayhi wa sallam)." (Al-Bazzār – with a good *isnād*)

In order to achieve the cooperation of the *shaytān* the magician has to perform deed such as asking the *shayātīn* for help, invoking them in things which they are not capable of, utter words of *kufr* in order to please them, slaughter for them, or to mock some of the things which Allāh has ordered us to venerate – such as the Qurān and other things – all of which is clear *kufr* from the one performing it. Add to these things if the one doing it or has it done for him believes

81

that the *shayatin* can benefit or harm without the permission of Allah or that they know the unseen.

So whoever performs magic according to what is described above, or has magic performed for him or is pleased with any of what has been mentioned, then he is *kafir* according to what has already gone forth of evidences and principles of the religion.

* *Al-I'rad* (turning away), which is the *kufr* that consist of turning away from learning the religion and performing what it necessitates and requires of the slave.

Allah – the Exalted – said:

﴿ وَالَّذِينَ كَفَرُوا عَمَّا أُنذِرُوا مُعْرِضُونَ ﴾

"And those who disbelieve turn away from what they were warned against." (Al-Ahqaf 46:3)

At-Tabari (d. 310h) said in his *tafsir* of the verse:

وَقَوْله : { وَالَّذِينَ كَفَرُوا عَمَّا أُنذِرُوا مُعْرِضُونَ } يَقُولُ تَعَالَى ذِكْره : وَالَّذِينَ جَحَدُوا وَحْدَانِيَّة اللَّه عَنْ إِنْذَار اللَّه إِيَّاهُمْ مُعْرِضُونَ , لَا يَتَّعِظُونَ بِهِ , وَلَا يَتَفَكَّرُونَ فَيَعْتَبِرُونَ

"And His words: "And those who disbelieve turn away from what they were warned against." He – Exalted is His mention – says: 'And those who rejected the Oneness of Allah are turning away from the warning of Allah to them. They do not take a warning, nor do they think, nor do they take a lesson." (Tafsir At-Tabari)

And He – the Exalted – said:

﴿ فَلَا صَدَّقَ وَلَا صَلَّى ۞ وَلَـٰكِنْ كَذَّبَ وَتَوَلَّى ﴾

"So he did not believe nor did he pray. Rather he rejected and he turned away." (Al-Qiyamah 75:31-32)

And the Prophet (*sallAllahu 'alayhi wa sallam*) said:

82

والذي نَفْسُ مُحَمَّدٍ بِيَدِهِ، لا يَسْمَعُ بِي أَحَدٌ مِن هذِهِ الأُمَّةِ يَهُودِيٌّ، ولا نَصْرانِيٌّ، ثُمَّ يَمُوتُ ولَمْ يُؤْمِنْ بِالَّذِي أُرْسِلْتُ به، إلَّا كانَ مِن أصْحابِ النَّارِ.

"By the One whose Hand Muhammad's soul is in, no-one from this Ummah, neither a Jew nor a Christian hears about me, and then do not believe in what I have been sent with, except that he is from the people of the fire." (Sahīh Muslim)

Everyone today who does not know the fundamental principles of Islām, nor does he perform the obligatory acts of worship due to not having sought to learn it, then he is not considered to be ignorant because the knowledge is present and accessible, rather he is considered to be among those who turned away from learning the religion of Allah, which is *kufr*.

The second testimony: *Muhammadun Rasūl-Allāh*

The testimony of **Muhammadun Rasūl-Allāh** includes the belief in
the Prophethood of Muhammad ibn 'Abdullāh ibn 'Abdul-
Muttalib ibn Hāshim ibn 'Abdi-Manāf ibn Qusayy ibn Kilāb ibn
Murrah ibn Ka'b ibn Luay ibn Ghālib ibn Fihr ibn Mālik ibn An-
Nadr ibn Kinānah ibn Khuzaymah ibn Mudrikah ibn Ilyās ibn
Mudar ibn Nazār ibn Ma'ad ibn 'Adnān, and 'Adnān is among the
children of Ismā'īl ibn Ibrāhīm (*alyhimā as-salām*), and that he
(*sallAllāhu 'alayhi wa sallam*) is the Messenger of Allāh. This
includes:

1. The general belief in his (*sallAllāhu 'alayhi wa sallam*)
   Message to all created beings, both *jinn* and mankind.
2. The belief in that he (*sallAllāhu 'alayhi wa sallam*) is the last
   messenger and that his Message is the seal of all the
   messages.
3. The belief in that his (*sallAllāhu 'alayhi wa sallam*) Message
   abrogates all previous messages and legislations.
4. The belief in that he (*sallAllāhu 'alayhi wa sallam*) conveyed
   the Message in its entirety, he fulfilled the *amānah* (trust), he
   gave advice to his *Ummah* until he left it on a clear path
   whose night is like its day.
5. The belief in that he (*sallAllāhu 'alayhi wa sallam*) is protected
   in what he conveys from Allāh the Exalted.
6. The belief in what he (*sallAllāhu 'alayhi wa sallam*) deserves
   of rights, such as loving him, respecting him, honoring him
   and holding him at high esteem.
7. The belief that he (*sallAllāhu 'alayhi wa sallam*) is dead and
   buried in Madīnah.

The testimony of **Muhammadun Rasūl-Allāh** furthermore includes
believing in everything which he (*sallAllāhu 'alayhi wa sallam*)
informed about, and the obedience of him in what he ordered. This
is because whatever the Messenger of Allāh (*sallAllāhu 'alayhi wa
sallam*) has informed about, regarding Allāh, His religion or the

unseen, then this is revelation from Allāh the Exalted, based upon His – the Exalted – words:

$$\lgroup\ وَالنَّجْمِ إِذَا هَوَى ، مَا ضَلَّ صَاحِبُكُمْ وَمَا غَوَى ، وَمَا يَنْطِقُ عَنِ الْهَوَى ، إِنْ هُوَ إِلَّا وَحْيٌ\ يُوحَى\ \rgroup$$

"By the star when it descends. Your companion (i.e. Muhammad) **has not gone astray nor has he erred. And he does not speak from** (his own) **desire. Rather it is revelation being revealed."**
(An-Najm 53:1-4)

So whatever he (sallAllāhu 'alayhi wa sallam) has informed about and established, then it is obligatory to establish it and believe in it, and whatever he negated, then it is obligatory to negate it. Thus it is obligatory for the believers to establish and believe in everything which the Messenger of Allāh (sallAllāhu 'alayhi wa sallam) informed about, regarding the Names and Attributes of Allāh. Likewise they must negate for Him whatever he (sallAllāhu 'alayhi wa sallam) negated for Allāh, such as similarity with the created being, and in this way they become free from ta'tīl (invalidating), takyīf (explaining), tashbīh (comparing) and tahrīf (distorting).

Furthermore there is no legislation, except the legislation which the Messenger of Allāh (sallAllāhu 'alayhi wa sallam) came with. Thus, accepting another legislation than the Sharī'ah is a breach of both the testimony of Lā ilāha illa Allāh and the testimony of Muhammadun Rasūl-Allāh. Allāh – the Exalted – says:

$$\lgroup\ فَلَا وَرَبِّكَ لَا يُؤْمِنُونَ حَتَّى يُحَكِّمُوكَ فِيمَا شَجَرَ بَيْنَهُمْ ثُمَّ لَا يَجِدُوا فِي أَنْفُسِهِمْ حَرَجًا مِمَّا\ قَضَيْتَ وَيُسَلِّمُوا تَسْلِيمًا\ \rgroup$$

"But no, by your Lord, they can have no Faith, until they make you (O Muhammad) **judge in all disputes between them, and find in themselves no resistance against your decisions, and accept** (them) **with full submission."** (An-Nisā 4:65)

So the true believers believe in the Messenger (*sallAllāhu 'alayhi wa sallam*) in what he has informed about Allāh, the Last Day, Islām, Īmān and Ihsān, and they obey him (*sallAllāhu 'alayhi wa sallam*) in what he has ordered and forbidden, they consider allowed what he has allowed and consider forbidden what he has forbidden, and they adopt the true religion based upon the Qurān and the *Sunnah*. Because there is no good except that the Messenger of Allāh (*sallAllāhu 'alayhi wa sallam*) has ordered it and no evil except that he forbade it.

The *ahādīth* of the Messenger of Allāh (*sallAllāhu 'alayhi wa sallam*) are referred to as the **Sunnah.** In the *Sunnah* issues from both the *usūl* (fundamental principles) of the religion and the *furū'* (branches) of the religion can be found. And no-one is saved from *bida'* (innovation) except the person who bases his religion upon the Qurān and the *Sunnah*.

After the death of the Messenger (*sallAllāhu 'alayhi wa sallam*), the groups of innovation such as the Khawārij, the Qadariyyah, the Murjiah, the Rāfidah, the Jahmiyyah and the Mu'tazilah emerged, and the people of truth became distinguished by a name indicating that they remained upon what the Messenger of Allāh (*sallAllāhu 'alayhi wa sallam*) came with; this name was **Ahlul-Hadīth** (the people of *hadīth*) or **Ahlus-Sunnah**. And the responsibility of aligning ones belief with the *understanding* of the *Salaf* is an individual obligation which no-one is free from adhering to.

The nullifiers of *Muhammadun Rasūl-Allāh*

Among that which nullifies and invalidates the testimony of *Muhammadun Rasūl-Allāh* are the following:

* Cursing him, swearing at him, belittling him and mocking him (*sallAllāhu 'alayhi wa sallam*). Included in this is speaking about him (*sallAllāhu 'alayhi wa sallam*) in a negative way, such as saying: "He was busy with women" or "I don't know if he was sane or insane" or other similar statements that has a negative connotation or mentioning some negative words in which the Prophet (*sallAllāhu 'alayhi wa sallam*) is intended without mentioning his (*sallAllāhu 'alayhi wa sallam*) name or title directly.

Allāh – the Exalted – said:

﴿ وَمِنْهُمُ الَّذِينَ يُؤْذُونَ النَّبِيَّ وَيَقُولُونَ هُوَ أُذُنٌ قُلْ أُذُنُ خَيْرٍ لَكُمْ يُؤْمِنُ بِاللَّهِ وَيُؤْمِنُ لِلْمُؤْمِنِينَ وَرَحْمَةٌ لِلَّذِينَ آمَنُوا مِنْكُمْ وَالَّذِينَ يُؤْذُونَ رَسُولَ اللَّهِ لَهُمْ عَذَابٌ أَلِيمٌ ﴾

"And among them are those who harm the Prophet and they say he is *udhun* (a person who believes everything he hears). Say: '(He is) a good *udhun* for you. He believes in Allāh and believes the believers and (he is) a mercy to those who believe among them.' And those who harm the Messenger of Allāh will have a painful punishment." (At-Tawbah 9:61)

At-Tabarī (d. 310h) mentioned in his *tafsīr* of the verse:

حَدَّثَنَا ابْنُ حُمَيْدٍ قَالَ : حَدَّثَنَا سَلَمَةُ عَنِ ابْنِ إِسْحَاقَ قَالَ : ذَكَرَ اللَّهُ غِشَّهُمْ يَعْنِي : الْمُنَافِقِينَ وَأَذَاهُمْ لِلنَّبِيِّ – صَلَّى اللَّهُ عَلَيْهِ وَسَلَّمَ – فَقَالَ : (وَمِنْهُمُ الَّذِينَ يُؤْذُونَ النَّبِيَّ وَيَقُولُونَ هُوَ أُذُنٌ) الْآيَةَ . وَكَانَ الَّذِي يَقُولُ تِلْكَ الْمَقَالَةَ ، فِيمَا بَلَغَنِي نَبْتَلُ بْنُ الْحَارِثِ أَحُو بَنِي عَمْرِو بْنِ عَوْفٍ ، وَفِيهِ نَزَلَتْ هَذِهِ الْآيَةُ ، وَذَلِكَ أَنَّهُ قَالَ: " إِنَّمَا مُحَمَّدٌ أُذُنٌ ! مَنْ حَدَّثَهُ شَيْئًا صَدَّقَهُ! " يَقُولُ اللَّهُ : (قُلْ أُذُنُ خَيْرٍ لَكُمْ) أَيْ : يَسْمَعُ الْخَيْرَ وَيُصَدِّقُ بِهِ .

"Ibn Humayd narrated to us and said: Salamah narrated to us from Ibn Ishāq who said: 'Allāh mentioned their betrayal – i.e. the munafiqūn – and their harm towards the Prophet (sallAllāhu 'alayhi wa sallam) when He

said: "And among them are those who harm the Prophet and they say he is *udhun* (a person who believes everything he hears)." *Until the rest of the verse. And the one said these words, according to what has reached me was Nabtal ibn Al-Hārith the brother of Banū 'Amr ibn 'Awf, and regarding him the verse was revealed. And this was because he said: 'Verily Muhammad is udhun (an ear). Whoever narrates something to him then he believes in him.' Allah says:* "Say: '(He is) a good *udhun* for you." *This means: He hears what is good and believes in it."* (Tafsīr At-Tabarī)

Another thing which is included in mocking the Prophet (*sallAllāhu 'alayhi wa sallam*) – and this is applicable for all of the prophets of Allāh (*alayhim as-salām*) – is playing, acting and portraying him (or them) in tv-movies and series. This is from the angle of belittling him. Because when an actor tries to portray any of the prophets he decreases them to his own lowly state while they (*alayhim as-salām*) are free from that.

The Prophet (*sallAllāhu 'alayhi wa sallam*) said:

لَا تَسُبُّوا أَصْحَابِي، لَا تَسُبُّوا أَصْحَابِي، فَوَالَّذِي نَفْسِي بِيَدِهِ لَوْ أَنَّ أَحَدَكُمْ أَنْفَقَ مِثْلَ أُحُدٍ ذَهَبًا، مَا أَدْرَكَ مُدَّ أَحَدِهِمْ، وَلَا نَصِيفَهُ.

"Do not swear at my companions. Do not swear at my companions. Because by the One in whose Hand my soul is in, if one of you spent an amount of gold at the size of (the mountain of) Uhud, then this would not be equal to the mudd[7] of any of them, and not even the half of it." (Sahīh Muslim)

If this is the comparison between the *Sahābah* and normal people, then how about someone portraying to be a prophet of Allāh, and then after that he goes and plays another role as a criminal or a homosexual or a sinner, or he returns to his own persona which

---

[7] The amount which fits in two hands gathered. So the *mudd* of gold of the *Sahābah* spent for Allāh is better than the amount of gold equal to the mountain of Uhud of anyone other than them spent for Allāh.

might be a sinning corrupt *kāfir* who has no right of being compared in any way with any of the prophets of Allāh (*alayhim as-salām*). This is the exact opposite of respecting them, honoring them and venerating them.

Allāh – the Exalted – said:

﴿ فَالَّذِينَ آمَنُوا بِهِ وَعَزَّرُوهُ وَنَصَرُوهُ وَاتَّبَعُوا النُّورَ الَّذِى أُنْزِلَ مَعَهُ أُولَئِكَ هُمُ الْمُفْلِحُونَ ﴾

"So those who believe and honored him (i.e. Muhammad) **and gave support to him and followed the Light which was revealed with him, these are the successful."** (Al-A'rāf 7:157)

And He – the Exalted – said:

﴿ لِتُؤْمِنُوا بِاللَّهِ وَرَسُولِهِ وَتُعَزِّرُوهُ وَتُوَقِّرُوهُ وَتُسَبِّحُوهُ بُكْرَةً وَأَصِيلًا ﴾

"In order for you to believe in Allāh and His Messenger, and honor him and respect him (i.e. the Messenger), **and praise Him** (i.e. Allāh) **in the morning and afternoon."** (Al-Fath 48:9)

So the Prophet (*sallAllāhu 'allayhi wa sallam*) is not like any man in history which can be portrayed in movies or series, nor are his words like the words of others that can be accepted or rejected as a person wish. Rather he is the Messenger and Prophet of Allāh (*sallAllāhu 'alayhi wa sallam*) and is not to be treated like an ordinary man.

Allāh – the Exalted – said:

﴿ لَا تَجْعَلُوا دُعَاءَ الرَّسُولِ بَيْنَكُمْ كَدُعَاءِ بَعْضِكُمْ بَعْضًا ﴾

"Do not make (your) **calling of the Messenger among you as the way you call each other."** (An-Nūr 24:63)

Mujāhid (d. after 104h) said regarding this verse:

أَمَرَهُمْ أَنْ يَدْعُوا يَا رَسُول الله , فِي لِين وَتَوَاضُع , وَلَا يَقُولُوا يَا مُحَمَّد , فِي جَهُّم.

"He ordered them to call him (by saying): 'O Messenger of Allāh', in softness and humility, and that they should not say: 'O Muhammad', while frowning." (Tafsīr At-Tabarī)

And Qatādah (d. 118h) said:

أَمَرَهُمْ أَنْ يُفَخِّمُوهُ وَيُشَرِّفُوهُ

"He ordered them to venerate him and hold him in high esteem (or honor)." (Tafsīr At-Tabarī)

Allāh has blessed the prophets in everything, from their bodies to their manners and their knowledge. So it is not possible for anyone – whether this is said while joking, being serious or acting – to say: 'I am this or this prophet', without him due to his faulty nature and low status compared to them, is belittling the prophet.

* Following a prophet or messenger after him, such as Musaylamah Al-Kadhdhāb, Al-Aswad Al-'Ansī or Ghulām Ahmad. Or accepting a legislation other than his legislation, either an abrogated legislation, or a newly invented legislation. Or that he claims that he or anyone else is exempt from following the legislation of Muhammad (sallAllāhu 'alayhi wa sallam).

Allāh – the Exalted – said:

﴿ فَلَا وَرَبِّكَ لَا يُؤْمِنُونَ حَتَّى يُحَكِّمُوكَ فِيمَا شَجَرَ بَيْنَهُمْ ثُمَّ لَا يَجِدُوا فِي أَنْفُسِهِمْ حَرَجًا مِمَّا قَضَيْتَ وَيُسَلِّمُوا تَسْلِيمًا ﴾

"But no, by your Lord, they can have no Faith, until they make you (O Muhammad) **judge in all disputes between them, and find in themselves no resistance against your decisions, and accept** (them) **with full submission."** (An-Nisā 4:65)

* Believing that he (sallAllāhu 'alayhi wa sallam) is not dead, or that he possesses aspects of divinity through which he can have affect upon the affairs from his grave, such as knowing the unseen, that he can benefit or harm, or that he hears and answers invocations.

Allah – the Exalted – said:

﴿ إِنَّكَ مَيِّتٌ وَإِنَّهُمْ مَيِّتُونَ ﴾

"You will verily die, and they will verily (also) die."
(Az-Zumar 39:30)

And He – the Exalted – said:

﴿ وَمَا مُحَمَّدٌ إِلَّا رَسُولٌ قَدْ خَلَتْ مِنْ قَبْلِهِ الرُّسُلُ أَفَإِنْ مَاتَ أَوْ قُتِلَ انْقَلَبْتُمْ عَلَى أَعْقَابِكُمْ
وَمَنْ يَنْقَلِبْ عَلَى عَقِبَيْهِ فَلَنْ يَضُرَّ اللَّهَ شَيْئًا وَسَيَجْزِى اللَّهُ الشَّاكِرِينَ ﴾

**"And Muhammad is nothing more than a messenger. Verily have
the messengers before him passed away. Then if he dies or is
killed will you then turn back on your heels? And whoever turns
back on his heels he does not harm Allah at all. And Allah will
reward the grateful."** (Āli 'Imrān 3:144)

And the Prophet (sallAllāhu 'alayhi wa sallam) said:

لَا تُطْرُونِي كَمَا أَطْرَتِ النَّصَارَى ابْنَ مَرْيَمَ، فَإِنَّمَا أَنَا عَبْدُهُ، فَقُولُوا عَبْدُ اللهِ وَرَسُولُهُ

*"Do not praise me with more than I am like the Christians praised
the Son of Maryam with more than he was. I am verily His slave,
so say: the slave of Allāh and His Messenger."* (Sahīh Al-Bukhārī)

91

The *Sunnah* and its rules

The term *Sunnah* covers over all issues in the religion, the evidences of which have come in the *hadīth* of the Messenger of Allāh (*sallAllāhu 'alayhi wa sallam*). As for this book, then it is confined to issues of *'aqīdah*. Nevertheless the rules of the *Sunnah* are general for all issues, and it is the **correct way of dealing with the *hadīth*** from the Prophet (*sallAllāhu 'alayhi wa sallam*). As for these rules then they are:

* The *Sunnah* is the *tafsīr* (interpretation) of the Qurān.

In order to remain upon *Sunnah* in the *'aqīdah* and protect one's self from *bida'* (innovation, which is the opposite of *Sunnah*) a person must interpret the Qurān with the *Sunnah*. The reason for this being mentioned is, that most of the people of innovation took verses from the Qurān and interpreted it in their own way while ignoring the correct *ahādīth* which was narrated on the subject, and by this they fell in innovation in their beliefs.[8]

Qatādah (d. 118h) said:

قُلْتُ يَا أُمَّ الْمُؤْمِنِينَ (عائشة) أَنْبِئِينِي عَنْ خُلُقِ رَسُولِ اللَّهِ صَلَّى اللَّهُ عَلَيْهِ وَسَلَّمَ قَالَتْ أَلَسْتَ تَقْرَأُ الْقُرْآنَ
قُلْتُ بَلَى قَالَتْ فَإِنَّ خُلُقَ نَبِيِّ اللَّهِ صَلَّى اللَّهُ عَلَيْهِ وَسَلَّمَ كَانَ الْقُرْآنَ

"I said to the Mother of the believers ('Āishah): 'Inform me about the manners (or behaviour) of the Messenger of Allāh (sallAllāhu 'alayhi wa sallam).' She said: 'Do you not read the Qurān?' I said: 'Yes.' She said: 'Verily the manners of the Prophet (sallAllāhu 'alayhi wa sallam) were the Qurān." (Sahīh Muslim)

* To adhere to what the Companions of the Messenger of Allāh (*sallAllāhu 'alayhi wa sallam*) were upon (*radiAllāhu 'anhum*).

This is because they are those who understood him (*sallAllāhu 'alayhi wa sallam*) best. So whoever wants to know how a *hadīth*

---

[8] Examples of this will be given later in this book.

92

should be understood and applied, then he should go to the sayings of the *Sahābah* (*radiAllāhu 'anhum*) and their students from the *tābi'ūn*, as this previously have been explained in the opening of this book.

The Prophet (*sallAllāhu 'alayhi wa sallam*) said:

فَإِنَّهُ مَنْ يَعِشْ مِنْكُمْ فَسَيَرَى اخْتِلَافًا كَثِيرًا، فَعَلَيْكُمْ بِسُنَّتِي وَسُنَّةِ الْخُلَفَاءِ الرَّاشِدِينَ الْمَهْدِيِينَ، عَضُّوا عَلَيْهَا بِالنَّوَاجِذِ، وَإِيَّاكُمْ وَمُحْدَثَاتِ الْأُمُورِ؛ فَإِنَّ كُلَّ بِدْعَةٍ ضَلَالَةٌ

"Verily, whoever among you that will live (after me) will verily see a lot of disagreement. So it is (obligatory) upon you to follow my Sunnah, and the Sunnah of the righteous and guided caliphs. Bite it with your molar teeth (i.e. grasp firmly onto it and don't let go). And be aware of every newly invented matter. Because every bid'ah (innovation) is misguidance." (At-Tirmidhī, Ibn Mājah, Abū Dāwūd and Imām Ahmad with a small difference – *thābit sahīh*)

* Leaving any opinion which opposes or contradicts the *hadīth*.

Anything which opposes or contradicts the meaning of a *hadīth* is an innovation. From the rights of the Messenger of Allāh, is to believe in him (*sallAllāhu 'alayhi wa sallam*) and believe in that he perfectly conveyed his Message in its entirety and that he did not leave anything unclear. Therefore whoever follows something which does not originate from the Messenger of Allāh (*sallAllāhu 'alayhi wa sallam*) then he is following innovations, lusts and desires. And this necessitates the claim the The Prophet (*sallAllāhu 'alayhi wa sallam*) has betrayed this Ummah, by not informing them about something from the religion.

Imām Mālik (d. 179h) said:

مَنْ أَحْدَثَ فِي هَذِهِ الْأُمَّةِ شَيْئًا لَمْ يَكُنْ عَلَيْهِ سَلَفُهَا فَقَدْ زَعَمَ أَنَّ رَسُولَ اللهِ صَلَّى اللهُ عَلَيْهِ وَسَلَّمَ خَانَ الدِّينَ ؛ لِأَنَّ اللهَ يَقُولُ : (الْيَوْمَ أَكْمَلْتُ لَكُمْ دِينَكُمْ) فَمَا لَمْ يَكُنْ يَوْمَئِذٍ دِينًا لَا يَكُونُ الْيَوْمَ دِينًا

"Whoever invents anything in this Ummah which our Salaf (predecessors) was not upon, then he has verily claimed that the Messenger of Allāh (sallAllāhu 'alayhi wa sallam) has betrayed the religion. Because Allāh says: "Today I have fulfilled for you your religion." (Al-Māidah 5:3) *So whatever was not from the religion at that time will never be from the religion today."* (Kitāb Al-I'tisām by Ash-Shātibī)

* There is no *qiyās* (analogy) in the *Sunnah*, nor are similitudes (or examples) put forth with it. The opinion or that which the intellect or desires leans towards are not taken into consideration when it comes to accepting the *Sunnah*. Rather it is solely to be followed and desires are left in it.

The *hadīth* is an undisputed source of legislation in the religion of Islām. One cannot, nor has the right to come with an example or an analogy from his opinion that renders the meaning of the *hadīth* invalid or inapplicable. The same way the *Sharī'ah* is not put up to a democratic voting for the people to chose it (because it is obligatory whether the people want it or not), then the *Sunnah* is not up for measuring or evaluation by anyone, whoever this might be. That which the *hadīth* states according to how the *Salaf* understood and applied it, is the only correct way of understanding and applying the *hadīth*, and that which opposes this is innovation and misguidance.

* Leaving the people of innovation and discussing with them about the beliefs, and in general leaving discussion, arguments and disputes in the religion.

The *Salaf* would consider it from the principles of the *Sunnah* itself that a person would leave discussion and arguing in the religion, even if the person himself is upon the right path. This is once again due to the fact that no-one from the people of *Sunnah* and *Jamā'ah* have ever debated, argued or discussed regarding the *Sunnah*. Rather all of them – from the *Sahābah* (*radiAllāhu 'anhum*) and until the end of what was of scholars of the *Salaf* – have submitted to the meaning of the *hadīth* without debating, arguing and discussing, all while following the above mentioned princples. This religion is based upon submission – thus the name Al-Islām (Submission) – and therefore contradicting this by indulging in discussions and arguing is an innovation not performed by the *Salaf*. Furthermore opening the door to discussing and debating the meaning of the *ahādīth* only opens the door to misguidance and mistakes, while submitting and remaining quiet is the way of staying safe.

Imām Ahmad (d. 241h) said:

أُصُولُ اَلسُّنَّةِ عِنْدَنَا: اَلتَّمَسُّكُ بِمَا كَانَ عَلَيْهِ أَصْحَابُ رَسُولِ اَللَّهِ ﷺ وَالْاِقْتِدَاءُ بِهِمْ، وَتَرْكُ اَلْبِدَعِ، وَكُلُّ بِدْعَةٍ فَهِيَ ضَلَالَةٌ، وَتَرْكُ اَلْخُصُومَاتِ، وَالْجُلُوسِ مَعَ أَصْحَابِ اَلْأَهْوَاءِ، وَتَرْكُ اَلْمِرَاءِ وَالْجِدَالِ وَالْخُصُومَاتِ فِي اَلدِّينِ.

"The fundamental principles of Sunnah for us are: Adhering to that which the Companions of the Messenger of Allāh (sallAllāhu 'alayhi wa sallam) were upon. And (it is) leaving innovations. And every innovation is misguidance. And leaving (both) the disputes (with the people of desires) and sitting with the people of desires (i.e. innovation). And leaving arguing, discussing and disputes in the religion." (Usūl As-Sunnah by Imām Ahmad – the *riwāyah* of 'Abdūs)

That which opposes the *Sunnah*

Everything which opposes the *Sunnah* is a *bid'ah* (innovation). The only disagreement in the religion which is allowed is that in which the *Sahābah* (*radiAllāhu 'anhum*) disagreed in. It is not allowed for anyone to come with an opinion or a verdict in the religion which oppose that which has been narrated in the *hadīth* and oppose the opinion regarding it narrated from the *Salaf*.

So everyone who falls in this mistake have fallen in innovation whether he likes it or not. The innovation in the religion is of two types:

* The first: *Al-Bid'ah Al-Mukaffirah*, which is the *innovation* which reaches the level of *kufr* and brings the person committing it or believing in it out of the fold of Islām.

Every *shirk* is a *bid'ah mukaffirah* which has not been legislated in the Qurān and *Sunnah*. So whoever claims that his *shirk* is from the religion, such as taking the people in the graves as intermediary between themselves and Allāh, then he has left the religion. Another example of a *bid'ah mukaffirah* could be the innovation of those who claimed that the Qurān is created, due to what this contains of rejecting the Attributes of Allāh, and the conclusion that the Attributes of Allāh – and thereby also Allāh – are created. Or those who claim that the slaves create their own deeds without the pre-existing knowledge of Allāh, and thereby ascribing a rival and partner with Allāh in the creation. Anyone who performs or believes in a *bid'ah mukaffirah* is *kāfir*.

* The second: *Al-Bid'ah ghayr Al-Mukaffirah*, which means the innovation which does not reach the level of *kufr* and thus does not bring the person committing it out of the fold of Islām.

Every way of worshipping or believing in Allāh which is not according to the Qurān and *Sunnah*, but it does not reach the limit of being a *nāqid* (nullifier) of Islām, is a *bid'ah ghayr mukaffirah*.

Whoever performs or believes in such a thing is an innovator who must be avoided until he returns to the truth. Examples of this could be those saying the *niyyah* (intention) for prayer out loud, or taking the birthday of the Prophet (*sallAllāhu 'alayhi wa sallam*) as a day of celebration, or making a specific amount of *dhikr* in specific place and times which are not prescribed in the *Sunnah* and making *dhikr in* congregation, all which have no basis in the Islāmic legislation etc. All these deeds are evil, but the one performing it does not become a *kāfir* merely by doing this.

And following are some of the methods which the innovators use to justify their innovation.

The methodologies of innovation

The innovators have many methods by which they reach to their *bid'ah*. The names might differ but the result is the same; namely leaving the narrations from the Messenger of Allāh (*sallAllāhu 'alayhi wa sallam*), the narrations from his Companions (*radiAllāhu 'anhum*) and the scholars who followed them in goodness. Below are some of these methods that all necessitate leaving the *Sunnah*.

* *Raī* (opinion)

The **criticized** *raī* (opinion) in Islām is that which opposes the *Sunnah* and have no basis in the Qurān or the *Sunnah*. Rather it is based upon personal opinion, lust and desires while it at the same time opposes the meaning which has come in the Qurān and *Sunnah*.

Allāh – the Exalted – said:

﴿ يَا أَيُّهَا الَّذِينَ آمَنُوا لَا تُقَدِّمُوا بَيْنَ يَدَيِ اللَّهِ وَرَسُولِهِ ۖ وَاتَّقُوا اللَّهَ ۚ إِنَّ اللَّهَ سَمِيعٌ عَلِيمٌ ﴾

"O you who believe. Do not prioritize anything over Allāh and His Messenger. And fear Allāh. Verily Allāh is All-Hearing and All-Knowing." (Al-Hujurat 49:1)

And the Messenger of Allāh (*sallAllāhu 'alayhi wa sallam*) said:

إِنَّ اللَّهَ لَا يَنْزِعُ العِلْمَ بَعْدَ أَنْ أَعْطَاكُمُوهُ انْتِزَاعًا، وَلَكِنْ يَنْتَزِعُهُ مِنْهُمْ مَعَ قَبْضِ العُلَمَاءِ بِعِلْمِهِمْ، فَيَبْقَى نَاسٌ جُهَّالٌ، يُسْتَفْتَوْنَ فَيُفْتُونَ بِرَأْيِهِمْ، فَيُضِلُّونَ وَيَضِلُّونَ

"Verily Allāh does not take away knowledge after having given it to you, by snatching it away (suddenly). Rather He takes it away from them by taking away the scholars and their knowledge. Then ignorant people will remain, who will be asked to give fatwā and so they will give fatwā with their own opinions, so they misguide and they are misguided." (Sahīh Al-Bukhārī)

And 'Umar ibn Al-Khattāb (*radiAllāhu 'anhu*) said:

إِنَّ أَصْحَابَ الرَّأْيِ أَعْدَاءُ السُّنَنِ أَعْيَتْهُمْ أَنْ يَحْفَظُوهَا وَتَفَلَّتَتْ مِنْهُمْ أَنْ يَعُوهَا ، وَاسْتَحْيَوْا حِينَ سُئِلُوا
أَنْ يَقُولُوا : لَا نَعْلَمُ ، فَعَارَضُوا السُّنَنَ بِرَأْيِهِمْ فَإِيَّاكُمْ وَإِيَّاهُمْ

"Verily the people of raī (opinion) are the enemies of the Sunan (pl. Sunnah). They were not able to memorize it, and understanding it also escaped them, and they were shy to say: 'I don't know', when they were asked. So they opposed the Sunan with their opinions. So beware of them." (Jāmi' Bayān Al-'Ilm by Ibn 'Abdul-Barr, and I'lām Al-Muwaqqi'īn by Ibn Al-Qaayim – the *isnād* is on the utmost level of correctness)

So every opinion – no matter who produced it or spoke well of it – which opposes the meaning found in the *hadīth*, then it is innovation and misguidance. And this opinion could be based upon the following, which all consists of leaving the narration of the *Salaf*:

* *Qiyās* (analogy)

The **criticized** *qiyās* in Islām is the one which is performed with the existence of evidence on the issue. The *qiyās* which results in something which opposes what the Messenger of Allāh (*sallAllāhu 'alayhi wa sallam*) has said or done is rejected and not taken into consideration at all.

Imam Ahmad (d. 241h) said:

وَلَيْسَ فِي السُّنَّةِ قِيَاسٌ، وَلَا تُضْرَبُ لَهَا الْأَمْثَالُ، وَلَا تُدْرَكُ بِالْعُقُولِ وَلَا الْأَهْوَاءِ، إِنَّمَا هُوَ الِاتِّبَاعُ وَتَرْكُ
الْهَوَى.

"And there is no qiyās (analogy) in the Sunnah, nor are similitudes (or examples) put forth with it. Nor is it comprehended through the intellect nor the desires. Rather it is (solely) to be followed and leaving desires in it." (Usul As-Sunnah, the *riwāyah* of 'Abdūs)

Al-Barbahārī (d. 329h) said:

واعلم رحمك الله أنه ليس في السنة قياس ولا تضرب لها الأمثال ولا تتبع فيها الأهواء بل هو التصديق
بآثار رسول الله ﷺ بلا كيف ولا شرح ولا يقال لم ولا كيف فالكلام والخصومة والجدال والمراء محدث
يقدح الشك في القلب وإن أصاب صاحبه الحق والسنة.

*"And know – may Allah have mercy upon you – that in the Sunnah there
is no qiyās (analogy), nor are similitudes (or examples) put forth with it,
nor are desires followed in it. Rather it is the belief in the narrations of the
Messenger of Allah (sallAllāhu 'alayhi wa sallam), without conditioning
or explaining, nor is it asked 'why' or 'how'. So speaking, disputing,
discussing and arguing are newly invented matter which cast doubt in the
heart, even if the one who does is correct upon the truth and the Sunnah."*
(Sharh As-Sunnah by Al-Barbahārī)

* Ijtihād (exertion)

The **rejected *ijtihād*** which in no way is acceptable is the one which
is performed with the existence of evidence on the issue. The *ijtihād*
which results in something which opposes what the Messenger of
Allāh (*sallAllāhu 'alayhi wa sallam*) has said or done is rejected, is not
taken into consideration, and the one performing it will not be
rewarded for that, rather he will lift the burden for it and for
everyone who followed him in his innovation.

* Falsafah (philosophy), hawā (desires) and 'ilm al-kalām

Philosphy and desires have no place in Islām. The evidences are
there to be submitted to and believed in. If a person's *nafs* (soul)
feels unease or has difficulties accepting the meaning which is
narrated in the *hadīth*, then it is still obligatory for him to accept the
narration and its meaning just as it has been narrated. As for the
Mutakallimūn (followers of *'ilm al-kalām*) then they – based upon
Greek philosophy – established some laws for which Allāh did not
sent down any authority, which they used to determine what from
the Islamic sources could be accepted, rejected or perhaps had to be
interpreted in order to be within the borders of their laws. Thus
their laws became a *tāghūt* for them which they sought *tahākum*
with and worshipped.

Imām Ahmad (d. 241 h) said:

عليكم بالسنَّة والحديث وما ينفعكم الله به وإياكم والخوض والجدال والمراء، فإنّه لا يفلح من أحب الكلام وكل من أحدث كلاماً لم يكن آخر أمره إلا إلى بدعة، لأن الكلام لا يدعو إلى خير

"It is upon you (to follow) the Sunnah, the hadīth and that through which Allah benefits you. And be aware of engaging (in discussions), disputing and arguing. Because verily the one who loves the kalām (philosophy) will not succeed, and everyone who invents some kalām then his affairs in the end will be nothing but innovation, because the kalām does not invite to goodness." (Al-Ibānah by Ibn Battah)

And Imām Ash-Shāfi'ī (d. 204h) said:

حكمي في أهل الكلام أن يضربوا بالجريد ويطاف بهم في العشائر ؛ ينادى عليهم هذا جزاء من ترك الكتاب والسنة وأقبل على الكلام

"My hukm (verdict) upon the people of kalām is that they are hit with palm-branches and circulated through the tribes while it is called out regarding them: 'This is the punishment for the one who leaves the Book and the Sunnah and turns to kalām.'" (Siyar A'lām An-Nubalā by Adh-Dhahabī)

* Tawīl bātil (false interpreation)

Interpreting the evidences in a wrong way is also not accepted in Islām. The Qurān and the *Sunnah* must be understood as the *Sahābah* (radiAllāhu 'anhum) and their students understood them. So whoever brings an interpretation of the evidences of Islām which is not in accordance with the understanding of the *Salaf*, then this is an innovation and misguidance.

Ibn Mandah (d. 295h):

التأويل عند أصحاب الحديث : نوع من التكذيب

"The tawīl (false interpretation) for people of hadīth is a type of rejection." (Ar-Radd 'alā Al-Jahmiyyah by Ibn Mandah)

The *Usūl* (fundamental principles) of the *Sunnah*

The scholars from the *Salaf* mentioned some issues from *'aqīdah* that have their basis in the *Sunnah*, and they referred to these issues as the *Usūl* (fundamental principles) of the *Sunnah*. Among the *Salaf* of this *Ummah* no-one would be considered a *Sunnī* (follower of the *Sunnah*) until he fulfilled and believed in all of these principles. Thus, every sect that opposed any of these principles – even if it was only one – was given a name to differentiate them from the people of truth.

Basically all innovations that exist today have their basis in the same types of misguided innovations which were mentioned by the *Salaf* in their books regarding the *Sunnah*. Only today they have become more extreme and more severe in their opposition to the Islāmic texts. But whatever of misguided innovative beliefs and principles that have survived from the time of the *Salaf* until today – and some people mentions these issues in their books as if they are an acceptable *manhaj* – then they are still misguided innovative beliefs which must be avoided before a person can call himself a follower of the *Sunnah*.

The truth is not known through men, rather the truth is known through the narrations.

Al-Barbahārī (d. 329h) said:

واحذر صغار المحدثات من الأمور فإن صغار البدع تعود حتى تصير كبارا وكذلك كل بدعة أحدثت في هذه الأمة كان أولها صغيرا يشبه الحق فاغتر بذلك من دخل فيها ثم لم يستطع المخرج منها فعظمت وصارت دينا يدان بها فخالف الصراط المستقيم فخرج من الإسلام فانظر رحمك الله كل من سمعت كلامه من أهل زمانك خاصة فلا تعجلن ولا تدخلن في شيء منه حتى تسأل وتنظر هل تكلم فيه أحد من أصحاب النبي ﷺ أو أحد من العلماء فإن أصبت فيه أثرا عنهم فتمسك به ولا تجاوزه لشيء ولا تختر عليه شيئا فتسقط في النار.

"And beware of the small innovations, because the small of innovations return until they become big. And every bid'ah which was innovated in

this Ummah began like this as something small that looked like the truth, so the one who entered it was deceived by that. Then he was not able to exit from it, and it grew and became a religion which he adopted. So he opposed the Straight Path and exited from Islām. So beware – may Allāh have mercy upon you – of everyone whose words you listen to specifically from the people of your time. Do not hasten and do not believe in anything until you ask and look; did anyone from the Companions of the Prophet (sallAllāhu 'alayhi wa sallam) speak about this or anyone from the scholars (of the Salaf)? Then if you find an athar (narration) regarding it from them, then hold on to it and do not deviate from it for anything, and do not chose anything over it, so you (if you do that) would fall in the fire" (Sharh As-Sunnah by Al-Barbahārī)

So the salvation lies in following the narrations.

An important thing to be aware of is – as it has already been mentioned – that the *Salaf* would not consider a person as a follower of the *Sunnah* until he believed in and adapted as his religion all the *usūl* of the *Sunnah*. Therefore it is important for the Muslim to study the books of the *Salaf* and learn the fundamental principles of the *Sunnah* in order to be free from innovation, just as he learns the fundamental principles of Tawhīd in order to be free from *shirk*.

Imām Ahmad (d. 241h) said:

وَمِنْ اَلسُّنَّةِ اَللَّازِمَةِ اَلَّتِي مَنْ تَرَكَ مِنْهَا خَصْلَةً – لَمْ يَقْبَلْهَا وَيُؤْمِنْ بِهَا – لَمْ يَكُنْ مِنْ أَهْلِهَا:

"And from the obligatory Sunnah, where the one who leaves one of them – by not accepting it and believing in it – then he is not from its people is…" (Usūl As-Sunnah by Imām Ahmad – the *riwāyah* of 'Abdūs)

And then he went on to mention some of the principles of the *Sunnah*.

And Sufyān ibn 'Uyaynah (d. 198h) said:

السُّنَّةُ عَشَرَةٌ ، فَمَنْ كُنَّ فِيهِ فَقَدِ اسْتَكْمَلَ السُّنَّةَ ، وَمَنْ تَرَكَ مِنْهَا شَيْئًا فَقَدْ تَرَكَ السُّنَّةَ.

103

"The Sunnah is ten. So whoever has these then he has completed the Sunnah, and whoever leaves any of it, then he has left the Sunnah." (Sharh Usūl I'tiqād Ahlus-Sunnah wal-Jamā'ah by Al-Lālakāī)

Harb ibn Ismā'īl Al-Karmānī (d. 280h) said:

فمن خالف شيئاً من هذه المذاهب أو طعن فيها أو عاب قائلها فهو مخالف مبتدع وخارج عن الجماعة زايل عن منهج السنة وسبيل الحق

"So whoever opposed anything from these madhāhib (i.e. ways or beliefs) or speak evil of it, or criticizes the one who says it, then he is a mukhālif (opposer) mubtadi' (innovator), (and he has) left the Jamā'ah and parted with the manhaj of Sunnah and the path of the Truth." (Kitāb As-Sunnah by Al-Karmānī)

And Al-Barbahārī (d. 329h) said:

ولا يحل لرجل أن يقول فلان صاحب سنة حتى يعلم أنه قد اجتمعت فيه خصال السنة فلا يقال له صاحب سنة حتى تجتمع فيه السنة كلها

"And it is not allowed for a man to say that fulān is a follower of Sunnah until he knows that the characteristics of Sunnah are gathered with him. So he is not called a follower of Sunnah until all of the Sunnah is gathered with him." (Sharh As-Sunnah by Al-Barbahārī)

Following is an introduction to some of the Usūl (principles) of the Sunnah and some of the fundamental beliefs which the scholars have mentioned in their books, but not all. The slave is encouraged to study the books of the Salaf[9] in order to become acquinted with the correct 'aqīdah and the religious principles of the Salaf in general, but also to achieve the love of the people whom Allāh – from above the seventh heaven – chose to preserve His religion.

---

[9] At the end of this book is a list of recommende books for the seeker of knowledge to study.

The reader is advised to notice how easy the religion becomes once the slave submits to the evidences. Just as the purpose and meaning of Tawhīd is very simple; worship Allah and do not associate partners with Him in anything, then the purpose of the *Sunnah* is equally simple and easy to understand; submit to and believe in what have been narrated in the *ahādīth* and *āthār* (narrations), and do not deviate from it for anything.

Tawhīd of Names and Attributes, and the description of Allāh

The *Salaf* mentioned the Tawhīd of Allāh and the description of Allāh and His Names and Attributes in their books of *Sunnah* due to the fact that the *hadīth* of the Messenger of Allāh is the way of interpreting the Qurān. So whoever wants to believe in Allāh and understand the Qurān in the correct way, he has to follow the *Sunnah* in its explanation. So whoever deviated (and deviates today) in the Tawhīd of *Al-Asmā was-Sifāt* (Names and Attributes) among the deviated sects, then the reason was (and is) their lack of believing in and following the correct *tafsīr* (interpretation) of the Qurān, which is the *Sunnah*.

And whoever looks into the *Sunnah* with regards to the description of Allāh and His Names and Attributes will find that the key to correct understanding and belief is the submittance to the words of Allāh and the words of His Messenger (*sallAllāhu 'alayhi wa sallam*) just as they have been narrated without changing even one letter for one reason or another. Thus it became a principle among the people of *Sunnah* that they believe in the description of Allāh – the Exalted – as this was informed about in the Qurān, from the Prophet (*sallAllāhu 'alayhi wa sallam*), from the Sahābah (*radiAllāhu 'anhum*) and those who followed them in goodness, without:

- *Tahrīf* (distortion) – this means to change the meaning of the words to something else, such as the meaning of hand to meaning power.
- *Ta'tīl* (invalidation) – this means to reject and invalidate the meaning of the words, such as saying Allāh does not speak.
- *Tashbīh* (comparison) – this means to compare the Creator with the created, such as saying the Sight of Allāh is like the sight of the creation.
- *Takyīf* (conditioning) – this means to explain the conditions of the Name or Attribute, such as explaining how Allāh descends to the lowest heaven.
- *Tafwīd* (relegation) – this means establishing the words themselves, such as Hand, Face, Shin etc. but then claiming that

106

the meaning of it is unknown, and thus not believing in the literal meaning of the Attribute.

The manhaj of the *Salaf* is summarized in the following words:

Al-Walīd ibn Muslim (d. 195h) said:

سألت سفيان الثوري، ومالك بن أنس، والأوزاعي، والليث بن سعد عن هذه الأحاديث التي في الرؤية والصفات قال : أمروها على ما جاءت، ولا تفسروها ".

"I asked Sufyān Ath-Thawrī, Mālik ibn Anas, Al-Awzā'ī and Layth ibn Sa'd about these ahādīth regarding the ruyah (seeing Allāh) and the Attributes (of Allāh). So they said: 'Let them pass (i.e. accept them) as they have been narrated and do not interpret them.'" (Al-Mu'jam by Ibn Al-Muqrī p. 111)

And Ahmad ibn Nasr (d. 231h) said:

سألت سفيان بن عيينة قلت : يا أبا محمد أريد أسألك ، قال : لا تسأل ، قلت : إذا لم أسألك فمن أسأل ، قال : سل قلت ما تقول في هذه الأحاديث التي رويت نحو : القلوب بين أصبعين ، وأن الله يضحك أو يعجب ممن يذكره في الأسواق ، فقال : « أمروها كما جاءت بلا كيف»

"I asked Sufyān ibn 'Uyaynah saying: 'O Abū Muhammad, I want to ask you something.' So he said: 'Do not ask.' I said: 'If I should not ask you, then who should I ask?' He said: '(Then) ask.' I said: 'What do you say about these ahādīth which were narrated regarding: The hearts are between Two Fingers, and that Allāh Laughs or is Amazed by the one who mentions Him in the markets?' So he said: 'Let them pass (i.e. accept them) just as they were narrated, without (describing) how.'" (Marāsil Abū Dāwūd p. 182, As-Siyar 8/467 and others)

And Abū Bakr Al-Marrūdhī (d. 275h) said:

سألت أبا عبد الله عن الأحاديث التي تردها الجهمية في الصفات، والرؤية، والإسراء، وقصة العرش، فصححها أبو عبد الله، وقال : « قد تلقتها العلماء بالقبول، نسلم الأخبار كما جاءت،

"I asked Abū 'Abdullāh (i.e. Imām Ahmad) about the ahādīth which the Jahmiyyah reject regarding the Attributes (of Allāh), the ruyah, the Isrā (night journey) and the story of the Throne. So Abū 'Abdullāh described them as being correct, and he said: 'Verily did the scholars receive these with acceptance. We submit to the reports just as they were narrated.'" (As-Sunnah by Abū Bakr Al-Khallāl, Ash-Sharī'ah by Al-Ājurrī and Tabaqāt Al-Hanābilah)

And Abū 'Īsā At-Tirmidhī (d. 279h) said:

هكذا رُوِي عن مالك، و سفيان بن عيينة، و عبد الله بن المبارك أنهم قالوا في هذه الأحاديث»: أمروها بلا كيف .«وهكذا قول أهل العلم من أهل السنة والجماعة، وأما الجهمية فأنكرت هذه الروايات وقالوا: هذا تشبيه. وقد ذكر الله عز وجل في غير موضع من كتابه: اليد والسمع والبصر، فتأولت الجهمية هذه الآيات ففسروها على غير ما فسر أهل العلم، وقالوا: إن الله لم يخلق آدم بيده. وقالوا: إن معنى اليد ههنا القوة.

"Such was it narrated from Mālik, Sufyān ibn 'Uyaynah and 'Abdullāh ibn Al-Mubārak that they said regarding these ahādīth: 'Let them pass (i.e. accept them) without (describing) how.' And this is the opinion of the people of knowledge from Ahlus-Sunnah wal-Jamā'ah. But the Jahmiyyah rejected these narrations and they said: 'This is comparing (the Creator with the creation).' And Allāh – 'azza wa jalla – has verily mentioned many places in His Book: the Hand, the Sight and the Hearing. So the Jahmiyyah interpreted these verses, and they explained them differently than what the people of knowledge have explained them. And they said: 'Allāh has not created Ādam with His Hand.' And they said: 'Verily the meaning of the Hand here is the Power.'" (Al-Jāmi' Al-Kabīr by At-Tirmidhī 2/42-43)

* The **Jahmiyyah** rejected the Names and Attributes of Allāh, under the argument that they necessitated *tashbih* (comparison) of the Creator with the creation. And by this rejection they are *kuffār*. Due to this belief they were also called the **Mu'attilah**, which means: those who invalidate (the Attributes of Allāh). **The Mu'tazilah** also rejected the Attributes. The **Matūrīdiyyah** and the **'Ashā'irah** also made a form of *ta'tīl* when they invalidated the reality of Allāh's

Speech and claimed that the *Kalām* (Speech) of Allāh is internal speech which is without voice or letters. Rather what is heard of recitation of the Qurān, then according to their claim this is merely an expression of the Word of Allāh, but not the Qurān itself. With this description of the *Kalām* of Allāh they continued from *ta'ṭīl* into *taḥrīf* by distorting the meaning of Attribute.

Many sects today, such as the 'Ashā'irah, the Ahbāsh and other hold the same beliefs as the Jahmiyyah when it comes to the Names and Attributes of Allāh, even though they might go under a different name. So whoever rejects any of the Names and Attributes of Allāh, then he is a *jahmi* in his beliefs whether he acknowledges this or not.

* The **Mushabbihah** compared the Names and Attributes of Allāh with those of the creation. So they said: 'My sight is like the Sight of Allāh', or 'My hand is like the Hand of Allāh', or 'My foot is like the foot of Allāh'. This constitutes *takyīf* (conditioning) from the aspect that they described how the Attributes of Allāh are, and it constitutes *tashbīh* (comparison) from the aspect that they compared the Attributes of Allāh with the attributes of the creation. And by this comparison they have ascribed partners to Allāh in His Attributes, and they are *kuffār*.

* Many different sects and persons have indulged in *taḥrīf* (distortion) of some of the Name and Attributes of Allāh. The **Jahmiyyah** said that *istawā* (rose above) the Throne in reality means *istawlā* (having authority or possession over) the Throne. Some claim that the *Raḥmah* (Mercy) of Allāh means wanting to bless, while the *Ghadab* (Anger) of Allāh means wanting to punish, while fleeing from the literal meanings of the two words. All of this is *taḥrīf* (distortion) of the literal meanings and this is *bāṭil* (falsehood). Rather the people of *Sunnah* believe that Allāh rose above His Throne, He has Mercy and Anger, and they do not describe the condition of these things, nor do they ask how.

* Another evil opinion claimed by the **Mufawwidah** was, that the words themselves of the Names and Attributes were to be established and believed in, but the meaning of them is unknown and the knowledge of it is only known by Allāh. For example would they accept and believe in the word *Yad* (Hand) made up by the letters *yā* and *dāl*, but they would claim having no idea what that word means. They claimed to follow the *Salaf* in this belief – which is false – but in reality they invented an hideous lie against Allāh and His Messenger (*sallAllāhu 'alayhi wa sallam*) when claiming that such a big part of the religion – namely the Names and Attributes of Allāh – was left unexplained to the slaves.

The scholars have written books and books describing the false and innovative beliefs of the deviators, and they have given them all a name in order for them to be recognized and warned against. Studying the right *'aqīdah* goes hand in hand with studying the misguidance and innovation. The Muslim is obliged to submit to the evidences of the Qurān and the *Sunnah*, according to the understanding and *manhaj* of the *Salaf*, because these issues are issues of *īmān* and *kufr*. So whoever denies an issue from the Tawhīd of Allāh and His Names and Attriubutes, and the issue is known from the *fitrah*, then he is a *kāfir* and he will remain in Hellfire for ever if he dies upon that. This is because rejecting anything from the Names and Attributes of Allāh in these kinds of issues, generally entails describing Him – the Exalted – with some form of deficiency, such as the one who claims that Allāh had no knowledge until He created it, because this claim necessitates that Allāh was ignorant until He created the knowledge. And this claim is clear *kufr*.

And whoever denies an issue in the Tawhīd of Allāh and His Names and Attriubutes, and the issue is only known through the texts – with the condition that the issue is not among the well-known issues – then if he rejects the truth when it comes to him then he is *kāfir*, and if he hangs on to a newly invented opinion of innovation which does not reach the level of *kufr*, or he is in a situation where he could be excused, then he is still considered a *mubtadi'* (innovator) whose good deeds will never be accepted from him until he repents, and along with this it is feared for him that he is considered among the *kuffār*.

The Qurān is the Word of Allāh

Rejecting the Attributes of Allāh lead the Jahmiyyah – led by and named after Jahm ibn Safwān – to claim that the Qurān is created. If Allāh – according to them – does not speak, then the Qurān cannot be the Speech and Word of Allāh, and so it must be created. Rather the people of *Sunnah* affirmed what the Qurān and *Sunnah* had already affirmed that the Qurān is the Word of Allāh and not created. And they declared *takfir* upon the one who says that the Qurān is created, due to what this saying contains of *kufr*. Among these types of *kufr* are:

- Rejecting that Allāh speaks.
- Claiming that Allāh did not have any knowledge until He created it. And this is based upon the fact that Allāh calls the Qurān knowledge. So this is a necessity of their claim.
- Allowing the invocation of something created. Allāh says (in the translation): **"Say call upon Allāh or call upon Ar-Rahmān."** And all the Names of Allāh according to them are created.
- Allowing seeking refuge with something created. The Prophet (*sallAllāhu 'alayhi wa sallam*) encouraged the believers to say: *"I seek refuge with the perfect words of Allāh, from the evil which He has created."* And these words according to them are created.

Allāh – the Exalted – said:

﴿ وَإِنْ أَحَدٌ مِنَ الْمُشْرِكِينَ اسْتَجَارَكَ فَأَجِرْهُ حَتَّى يَسْمَعَ كَلَامَ اللَّهِ ﴾

"And if anyone from the *mushrikūn* seek your protection, then protect him so he may hear the words of Allāh." (At-Tawbah 9:6)

And He – the Exalted – said:

﴿ وَكَلَّمَ اللَّهُ مُوسَى تَكْلِيمًا ﴾

"And Allāh spoke to Musa directly." (An-Nisā 4:164)

Jābir ibn 'Abdullāh – *radiAllāhu 'anhu* – said:

كَانَ النَّبِيُّ صَلَّى اللهُ عَلَيْهِ وَسَلَّمَ يَعْرِضُ نَفْسَهُ عَلَى النَّاسِ بِالْمَوْقِفِ فَيَقُولُ: «هَلْ مِنْ رَجُلٍ يَحْمِلُنِي إِلَى قَوْمِهِ؛ فَإِنَّ قُرَيْشًا قَدْ مَنَعُونِي أَنْ أُبَلِّغَ كَلَامَ رَبِّي عَزَّ وَجَلَّ

"The Prophet (sallAllāhu 'alayhi wa sallam) used to present himself at the stopping place (for the pilgrims) and then say: 'Is there a man who will carry me to his people. For verily Quraysh have forbidden me to declare the words of my Lord the Mighty and Majesty.'" (At-Tirmidhī, Ahmad, An-Nasāī – *sahīh* according to the conditions of Al-Bukhārī)

And 'Umar ibn Al-Khattāb (*radiAllāhu 'anhu*) said:

إِنَّ هَذَا الْقُرْآنَ كَلَامُ اللهِ عَزَّ وَجَلَّ فَضَعُوهُ عَلَى مَوَاضِعِهِ

"Verily this Qurān is the Word of Allāh – the Mighty and Majestic – so put it in its right place." (Ar-Rad 'alā Al-Jahmiyyah by Ad-Dārimī)

And Al-Lālakāī (d. 418h) after having mentioned the names of the scholars of the *Salaf* from different cities and countries by name, he said:

قَالُوا كُلُّهُمْ: الْقُرْآنُ كَلَامُ اللهِ غَيْرُ مَخْلُوقٍ , وَمَنْ قَالَ مَخْلُوقٌ فَهُوَ كَافِرٌ. فَهَؤُلَاءِ خَمْسُ مِائَةٍ وَخَمْسُونَ نَفْسًا أَوْ أَكْثَرُ مِنَ التَّابِعِينَ وَأَتْبَاعِ التَّابِعِينَ وَالْأَئِمَّةِ الْمَرْضِيِّينَ سِوَى الصَّحَابَةِ الْخَيِّرِينَ عَلَى اخْتِلَافِ الْأَعْصَارِ وَمُضِيِّ السِّنِينَ وَالْأَعْوَامِ. وَفِيهِمْ نَحْوٌ مِنْ مِائَةِ إِمَامٍ مِمَّنْ أَخَذَ النَّاسُ بِقَوْلِهِمْ وَتَدَيَّنُوا بِمَذَاهِبِهِمْ , وَلَوِ اشْتَغَلْتُ بِنَقْلِ قَوْلِ الْمُحَدِّثِينَ لَبَلَغَتْ أَسْمَاؤُهُمْ أُلُوفًا كَثِيرَةً , لَكِنِّي اخْتَصَرْتُ وَحَذَفْتُ الْأَسَانِيدَ لِلِاخْتِصَارِ , وَنَقَلْتُ عَنْ هَؤُلَاءِ عَصْرًا بَعْدَ عَصْرٍ لَا يُنْكِرُ عَلَيْهِمْ مُنْكِرٌ

"They all said: 'The Qurān is the Word of Allāh and not created, and whoever says (that it is) created then he is kāfir.' And these are five hundred and fifty persons or more from the tābi'ūn and the followers of the tābi'ūn and the accepted leaders besides the good-doing Sahābah, opposite of (what has occurred in) the times and with the passing of years. And among them there are around hundred leaders whose words were accepted and they (i.e. the people) adopted their religion according to their

madhhab. And if I had busied myself with narrating the words of the people of hadīth then their names would have reached many thousands. But I summarized and I deleted the chains of narration due to the summarization. And I narrated from these (scholars) time after time while no-one would reject anything from them." (Sharh Usūl Al-I'tiqād by Al-Lālakāī 2/312)

So saying that the Qurān is created is an abominable innovation which without a doubt contains *kufr* to Allāh from several angles, and whoever claims this is a *kāfir*.

The belief in the *Qadar* (Divine Decree)

Allāh – the Exalted – said:

﴿ إِنَّا كُلَّ شَيْءٍ خَلَقْنَاهُ بِقَدَرٍ ﴾

"Verily, everything We have created with Qadar."
(Al-Qamar 54:49)

And the Prophet (*sallAllāhu 'alayhi wa sallam*) explained how to belief in the *Qadar*, when he said:

قَدَّرَ اللهُ الْمَقَادِيرَ قَبْلَ أَنْ يَخْلُقَ السَّمَاوَاتِ وَالْأَرْضَ بِخَمْسِينَ أَلْفَ سَنَةٍ

"Allāh decided the maqādīr (decrees) fifty thousand years before he created the heavens and the earth." (Saḥīḥ Ibn Hibbān)

And the Prophet (*sallAllāhu 'alayhi wa sallam*) said:

إِنَّ اللهَ وَكَّلَ بِالرَّحِمِ مَلَكًا فَقَالَ: أَيْ رَبِّ نُطْفَةٌ، أَيْ رَبِّ عَلَقَةٌ، أَيْ رَبِّ مُضْغَةٌ، فَإِذَا قَضَى اللهُ عَزَّ وَجَلَّ خَلْقَهَا قَالَ: أَيْ رَبِّ شَقِيٌّ أَوْ سَعِيدٌ ذَكَرٌ أَوْ أُنْثَى فَمَا الرِّزْقُ وَمَا الْأَجَلُ؟ فَيُكْتَبُ ذَلِكَ فِي بَطْنِ أُمِّهِ

"Verily Allāh has delegated an angel in the womb who says: 'O my Lord, a semen drop. O my Lord, a clot. O my Lord, a lump of flesh.' Then when Allāh – 'azza wa jalla – has finished its creation, he (i.e. the angel) says: 'O my Lord, unhappy or happy, male or female, and what is the provisions and when is the death?' Then this is written (when he is still) in the stomach of the mother." (Saḥīḥ Muslim)

And Al-Walīd ibn 'Ubādah ibn As-Sāmit (*radiAllāhu 'anhumā*) said:

أَوْصَانِي أَبِي رَحِمَهُ اللهُ تَعَالَى فَقَالَ يَا بُنَيَّ أُوصِيكَ أَنْ تُؤْمِنَ بِالْقَدَرِ خَيْرِهِ وَشَرِّهِ فَإِنَّكَ إِنْ لَمْ تُؤْمِنْ أَدْخَلَكَ اللهُ تَبَارَكَ وَتَعَالَى النَّارَ قَالَ وَسَمِعْتُ النَّبِيَّ صَلَّى اللَّهُمَّ عَلَيْهِ وَسَلَّمَ يَقُولُ أَوَّلُ مَا خَلَقَ اللهُ تَبَارَكَ وَتَعَالَى الْقَلَمَ ثُمَّ قَالَ لَهُ اكْتُبْ قَالَ وَمَا أَكْتُبُ قَالَ فَاكْتُبْ مَا يَكُونُ وَمَا هُوَ كَائِنٌ إِلَى أَنْ تَقُومَ السَّاعَةُ

"My father – rahimahullāh – advised me and said: 'O my son. I advise you to believe in the Qadar, the good of it and the bad of it, because if you don't believe in it, then Allāh will enter you into Hellfire.' He said: And I heard

the Prophet (sallAllāhu 'alayhi wa sallam) say: 'The first thing Allāh created was the pen, then He said to it: 'Write.' It said: 'And what should I write.' He said: 'So write what is now, and what will happen until the Hour is established.'" (Abū Dāwūd, Ahmad, and At-Tirmidhī with a small difference – *sahīh*)

Among that which the people of *Sunnah* believe in regarding the *Qadar* is:

1. The belief that Allāh knows all things, in general and in detail, in all times, whether that has to do with His actions or the actions of His slaves.
2. The belief that Allāh has written the *Qadar* in *Al-Lawh Al-Mahfūdh* (the Book of Decrees).
3. The belief that whatever happens – of both good and evil – only happens by the Will of Allāh.
4. The belief that everything from the creation is created by Allāh, and among this are the deeds of the slaves, just as the evidences have proved.

The people who innovated false beliefs regarding the *Qadar* were called the **Qadariyyah**, and among their beliefs are:

* To reject that Allāh has pre-existing knowledge about everything and claiming that Allāh does not know what will happen until it occurs, including the deeds of the slave. Whoever says this he is a *kāfir*, due to rejecting the *Qadar* of Allāh.

* That the deeds of the slaves are created by the slave himself and not by Allāh. Whoever says this he is a *kāfir*, due to ascribing the attribute of creation to the slaves.

* To negate that Allāh has predetermined that which is evil and that He has only predetermined the good. Whoever says this he is a *kāfir*, due to rejecting a part of the *Qadar*.

* Then there were those who did not reject any of the four pillars of the *Qadar*, but due to wanting to exalt Allāh they would refrain

116

from saying: *'A person commits zinā, and steals, and drinks alcohol with Qadar (i.e. according to what Allāh has predestined for him).'* Whoever refrains from saying this is a *mubtadi'* (innovator).

Some people – as a refutation to the Qadariyyah – said that the deed of the slave is not even ascribed to the slave and that he has no will in that, rather the deeds of the slaves are ascribed to Allāh. These are the **Jabriyyah**, and this saying is clear *kufr*.

Rather the people of *Sunnah* are in between the two extremes. *Ahlus-Sunnah* does not negate the will for the slave; rather the will exists <u>subject</u> to the *Qadar* and *Mashīah* (Will) of Allāh the Exalted. Whatever Allāh wants then it will occur, and whatever He does not want, then it will never occur.

﴿ وَمَا تَشَاءُونَ إِلَّا أَنْ يَشَاءَ اللَّهُ رَبُّ الْعَالَمِينَ ﴾

"And you do not will except that Allāh wills, Lord of the worlds."
(At-Takwīr 81:29)

And verily has the correct understanding of this issue already been explained in the narrations from the *Salaf*.

'Abdullāh ibn 'Umar (*radiAllāhu 'anhumā*) said:

قَالَ عُمَرُ رَضِيَ اللَّهُ عَنْهُ: يَا رَسُولَ اللَّهِ أَرَأَيْتَ مَا نَعْمَلُ فِيهِ أَفِي أَمْرٍ قَدْ فُرِغَ مِنْهُ، أَوْ أَمْرٍ مُبْتَدَإٍ أَوْ مُبْتَدَعٍ؟ قَالَ: «فِيمَا قَدْ فُرِغَ مِنْهُ، فَاعْمَلْ يَا ابْنَ الْخَطَّابِ فَإِنَّ كُلًّا مُيَسَّرٌ، أَمَّا مَنْ كَانَ مِنْ أَهْلِ السَّعَادَةِ فَإِنَّهُ يَعْمَلُ لِلسَّعَادَةِ، وَأَمَّا مَنْ كَانَ مِنْ أَهْلِ الشَّقَاءِ فَإِنَّهُ يَعْمَلُ لِلشَّقَاءِ»

"'Umar (radiAllāhu 'anhu) said: 'O Messenger of Allāh. Do you see these deeds which we do, are they a matter which has been determined or are they a new matter or an invented matter?' So he said: 'It is something which has already been determined. So make deeds O son of Al-Khattāb, because it has all been made easy (in accordance with what has already been decided). The one who is (decreed to be) from the people of happiness then he will make deeds for the happiness, and whoever is (decreed to be) from the people of

unhappiness then he will make deeds for the unhappiness.'" (Saḥīḥ At-Tirmidhī)

Abū Yaḥyā Al-A'raj (d. around 80h) the *mawlā* of Ibn 'Ifrā (*radiAllāhu 'anhu*) said:

أَتَيْتُ ابْنَ عَبَّاسٍ رَضِيَ اللَّهُ عَنْهُمَا، وَمَعِي رَجُلَانِ مِنَ الَّذِينَ يَذْكُرُونَ الْقَدَرَ أَوْ يُنْكِرُونَهُ، فَقُلْتُ: يَا ابْنَ عَبَّاسٍ، مَا تَقُولُ فِي الْقَدَرِ لَوْ أَنَّ هَؤُلَاءِ أَتَوْكَ يَسْأَلُونَكَ؟ وَقَالَ إِسْمَاعِيلُ مَرَّةً يَسْأَلُونَكَ عَنِ الْقَدَرِ إِنْ زَنَا وَإِنْ سَرَقَ أَوْ شَرِبَ الْخَمْرَ، فَحَسَرَ قَمِيصَهُ حَتَّى أَخْرَجَ مَنْكِبَهُ، وَقَالَ: «يَا أَبَا يَحْيَى لَعَلَّكَ مِنَ الَّذِينَ يُنْكِرُونَ الْقَدَرَ وَيُكَذِّبُونَ بِهِ، وَاللَّهِ لَوْ أَنِّي أَعْلَمُ أَنَّكَ مِنْهُمْ أَوْ هَذَيْنِ مَعَكَ لَجَاهَدْتُكُمْ، إِنْ زَنَا فَبِقَدَرٍ، وَإِنْ سَرَقَ فَبِقَدَرٍ، وَإِنْ شَرِبَ الْخَمْرَ فَبِقَدَرٍ»

"I came to Ibn 'Abbās (radiAllāhu 'anhumā) and with me was two men from those who mention the Qadar or reject it. So I said: 'O Ibn 'Abbās. What do you say about the Qadar, because these two have come to ask you.'" And Ismā'īl said one time: "(They have come) to ask you about the Qadar. If he fornicates, and if he steals or drinks alcohol (is it then with Qadar)?' So he (i.e. Ibn 'Abbās) pulled away his shirt until he brought out his shoulder, and he said: 'O Abū Yaḥyā. Maybe you are from those who reject the Qadar and deny it. By Allāh, if I knew that you were from them or these two who are with you then I would have fought you. If he fornicates then it is with Qadar, and if he steals then it is with Qadar and if he drinks alcohol then it is with Qadar." (Kitāb As-Sunnah by 'Abdullāh)

Finally, there are some things to be aware of when it comes to the *Qadar* of Allāh. First and foremost is that Allāh is Just and He does not make injustice to anyone. Thus, everyone who enters Hellfire, then that will be justified and deserved, and only after Allāh have sent messengers and prophets to them in order to warn them about the punishment of Allāh and inform them about what is obligatory and forbidden for them to perform.

Allāh – Exalted – said:

﴿ فَرِيقًا هَدَىٰ وَفَرِيقًا حَقَّ عَلَيْهِمُ الضَّلَالَةُ إِنَّهُمُ اتَّخَذُوا الشَّيَاطِينَ أَوْلِيَاءَ مِنْ دُونِ اللَّهِ وَيَحْسَبُونَ أَنَّهُمْ مُهْتَدُونَ ﴾

"A group He guided, and for a group the misguidance became a reality. They verily took the *shayatin* (devils) as allies (or protectors) besides Allāh, while they think that they are guided." (Al-A'rāf 7:30)

And He – the Exalted – said:

﴿ وَمَا كُنَّا مُعَذِّبِينَ حَتَّىٰ نَبْعَثَ رَسُولًا ﴾

"And We do not punish (anyone) before We send a messenger (to warn)." (Al-Isrā 17:15)

And He – the Exalted – said:

﴿ وَوُضِعَ الْكِتَابُ فَتَرَى الْمُجْرِمِينَ مُشْفِقِينَ مِمَّا فِيهِ وَيَقُولُونَ يَا وَيْلَتَنَا مَالِ هَذَا الْكِتَابِ لَا يُغَادِرُ صَغِيرَةً وَلَا كَبِيرَةً إِلَّا أَحْصَاهَا وَوَجَدُوا مَا عَمِلُوا حَاضِرًا وَلَا يَظْلِمُ رَبُّكَ أَحَدًا ﴾

"And the book (of deeds) will be placed. Then you will see the criminals fearful for what is in it, and they will say: 'Woe to us. What is this book which does not leave out any small things or any big things, except that it has counted it.' And they will find what they have done (of deeds) present in it. And your Lord does not make injustice to anyone." (Al-Kahf 18:49)

We as slaves cannot fully comprehend the *Qadar* of Allāh. Despite of this it is still obligatory to believe in it and it is strictly forbidden to ask questions like 'how' and 'why' when it comes to issues from the *Qadar* of Allāh. This is because the *Qadar* is among the secrets of Allāh, and doubting or rejecting anything from it only leads the slave to misguidance. Allah – the Exalted – said:

﴿ لَا يُسْأَلُ عَمَّا يَفْعَلُ وَهُمْ يُسْأَلُونَ ﴾

"He (i.e. Allah) is not asked about what He does, but they (i.e. the slaves) will be asked." (Al-Anbiyā 21:23)

And the Prophet (sallAllāhu 'alayhi wa sallam) said:

لاَ يُؤْمِنُ عَبْدٌ حَتَّى يُؤْمِنَ بِالْقَدَرِ خَيْرِهِ وَشَرِّهِ

"The slave does not believe before he believes in the Qadar, both the good of it and the bad." (Musnad Imām Ahmad - sahīh)

Al-Barbahārī (d. 329h) said:

والكلام والجدل والخصومة في القدر خاصة منهيّ عنه عند جميع الفرق؛ لأن القدر سر الله، ونهى الرب تبارك وتعالى الأنبياء عن الكلام في القدر

"And speaking about, arguing and disagreeing regarding the Qadar specifically is prohibited according to all the groups, because the Qadar is the secret of Allāh. And the Lord – tabāraka wa ta'ālā – prohibited the prophets from speaking about the Qadar." (Sharh As-Sunnah by Al-Barbahārī)

Al-Ājurrī (d. 320h) said:

لا يحسن بالمسلمين التنقير والبحث في القدر، لأن القدر سر من أسرار الله عز وجل، بل الإيمان بما جرت به المقادير من خير أو شر واجب على العباد أن يؤمنوا به، ثم لا يأمن العبد أن يبحث عن القدر فيكذب بمقادير الله الجارية على العباد، فيضل عن طريق الحق

"It is not befitting for the Muslims to investigate and examine the Qadar. Because the Qadar is a secret from the secrets of Allāh – 'azza wa jalla. Rather to believe in what the maqādīr (pl. qadar) has brought of both good and evil is obligatory upon the slaves. After that the slave cannot feel secure from – if he searches in the Qadar – that he rejects the maqādīr of Allāh which are occurring upon the slaves, by which he deviates from the truth." (Ash-Sharī'ah by Al-Ājurrī 2/702)

The status of the *Sahābah* (*radiAllāhu 'anhum*)

The Companions of Muhammad (*sallAllāhu 'alayhi wa sallam*) are the best people to walk the face of the earth after the Prophets (*'alayhim as-salam*). Allāh – the Exalted – chose them to be the carriers of His religion and He praised them and approved of them in the Qurān. Thus, the correct belief regarding them is holding them at high esteem and witnessing for them what Allāh and His Messenger (*sallAllāhu 'alayhi wa sallam*) have witnessed for them of high rank and excellence, and not speaking bad about them or mentioning their faults.

Allāh – the Exalted – said:

﴿ مُحَمَّدٌ رَسُولُ اللَّهِ وَالَّذِينَ مَعَهُ أَشِدَّاءُ عَلَى الْكُفَّارِ رُحَمَاءُ بَيْنَهُمْ تَرَاهُمْ رُكَّعًا سُجَّدًا يَبْتَغُونَ فَضْلًا مِنَ اللَّهِ وَرِضْوَانًا سِيمَاهُمْ فِي وُجُوهِهِمْ مِنْ أَثَرِ السُّجُودِ ذَلِكَ مَثَلُهُمْ فِي التَّوْرَاةِ وَمَثَلُهُمْ فِي الْإِنْجِيلِ كَزَرْعٍ أَخْرَجَ شَطْأَهُ فَآزَرَهُ فَاسْتَغْلَظَ فَاسْتَوَى عَلَى سُوقِهِ يُعْجِبُ الزُّرَّاعَ لِيَغِيظَ بِهِمُ الْكُفَّارَ وَعَدَ اللَّهُ الَّذِينَ آمَنُوا وَعَمِلُوا الصَّالِحَاتِ مِنْهُمْ مَغْفِرَةً وَأَجْرًا عَظِيمًا ﴾

"Muhammad is the Messenger of Allāh, and those who are with him are severe against disbelievers, and merciful among themselves. You see them bowing and prostrating, seeking bounty from Allāh and (His) Good Pleasure. Their sign is on their faces from the traces of (their) prostration (during prayers). This is their description in the *Tawrāh*. But their description in the *Injīl* is like a (sown) seed which sends forth its shoot, then makes it strong, it then becomes thick, and it stands straight on its stem, delighting the sowers that He may enrage the disbelievers with them. Allāh has promised those among them who believe and do righteous good deeds, forgiveness and a mighty reward." (Al-Fath 48:29)

And He – the Exalted – said:

121

﴿ وَالسَّابِقُونَ الْأَوَّلُونَ مِنَ الْمُهَاجِرِينَ وَالْأَنْصَارِ وَالَّذِينَ اتَّبَعُوهُمْ بِإِحْسَانٍ رَضِيَ اللَّهُ عَنْهُمْ وَرَضُوا عَنْهُ وَأَعَدَّ لَهُمْ جَنَّاتٍ تَجْرِى تَحْتَهَا الْأَنْهَارُ خَالِدِينَ فِيهَا أَبَدًا ذَلِكَ الْفَوْزُ الْعَظِيمُ ﴾

"And the first forerunners (in _īmān_) among the _Muhājirīn_ and the _Ansār_ and those who followed them in goodness. Allāh is pleased with them and they are pleased with Him, and He has prepared for them gardens beneath which rivers flow, wherein they will abide forever. That is the great attainment."
(At-Tawbah 9:100)

And the Prophet (_sall Allāhu 'alayhi wa sallam_) said:

لا تَسُبُّوا أَصْحَابِي، لا تَسُبُّوا أَصْحَابِي، فَوَالذي نَفْسِي بِيَدِهِ لو أَنَّ أَحَدَكُمْ أَنْفَقَ مِثْلَ أُحُدٍ ذَهَبًا، ما أَدْرَكَ مُدَّ أَحَدِهِمْ، ولا نَصِيفَهُ.

"Do not swear at my companions. Do not swear at my companions. Because by the One in whose Hand my soul is in, if one of you spent an amount of gold at the size of (the mountain of) Uhud, then this would not be equal to the mudd[10] of any of them, and not even the half of it." (Sahīh Muslim)

Ibn Battah (d. 387h) narrated the agreement on not mentioning anything negative which occurred among the _Sahābah_, and testifying to their virtues and good deeds:

ومن بعد ذلك نكف عما شجر بين أصحاب رسول الله – صلى الله عليه وسلم – فقد شهدوا المشاهد معه، وسبقوا الناس بالفضل فقد غفر الله لهم وأمرك بالاستغفار لهم والتقرب إليه بمحبتهم وفرض ذلك على لسان نبيه وهو يعلم ما سيكون منهم وأنهم سيقتتلون وإنما فضلوا على سائر الخلق لأن الخطأ والعمد قد وضع عنهم وكل ما شجر بينهم مغفور لهم ولا تنظر في كتاب صفين والجمل ووقعة الدار وسائر المنازعات التي جرت بينهم ولا تكتبه لنفسك ولا لغيرك ولا تروه عن أحد ولا تقرأه على غيرك ولا تسمعه ممن يرويه فعلى ذلك اتفق سادات علماء هذه الأمة من النهي عما وصفناه

---

[10] The amount which fits in two hands gathered. So the _mudd_ of gold of the _Sahābah_ spent for Allāh is better than the amount of gold equal to the mountain of Uhud of anyone other than them spent for Allāh.

منهم: حماد بن زيد ويونس بن عبيد وسفيان الثوري وسفيان بن عيينة وعبدالله بن إدريس ومالك بن أنس وابن أبي ذئب وابن المنكدر وابن المبارك وشعيب بن حرب وأبو إسحاق الفزاري ويوسف بن أسباط وأحمد بن حنبل وبشر بن الحارث وعبدالوهاب الوراق. كل هؤلاء قد رأوا: النهي عنها والنظر فيها والاستماع إليها وحذروا من طلبها والاهتمام بجمعها.

"And after that we refrain from that which occurred of disputes between the Companions of the Messenger of Allāh (sallAllāhu 'alayhi wa sallam). Because they verily testified the battles with him and they preceded the people in virtues. So Allāh has verily forgiven them and ordered you to ask for forgiveness for them, and seeking nearness to Him by loving them. He made this obligatory upon the tongue of His Prophet while He knew what would occur among them and that they would fight against each other. They were given precedence over all of the creation because (the burden of) the mistake and (what was done with) intent was removed from them, and every dispute which they had was forgiven for them. And do not look in the book 'Siffin' and 'Al-Jamal' and 'Waq'ah Ad-Dār' and all other disagreements which occurred among them. And do not write it down for your self or for anyone else. And do not narrate it from anyone, do not read it for others, and do not listen to it from the one who narrates it. The leaders of the scholars of this Ummah agreed upon this, of prohibition of that which we have described. Among them are: Hammād ibn Zayd, Yūnus ibn 'Ubayd, Sufyān Ath-Thawrī, Sufyān ibn 'Uyaynah, 'Abdullāh ibn Idrīs, Mālik ibn Anas, Ibn Abī Dhib, Ibn Al-Munkadir, Ibn Al-Mubārak, Shu'ayb ibn Harb, Abu Ishaq Al-Fazari, Yusuf ibn Asbat, Ahmad ibn Hanbal, Bishr ibn Al-Hārith and 'Abdul-Wahhāb Al-Warrāq. All of these believed in: the prohibition of (narrating) it, and looking into it, and listening to it. And they warned against seeking it and dedicating (ones self) to gathering it." (Al-Ibānah As-Sughrā by Ibn Battah)

And as for who is the best among the Companions (radiAllāhu 'anhum) internally, then the best of them is Abū Bakr, then 'Umar, then 'Uthmān (radiAllāhu 'anhum) according to the hadīth of Ibn 'Umar (radiAllāhu 'anhumā) who said:

كُنَّا نَعُدُّ وَرَسُولُ اللهِ ﷺ حَيٌّ وَأَصْحَابُهُ مُتَوَافِرُونَ أَبُو بَكْرٍ ثُمَّ عُمَرُ ثُمَّ عُثْمَانُ ثُمَّ نَسْكُتُ

"We used to consider (as the best), when the Messenger of Allāh (sallAllāhu 'alayhi wa sallam) was alive and his Companions were great in numbers, Abū Bakr, then 'Umar, then 'Uthmān, and then we would remain silent." (Takhrīj Al-Musnad – its *isnād* is *sahīh* according to the conditions of Muslim)

And these three, along with 'Alī (*radiAllāhu 'anhu*), are *Al-Khulafā Ar-Rāshidīn* (the rightly guided caliphs).

Then comes the ten who were given the glad tidings of Paradise by the Prophet (*sallAllāhu 'alayhi wa sallam*) when he said:

عَشَرَةٌ فِي الجَنَّةِ : أَبُو بكرٍ فِي الجَنَّةِ وعُمَرُ فِي الجَنَّةِ وعُثْمانُ فِي الجَنَّةِ وعليٌّ فِي الجَنَّةِ والزُّبيرُ فِي الجَنَّةِ وطَلحةُ فِي الجَنَّةِ وابنُ عوفٍ فِي الجَنَّةِ وسعدٌ فِي الجَنَّةِ وسعيدُ بنُ زيدٍ فِي الجَنَّةِ وأَبُو عُبَيدةَ بنُ الجَرَّاحِ فِي الجَنَّةِ

"Ten are in Paradise: Abū Bakr is in Paradise. 'Umar is in Paradise. 'Uthmān is in Paradise. 'Alī is in Paradise. Az-Zubayr is in Paradise. Talhah is in Paradise. ('Abdur-Rahmān) ibn 'Awf is in Paradise. Sa'd (ibn Abī Waqqās) is in Paradise. Sa'īd ibn Zayd is in Paradise. Abū 'Ubaydah ibn Al-Jarrāh is in Paradise." (Sahīh Ibn Hibbān)

And then in general the *Muhājirūn* – who were those who emigrated with the Prophet (*sallAllāhu 'alayhi wa sallam*) from Makkah to Madīnah – and the *Ansār*, who were the inhabitants of Madinah who received and gave support to the Prophet (*sallAllāhu 'alayhi wa sallam*) and Islām, may Allāh be pleased with all of them.

Those who oppose these principles are the **Shī'ah** and the **Rāfidah**. Among their misguided beliefs of innovation are:

* Believing that 'Alī was better than 'Uthmān. These people fell into an innovation.

* Hating and cursing the Companions (*radiAllāhu 'anhum*) of the Messenger of Allāh (*sallAllāhu 'alayhi wa sallam*). These people are

kuffār, due to cursing the people whom Allāh chose to carry His message, those He gave the stamp of approval and those whom He is pleased with.

* Ascribing divine Attributes to the household of the Prophet (*sallAllāhu 'alayhi wa sallam*) and ascribing them as partners with Allāh in worship. Among these are:

- Those who invoke or ask for help from 'Alī, Fātimah, Husayn (*radiAllāhu 'anhum*) and others.
- Those who claim that their 12 Imāms have knowledge about the unseen, or can arrange or have influence upon the affairs of the creation.

* Those who claim that parts of the Qurān are missing, or it has been substituted or changed or similar to this. These people are *kuffār*.

* Some claim that the latecomers have more knowledge and understanding in the religion that the *Sahābah* and the scholars of the *Salaf*.

* Some claim that Jibrīl (*'alayhi as-salām*) made a mistake when he brought the message and prophethood from Allāh to Muhammad (*sallAllāhu 'alayhi wa sallam*). These are *kuffār*.

Ibn 'Abbās (*radiAllāhu 'anhu*) said:

كُنْتُ عندَ النَّبِيّ صلَّى اللهُ عليه وسلَّم وعندَه عليٌّ فقال النَّبِيُّ صلَّى اللهُ عليه وسلَّم يا عليُّ سيكونُ في أُمَّتي قومٌ ينتَحِلونَ حبَّ أهلِ البيتِ لهم نَبْزٌ يُسمَّونَ الرَّافضةَ قاتِلُوهم فإنَّهم مشرِكونَ

"I was with the Prophet (sallAllāhu 'alayhi wa sallam) while 'Alī was with him. Then the Prophet (sallAllāhu 'alayhi wa sallam) said: 'O 'Alī. In my Ummah there will come a people who unrightfully will claim to love Ahlul-Bayt (the household of the Prophet). They have a nickname and are called the Rāfidah. Fight against them, for verily they are mushrikūn.'" (Majma' Az-Zawāid by Al-Haythamī – its *isnād* is *hasan*)

And 'Alī (*radiAllāhu 'anhu*) said:

سيكون بعدنا قوم ينتحلون مودتنا، يكذبون علينا، مارقة، آية ذلك، أنهم يسبون أبا بكر وعمر

"*After us there will come a people who unrighfully claim to love us. They are lying against us (and there are) māriqah (i.e. people who have left the religion). The sign of this is, that they curse Abū Bakr and 'Umar.*" (Sharh Usūl I'tiqād Ahlus-Sunnah by Al-Lālakāī)

Īmān is in speech and deeds, it increases and decreases

The people of *Sunnah* define *īmān* as being both in words and deeds[11], and that the *īmān* of the slave increases when he performs good deeds and it decreases when he performs sins.

Allah – the Exalted – said:

﴿ الَّذِينَ قَالَ لَهُمُ النَّاسُ إِنَّ النَّاسَ قَدْ جَمَعُوا لَكُمْ فَاخْشَوْهُمْ فَزَادَهُمْ إِيمَانًا وَقَالُوا حَسْبُنَا اللَّهُ وَنِعْمَ الْوَكِيلُ ﴾

"Those to whom the people said: 'Verily have the people gathered against you, so fear them.' But this (only) increased them in *īmān* and they said: 'Allāh is sufficient for us, and (He is) the Best Disposer of affairs." (Āli 'Imrān 3:173)

The Prophet (*sallAllāhu 'alayhi wa sallam*) said:

الإِيمَانُ بِضْعٌ وَسَبْعُونَ، أَوْ بِضْعٌ وَسِتُّونَ، شُعْبَةً، فَأَفْضَلُهَا قَوْلُ لا إِلَهَ إِلَّا اللَّهُ، وَأَدْنَاهَا إِمَاطَةُ الأَذَى عَنِ الطَّرِيقِ، والْحَيَاءُ شُعْبَةٌ مِنَ الإِيمَانِ.

"Īmān is seventy odd or sixty odd categories. The best of them is Lā ilāha illa Allāh and the lowest of them is removing the harm from the road. And hayā (shyness) is from īmān." (Sahīh Muslim)

And the Prophet (*sallAllāhu 'alayhi wa sallam*) also said:

أَكْمَلُ المؤمِنِينَ إِيمَاناً أَحْسَنُهُم خُلُقاً، وخِيَارُكُم خِيَارُكُمْ لِنِسَائِهِمْ

"The believers with the most complete īmān are those with the best manners. And the best of you are those who behave best towards their women." (Ahmad, At-Tirmidhī and Abū Dāwūd – *hasan sahīh*)

---

[11] When the *Salaf* said *īmān* is in speech and deeds, then they intented: the speech of the heart and the tongue, and the deeds of the heart and the limbs. The speech of the heart is the belief and the conviction, while the deeds of the heart are the likes of hope, fear, longing etc. As for the speech of the tongue and the deeds of the limbs, then this is clear.

And Jundub ibn ʿAbdullāh (radiAllāhu ʿanhu) said:

كُنَّا مَعَ النَّبِيِّ – صَلَّى اللَّهُ عليهِ وعلى آلِهِ وسلَّمَ – ونحنُ فِتيانٌ حَزاوِرَةٌ ، فتعلَّمنا الإِيمانَ قبْلَ أنْ
نتعلَّمَ القرآنَ ثُمَّ تعلَّمنا القرآنَ فازدَدنا بِهِ إِيمانًا

"We were with the Messenger of Allāh (sallAllāhu ʿalayhi wa ʿala alihi wa sallam) and we were young boys, so we would learn about īmān before we would learn the Qurān. And then we would learn the Qurān, and by that we would increase in īmān." (Ibn Mājah - sahīh)

And ʾAbdullāh ibn Masʿūd (radiAllāhu ʿanhu) use to make the *duʿā* (invocation):

اللَّهُمَّ زِدْنَا إِيمانًا وَيَقِينًا وَفِقْهًا

"O Allāh, increase us in iman, in certainty and in understanding." (As-Sharīʿah by Al-Ājurrī 7/262)

These narrations – along with many many more – all give evidence to the fact that deeds are a part of *īmān*, and that the *īmān* can increase and thereby also decrease.

A misguided group called the **Murjiah** innovated the claim that the deeds of the limbs are not included in *īmān*, which meant that whoever believes in his heart and testifies to *īmān* with his words, then he has a complete *īmān* and no sin would harm him in his *īmān*. **And with this they opened the door for sinning for the *Ummah*.** Because according to their claim sins had no consequences upon the completeness of *īmān*. The *Salaf* would refute and disagree with the claim of the Murjiah, warn against them and consider them as innovators.

ʾAbdullāh ibn Imām Ahmad (d. 290h) narrated:

حَدَّثَنِي سُوَيْدُ بْنُ سَعِيدٍ، نا عَبْدُ اللهِ بْنُ مَيْمُونٍ، قَالَ: سَمِعْتُ ابْنَ مُجَاهِدٍ، قَالَ: كُنْتُ عِنْدَ عَطَاءِ بْنِ أَبِي
رَبَاحٍ فَجَاءَ ابْنُهُ يَعْقُوبُ، فَقَالَ: يَا أَبَتَاهُ إِنَّ أَصْحَابًا لَنَا يَزْعُمُونَ أَنَّ إِيمَانَهُمْ كَإِيمَانِ جِبْرِيلَ عَلَيْهِ السَّلَامُ،
فَقَالَ: «يَا بُنَيَّ كَذَبُوا لَيْسَ إِيمَانُ مَنْ أَطَاعَ اللهَ عَزَّ وَجَلَّ كَإِيمَانِ مَنْ عَصَى اللهَ تَعَالَى»

128

"Suwayd ibn Sa'īd narrated to me, from 'Abdullāh ibn Maymūn who said: I heard Ibn Mujāhid say: 'I was with 'Atā ibn Abī Rabāh when his son Ya'qūb came, and then said: 'O father, some of our companions claim that their īmān is like the īmān of Jibrīl ('alayhi as-salām).' So he said: 'O my son. They have lied. The īmān of the one who obeys Allāh – 'azza wa jalla – is not like the īmān of the one who disobeys Allāh the Exalted.'"(Kitāb As-Sunnah by 'Abdullāh)

And Fudayl ibn 'Iyyād (d. 187h) said:

أَصْلُ الْإِيمَانِ عِنْدَنَا وَفَرْعُهُ بَعْدَ الشَّهَادَةِ وَالتَّوْحِيدِ وَبَعْدَ الشَّهَادَةِ لِلنَّبِيِّ صَلَّى اللهُ عَلَيْهِ وَسَلَّمَ بِالْبَلَاغِ وَبَعْدَ أَدَاءِ الْفَرَائِضِ صِدْقُ الْحَدِيثِ، وَحِفْظُ الْأَمَانَةِ، وَتَرْكُ الْخِيَانَةِ، وَالْوَفَاءُ بِالْعَهْدِ، وَصِلَةُ الرَّحِمِ، وَالنَّصِيحَةُ لِجَمِيعِ الْمُسْلِمِينَ، وَالرَّحْمَةُ لِلنَّاسِ عَامَّةً

"The foundation of īmān for us and its branches – after the Shahādah and the Tawhīd, and after the testimony to the Prophet (sallAllāhu alayhi wa sallam) that he brought the Message, and after performing the obligatory acts of worship, is speaking truthfully, preserving the trust, leaving betrayal, fulfilling the promise, keeping the bond of kinship, giving advice to all of the Muslims and being merciful with all people in general." (As-Sunnah by 'Abdullāh)

So the belief of the *Salaf* is in accordance with the Qurān and *Sunnah*, which states that the deeds of the limbs all are included in *īmān*.

The **Jahmiyyah** went even further astray when they claimed that *īmān* merely is the knowledge or acknowledgement of the heart, without any speech or apparent deeds. And the *Salaf* declared them as *kuffār* because of this, due to claiming that whoever curses Allāh or performs a *nāqid* (nullifier) from the *nawāqid* of Islām, then even if he gets the *hukm* of a *kāfir* in *dunyā*, then he could still be a believer in the sight of Allāh due to the *īmān* of his heart. And this necessitate that the Jews, Christians and even Iblīs all could be believers.

129

Wakī' ibn Al-Jarrāh (d. 197h) said:

قَدْ قَالَتِ الْمُرْجِئَةُ: الْإِقْرَارُ بِمَا جَاءَ مِنْ عِنْدِ اللَّهِ عَزَّ وَجَلَّ يُجْزِئُ مِنَ الْعَمَلِ، وَقَالَتِ الْجَهْمِيَّةُ الْمَعْرِفَةُ بِالْقَلْبِ بِمَا جَاءَ مِنْ عِنْدِ اللَّهِ يُجْزِئُ مِنَ الْقَوْلِ وَالْعَمَلِ وَهَذَا كُفْرٌ

"Verily did the Murjiah say: 'The acknowledgement (with the heart and tongue) of that which has come from Allāh – 'azza wa jalla – is sufficient from the deeds.' And the Jahmiyyah said: 'The knowledge in the heart regarding that which has come from Allāh, is sufficient from the words and the deeds', and this is kufr." (As-Sunnah by 'Abdullāh)

Harb ibn Ismā'īl Al-Karmānī (d. 280h) said:

ومن زعم إن المعرفة تنفع في القلب و إن لم يتكلم بها فهو جهمي

"And whoever claims that the knowledge (or acknowledgement) of the heart benefits, even if he does not utter it, then he is a jahmī." (As-Sunnah by Al-Karmānī)

And they verily agreed upon the *kufr* of the Jahmiyyah.

The *bid'ah* of the Murjiah – i.e. excluding the deeds of the limbs from *īmān* – is the starting point of many innovations as it will be clear.

The one who leaves the prayer is *kāfir*

As a consequence of the saying of the Murjiah – that the deeds of the limbs are not from *īmān* – these innovators would not declare *takfīr* upon the one who leaves the prayer. The scholars included the issue of declaring *takfīr* upon the one who leaves the prayer among the principles of the *Sunnah*, due to the clear evidences narrated regarding it, and the innovators turning away from it.

The Prophet (*sallAllāhu 'alayhi wa sallam*) said:

ليسَ بينَ العبدِ والشِّركِ إلَّا تركُ الصَّلاةِ فإذا تَرَكَها فقد أشرَكَ

"There is nothing between the slave and shirk, except leaving the prayer. So whoever leaves it has verily committed shirk." (Sahīh Ibn Mājah)

And he (*sallAllāhu 'alayhi wa sallam*) said:

إنَّ الْعَهْدَ الَّذِي بَيْنَنَا وَبَيْنَهُمُ الصَّلَاةُ فَمَنْ تَرَكَهَا فَقَدْ كَفَرَ

"The covenant which stands between us and them is the prayer, so whoever leaves it he has verily committed kufr." (At-Tirmidhī, Ahmad, Ibn Hibbān, An-Nasāī - *sahīh*)

And it is narrated with a *hasan* chain of narration:

عن مجاهد أبي الحجاج أنه سأل جابر بن عبد الله رضي الله عنه : ما كان يفرق بين الكفر والإيمان عندكم في عهد رسول الله صلى الله عليه وسلم ؟ فقال : الصلاة

"From Mujāhid Abū Al-Hajjāj, that he asked Jābir ibn 'Abdullāh (radiAllāhu 'anhu): 'What used to differentiate between kufr and īmān for you (i.e. the Sahābah) in the time of the Messenger of Allāh (sallAllāhu 'alayhi wa sallam)?' He (i.e. Jābir) said: 'The prayer.'" (Sharh Usūl Al-I'tiqād Ahlus-Sunnah by Al-Lālakāī 4/829)

131

And Abū Hurayrah (radiAllāhu 'anhu) said:

كان أصحاب رسول الله صلى الله عليه وسلم لا يرون شيئا من الأعمال تركه كفرا غير الصلاة

"The Companions of the Messenger of Allāh (sallAllāhu 'alayhi wa sallam) would not consider leaving any of the deeds as kufr, except the prayer." (Al-Hākim – sahīh according to the conditions of Al-Bukhārī and Muslim)

And Ayyūb As-Sikhtiyānī (d. 131h) said:

تَرْكُ الصلاة كُفْر، لا يُختلَفُ فيه

"Leaving the prayer is kufr. There is no disagreement regarding this." (Ta'dhīm Qadr As-Salāh by Al-Marwazī)

And Ishāq ibn Rāhūyah (d. 238h) said:

قد صح عن رسول الله صلى الله عليه وسلم أن تارك الصلاة كافر، وكذلك كان رأي أهل العلم من لدن النبي صلى الله عليه وسلم إلى يومنا هذا أن تارك الصلاة عمدا من غير عذر حتى يذهب وقتها كافر.

"It has verily correctly been narrated from the Messenger of Allāh (sallAllāhu 'alayhi wa sallam) that the one who leaves the prayer is kāfir. And likewise was the opinion of the people of knowledge from the time of the Prophet (sallAllāhu 'alayhi wa sallam) until this day of ours; that the one who leaves the prayer on purpose without an excuse, until its (prescribed) time leaves, he is kāfir." (Ta'dhīm Qadr As-Salāh by Al-Marwazī 2/929)

And Al-Hasan Al-Basrī (d. 110h) said:

بلغني أن أصحاب رسول الله صلى الله عليه وسلم كانوا يقولون: بين العبد وبين أن يشرك فيكفر أن يدع الصلاة من غير عذر

"It has reached me that the Companions of the Messenger of Allāh (sallAllāhu 'alayhi wa sallam) used to say: 'Between the slave and between

him committing shirk whereby he commits kufr, is that he leaves the prayer without any excuse." (Sharh Usūl I'tiqād Ahlus-Sunnah by Al-Lalakai)

And Imām Ahmad (d. 241h) said:

وَلَيْسَ مِنْ اَلْأَعْمَالِ شَيْءٌ تَرْكُهُ كُفْرٌ إِلَّا اَلصَّلَاةُ، مَنْ تَرَكَهَا فَهُوَ كَافِرٌ.

"And there is nothing from the deeds where leaving it is kufr, except the prayer. Whoever leaves it, then he is kāfir." (Usūl As-Sunnah by Imām Ahmad – the riwāyah of 'Abdūs)

Thus, the so-called "disagreement" which has occurred regarding the one who leaves the prayer, whether he commits *kufr* or not by this, is a disagreement that did not exist between the Companions of the Messenger of Allāh (*sallAllāhu 'alayhi wa sallam*), nor those who followed them in goodness. And the opinion that the one who leaves the prayer does not commit *kufr* and leave Islām has its basis in the *'aqīdah* of the Murjiah, and therefore it is an innovation which is not to be taken into consideration.

The one who leaves the prayer is *kāfir*, and the one who excuses him is following a *shubah* (doubt) which originates from *irjā* (i.e. the belief of the Murjiah). The correct *ahādīth* have already refuted the claim that the one who leaves the prayer is still a Muslim. The Prophet (*sallAllāhu 'alayhi wa sallam*) said:

إِنَّه يُسْتَعْمَلُ عَلَيْكُم أُمَرَاءُ، فَتَعْرِفُونَ وتُنْكِرُونَ، فَمَن كَرِهَ فَقَدْ بَرِئَ، ومَن أَنْكَرَ فَقَدْ سَلِمَ، ولَكِنْ مَن رَضِيَ وتابَعَ، قالوا: يا رَسولَ اللهِ، ألا نُقاتِلُهُمْ؟ قالَ: لا، ما صَلَّوا.

"Verily leaders will be appointed over you (from which) you will acknowledge (some of their deeds) and reject (others). So whoever hates (their bad deeds) is innocent. And whoever rejects it is safe. But whoever is pleased and follows it (is destroyed). They said: 'O Messenger of Allāh, should we not fight against them?' He said: 'No, not as long as they pray (the five prayers).'" (Sahīh Muslim)

Ishāq ibn Rāhūyah (d. 238h) said about this *hadīth*:

وفيها هلاك المرجئة

"And in it is the destruction of the Murjiah." (Musnad Ibn 'Awānah)

This is because the Prophet (*sallAllāhu 'alayhi wa sallam*) made the prayer the distinguishing factor between Islām and *kufr* in this life (as long as no *nawāqid* are performed), and by leaving the prayer the leader is no longer obeyed, which means he becomes a *kāfir*.

The Prophet (*sallAllāhu 'alayhi wa sallam*) also said in a longer *hadīth* about the events of the Day of Judgment after some people have entered Hellfire:

أَمَرَ الملَائِكَةَ أَنْ يُخْرِجُوا مِنَ النَّارِ، مَن كانَ لا يُشْرِكُ بِاللَّهِ شيئًا، مِمَّنْ أَرَادَ اللَّهُ أَنْ يَرْحَمَهُ، مِمَّنْ يَشْهَدُ أَنْ لا إِلَهَ إِلَّا اللَّهُ، فَيَعْرِفُونَهُمْ في النَّارِ بِأَثَرِ السُّجُودِ، تَأْكُلُ النَّارُ ابْنَ آدَمَ إِلَّا أَثَرَ السُّجُودِ، حَرَّمَ اللَّهُ عَلَى النَّارِ أَنْ تَأْكُلَ أَثَرَ السُّجُودِ

"Then He orders the angels to bring out from Hellfire whoever who did not associate partners with Allāh in worship (in dunyā), among those whom Allāh wants to show mercy, from those who testify to Lā ilāha illa Allāh. So they (i.e. the angels) will recognize them in the fire by their trace of prostration. The fire eats (all of) the son of Adam except the trace of prostration, (because) Allāh forbade the fire to eat the trace of prostration." (Sahīh Al-Bukhārī)

This *hadīth* also proves – in accordance with all the other evidence – that whoever wants a hope of exiting the fire after having being thrown in it, must be from the people of the prayer, since the trace of prostration only appears on the one who used to pray.

The one who performs a major sin is a Muslim with faulty *īmān*

Ahlus-Sunnah believes that the person who performs a major sin – which is lesser than major *shirk* and major *kufr* – deserves the threat which is connected to the sin performed, just as this has been narrated in the texts from the Qurān and *Sunnah*. But he does not leave Islām by this, nor is he judged as being in Hellfire forever if he dies without having repented. Rather he is a Muslim with the basis of his *īmān* (i.e. its basis is there but his *īmān* is faulty due to his sin), and a *fāsiq* (sinner) due to his major sin. And he is under the *Mashīah* (Will) of Allāh; if He wants He will punish him according to his sin, and if He wants to He will forgive and pardon him.

Muhammad ibn Ismāʿīl Al-Bukhārī (d. 256h) said:

بَابُ الْمَعَاصِي مِنْ أَمْرِ الْجَاهِلِيَّةِ وَلَا يُكَفَّرُ صَاحِبُهَا بِارْتِكَابِهَا إِلَّا بِالشِّرْكِ لِقَوْلِ النَّبِيِّ صَلَّى اللهُ عَلَيْهِ وَسَلَّمَ إِنَّكَ امْرُؤٌ فِيكَ جَاهِلِيَّةٌ وَقَوْلِ اللهِ تَعَالَى إِنَّ اللهَ لَا يَغْفِرُ أَنْ يُشْرَكَ بِهِ وَيَغْفِرُ مَا دُونَ ذَلِكَ لِمَنْ يَشَاءُ

30 - حَدَّثَنَا سُلَيْمَانُ بْنُ حَرْبٍ قَالَ حَدَّثَنَا شُعْبَةُ عَنْ وَاصِلٍ الْأَحْدَبِ عَنِ الْمَعْرُورِ بْنِ سُوَيْدٍ قَالَ لَقِيتُ أَبَا ذَرٍّ بِالرَّبَذَةِ وَعَلَيْهِ حُلَّةٌ وَعَلَى غُلَامِهِ حُلَّةٌ فَسَأَلْتُهُ عَنْ ذَلِكَ فَقَالَ إِنِّي سَابَبْتُ رَجُلًا فَعَيَّرْتُهُ بِأُمِّهِ فَقَالَ لِي النَّبِيُّ صَلَّى اللهُ عَلَيْهِ وَسَلَّمَ يَا أَبَا ذَرٍّ أَعَيَّرْتَهُ بِأُمِّهِ إِنَّكَ امْرُؤٌ فِيكَ جَاهِلِيَّةٌ إِخْوَانُكُمْ خَوَلُكُمْ جَعَلَهُمُ اللهُ تَحْتَ أَيْدِيكُمْ فَمَنْ كَانَ أَخُوهُ تَحْتَ يَدِهِ فَلْيُطْعِمْهُ مِمَّا يَأْكُلُ وَلْيُلْبِسْهُ مِمَّا يَلْبَسُ وَلَا تُكَلِّفُوهُمْ مَا يَغْلِبُهُمْ فَإِنْ كَلَّفْتُمُوهُمْ فَأَعِينُوهُمْ

"Chapter: The sins are from the affairs of jāhiliyyah, and takfīr is not declared upon the one performing them, except if it is shirk. Due to the saying of the Prophet (sallAllāhu ʿalayhi wa sallam): **'You are verily a person in which there is some jāhiliyyah.'** *And the words of Allāh the Exalted:* **"Verily Allāh does not forgive that partners are associated with Him** (in worship), **and He forgives whatever is besides this for whomever He wants."**

30 – *Sulaymān ibn Harb narrated to us and said: Shu'bah narrated to us, from Wāsil Al-Ahdab, from Al-Ma'rūr ibn Suwayd who said: I met Abū Dhar in Ar-Rabdhah and he was wearing a cloak and his slaveboy was also wearing a cloak. So I asked him regarding this. So he said: "I verily cursed at a man by and dishonored him by (saying evil words about) his mother. So the Prophet (sallAllāhu 'alayhi wa sallam) said to me:* **'O Abū Dhar. Did you dishonor him by his mother? You are verily a person in which there is some jāhiliyyah. Your slaves are your brothers. Allāh has made them under your hands (i.e. authority). So whoever has his brother under his hand, then let him feed him with what he feeds himself, and clothe him with what he clothes himself. And do not burden them with what is too much for them, and if you burden them (with hard work) then help them.'"** (Sahīh Al-Bukhārī)

Imām Ahmad (d. 241h) said:

وَمَنْ مَاتَ مِنْ أَهْلِ الْقِبْلَةِ مُوَحِّدًا يُصَلَّى عَلَيْهِ، وَيُسْتَغْفَرُ لَهُ وَلَا يُحْجَبُ عَنْهُ الِاسْتِغْفَارُ، وَلَا تُتْرَكُ اَلصَّلَاةُ عَلَيْهِ لِذَنْبٍ أَذْنَبَهُ صَغِيرًا كَانَ أَوْ كَبِيرًا، أَمْرُهُ إِلَى اَللَّهِ تَعَالَى.

"And whoever dies from the Ahlul-Qiblah (i.e. those who pray) as a muwahhid then he is prayed upon, and forgiveness is asked for him and asking for forgiveness for him is not forsaken. Nor is the prayer upon him left due to a sin which he committed, whether it is small or big. His affairs are with Allāh the Exalted." (Usūl As-Sunnah by Imām Ahmad – the riwāyah of 'Abdūs)

The **Murjiah** – as this has already gone forth – claims that sins have no effect upon *īmān*, and that whoever commits a major sin still has a complete *īmān* as long as his *īmān* in speech and the heart remains. And these people are innovators if their claim does not exceed this claim.

The **Khawārij** deviated by claiming that the one who commits a major sin is a *kāfir* and will remain in Hellfire forever if he dies without having repented from the sin. The **Mu'tazilah** took from the Khawārij that the one who commits major sin remains in Hellfire forever without the possibility of Allāh forgiving and pardoning him, but they differed with the Khawārij in what they named him in *dunyā*. While Khawārij says he is *kāfir*, the Mu'tazilah claimed that the one who commits a major sin is neither a Muslim nor a *kāfir*, rather he is in *al-manzilah bayn al-mazilatayn* (the position between the two positions).

These beliefs are all innovations that oppose the Qurān and the *Sunnah* in accordance with the understanding of the *Salaf*, and the evidences have already refuted all of these claims.

The Prophet (*sallAllāhu 'alayhi wa sallam*) said:

يَدْخُلُ أَهْلُ الجَنَّةِ الجَنَّةَ، وَأَهْلُ النَّارِ النَّارَ، ثُمَّ يقولُ اللَّهُ تَعَالَى: أَخْرِجُوا مِنَ النَّارِ مَن كانَ في قَلْبِهِ مِثْقَا

لُ حَبَّةٍ مِن خَرْدَلٍ مِن إِيَمَانٍ. فيُخْرَجُونَ منها قَدِ اسْوَدُّوا

"The people of Paradise will enter Paradise and the people of Hellfire will enter Hellfire. Then Allāh – the Exalted – will say: 'Bring out from Hellfire anyone who had īmān at the size of a mustard seed in his heart. Then they will come out of it, when they (already) have become black (like coals)." (Sahīh Al-Bukhārī)

So this *hadīth* with clarity proves that some believers will enter Hellfire due to their sins, and then they will be brought out of it due to their *īmān*.

Al-Istithnā (the exception)

Ahlus-Sunnah refrain from describing themselves or others as believers (*muminūn*) without adding: '*In shā Allāh*' or 'I hope' or something similar to this. This is referred to as *al-istithnā* (the exception) in *īmān*. The reasons for this exception is that a Muslim should not purify himself, nor should he claim to be guaranteed the entrance into Paradise, nor does he know about his *īmān* whether it is complete or not, since this would mean that he has fulfilled all the obligatory acts of worship without the slightest flaw along with having avoided everything of the forbidden, and this all then have been accepted by Allāh. And they followed the Prophet (*sallAllāhu 'alayhi wa sallam*) and the Sahābah (*radiAllāhu 'anhum*) in this belief and practice.

The Prophet (*sallAllāhu 'alayhi wa sallam*) said to the people in the graves:

السَّلامُ عليكم دارَ قومٍ مؤمنينَ وإنَّا إنْ شاء اللهُ بكم لاحِقونَ

"As-Salāmu 'alaykum the abode of a believing people. And verily will we in sha Allāh (if Allāh wills) follow you." (Sahīh Ibn Hibbān)

And the Prophet (*sallAllāhu 'alayhi wa sallam*) said in a longer *hadīth* in which he described the testing in the grave:

فيقالُ لَه انظُرْ إلى ما وقاكَ اللهُ عزَّ وجلَّ ثمَّ يُفرَجُ لَه فرجةٌ إلى الجنَّةِ فينظُرُ إلى زَهرتِها وما فيها فيقالُ لَه هذا مقعدُك منها ويقالُ علَى اليقينِ كنتَ وعليهِ مُتَّ وعليهِ تُبعَثُ إن شاءَ اللهُ

"Then it will be said to him: 'Look at what Allāh – 'azza wa jalla – has preserved for you.' And then an opening will be opened for him to Paradise and he will look at its beauty and whatever is in it. Then it will be said to him: 'This is your place in it.' And it will be said: 'Upon certainty were you, and upon did you die, and upon it you will be resurrected in sha Allāh." (Musnad Imām Ahmad – sahīh)

And 'Alqamah (d. between 60h and 73h) said:

قَالَ رَجُلٌ عِنْدَ عَبْدَاللَّهِ: إِنِّي مُؤْمِنٌ. قَالَ: قُلْ: إِنِّي فِي الْجَنَّةِ، وَلَكِنَّا نَقُولُ: آمَنَّا بِاللَّهِ وَمَلَائِكَتِهِ وَكُتُبِهِ وَرُسُلِهِ

*"A man said in front of 'Abdullāh (ibn Mas'ud): 'I am verily a believer.'
So he said: '(Why don't you) say: 'I will verily be in Paradise.' Rather we
say: We have believed in Allah, His angels, His Books and His
messengers.'"* (Al-Musannaf by Ibn Abī Shaybah, and As-Sunnah by
'Abdullāh)

And 'Abdullāh ibn Ahmad (d. 290h) narrated:

حَدَّثَنِي أَبُو بَكْرِ بْنُ أَبِي شَيْبَةَ، نا جَرِيرُ بْنُ عَبْدِ الْحَمِيدِ، عَنْ مُغِيرَةَ، عَنْ سِمَاكِ بْنِ سَلَمَةَ الضَّبِّيِّ، عَنْ
عَبْدِ الرَّحْمَنِ بْنِ عِصْمَةَ، قَالَ: كُنْتُ عِنْدَ عَائِشَةَ رَضِيَ اللَّهُ عَنْهَا فَأَتَاهَا رَسُولُ مُعَاوِيَةَ رَضِيَ اللَّهُ عَنْهُ
بِهَدِيَّةٍ فَقَالَ: أَرْسَلَ بِهَا إِلَيْكِ أَمِيرُ الْمُؤْمِنِينَ فَقَالَتْ: «أَنْتُمُ الْمُؤْمِنُونَ إِنْ شَاءَ اللَّهُ تَعَالَى وَهُوَ أَمِيرُكُمْ وَقَدْ
قَبِلْتُ هَدِيَّتَهُ»

*"Abū Bakr ibn Abī Shaybah narrated to me, from Jarīr ibn 'Abdul-Hamīd,
from Mughīrah, from Simāk ibn Salamah Ad-Dabbī, from 'Abdur-
Rahmān ibn 'Ismah who said: "I was with 'Āishah (radiAllāhu 'anhā)
when the messenger of Mu'āwiyah (radiAllāhu 'anhu) came to her with a
gift. So he said: 'Amīr Al-Muminīn has sent this for you.' So she said:
'You are the believers in shā Allāh ta'ālā, and he is your amīr, and I have
verily accepted his gift.'"* (As-Sunnah by 'Abdullāh)

The **Murjiah** negated the *istithnā* and forbade it and called it
doubting in ones *īmān*. This is because *īmān* for them is only in belief
and speech, so whoever professes to *īmān* – according to them – has
complete *īmān*.

The people of *Sunnah* disagreed with them on this issue, and some
took a softer stance in this issue, under the condition that the person
not making *istithnā* otherwise had the correct *'aqīdah* regarding the
definition of *īmān*.

'Abdullāh ibn Ahmad (d. 290h) narrated:

حَدَّثَنِي مُحَمَّدُ بْنُ سُلَيْمَانَ لُوَيْنٌ الْأَسَدِيُّ، قَالَ: قِيلَ لِسُفْيَانَ: رَجُلٌ يَقُولُ مُؤْمِنٌ أَنْتَ؟ قَالَ: «مَا أَشُكُّ فِي إِيمَانِي وَسُؤَالُكَ إِيَّايَ بِدْعَةٌ مَا أَدْرِي مَا أَنَا عِنْدَ اللهِ عَزَّ وَجَلَّ شَقِيٌّ أَوْ مَقْبُولُ الْعَمَلِ أَوْ لَا؟»

"Muhammad ibn Sulaymān Luwayn Al-Asadī narrated to me and said: "It was said to Sufyān: 'Are you a believer?' So he said: 'I do not doubt in my īmān, and your question to me is a bid'ah. I do not know what status I have with Allāh, if I am unhappy or my deeds have been accepted or not?" (Kitab As-Sunnah by 'Abdullāh)

And he also narrated from his father Imām Ahmad:

سَأَلْتُ أَبِي عَنْ رَجُلٍ، يَقُولُ: الْإِيمَانُ قَوْلٌ وَعَمَلٌ يَزِيدُ وَيَنْقُصُ وَلَكِنْ لَا يَسْتَثْنِي أَمُرْجِئٌ؟ قَالَ: «أَرْجُو أَنْ لَا يَكُونَ مُرْجِئًا»

"I asked my father about a man who says: Īmān is in speech and deeds, and it increases and decreases, but he does not make istithnā, is he a murjī? He said: 'I hope that he is not a murjī.'"[12]

---

[12] The one who has the correct fundamental beliefs, but refrains from performing the istihnā, then Imām Ahmad here said that he hopes that he is not a murjī, while other scholars would declare him a murjī based upon this only. This shows the importance and obligation of al-istithnā, and that it is an issue which should not be underestimated.

Belief in the Books and the Messengers

Allāh – the Exalted – sent messengers and revealed books as a guidance, a mercy and an argument upon mankind and *jinn*. The people of *Sunnah* believe in all the messengers and prophets of Allāh, and they believe in all the books sent from Allāh, except that the Qurān which was revealed to the final Messenger Muhammad (*sallAllāhu 'alayhi wa sallam*) rendered the previous legislations abrogated and no longer to be followed.

Allāh – the Exalted – said:

﴿ يَا أَيُّهَا الَّذِينَ آمَنُوا آمِنُوا بِاللَّهِ وَرَسُولِهِ وَالْكِتَابِ الَّذِي نَزَّلَ عَلَى رَسُولِهِ وَالْكِتَابِ الَّذِي أَنْزَلَ مِنْ قَبْلُ وَمَنْ يَكْفُرْ بِاللَّهِ وَمَلَائِكَتِهِ وَكُتُبِهِ وَرُسُلِهِ وَالْيَوْمِ الْآخِرِ فَقَدْ ضَلَّ ضَلَالًا بَعِيدًا ﴾

"O you who believe, believe in Allāh and His Messenger and the Book which was revealed to His Messenger and the book which was revealed before. And whoever rejects Allāh, His angels, His books, His messengers and the Last Day, then he has verily gone far astray." (An-Nisā 4:136)

And He – the Exalted – said:

﴿ آمَنَ الرَّسُولُ بِمَا أُنْزِلَ إِلَيْهِ مِنْ رَبِّهِ وَالْمُؤْمِنُونَ كُلٌّ آمَنَ بِاللَّهِ وَمَلَائِكَتِهِ وَكُتُبِهِ وَرُسُلِهِ لَا نُفَرِّقُ بَيْنَ أَحَدٍ مِنْ رُسُلِهِ وَقَالُوا سَمِعْنَا وَأَطَعْنَا غُفْرَانَكَ رَبَّنَا وَإِلَيْكَ الْمَصِيرُ ﴾

"The Messenger belives in what have been revealed to him from his Lord, and (so do) the believers. They all believe in Allāh, His angels, His books and His messengers. We do not differentiate between any of His messengers." (Al-Baqarah 2:285)

Ibn Zayd (d. 159h) said:

لَا نُفَرِّقُ بَيْنَ أَحَدٍ مِنْ رُسُلِهِ " كَمَا صَنَعَ الْقَوْمُ – يَعْنِي بَنِي إِسْرَائِيلَ – قَالُوا : فُلَانٌ نَبِيٌّ ، وَفُلَانٌ لَيْسَ نَبِيًّا ، وَفُلَانٌ نُؤْمِنُ بِهِ ، وَفُلَانٌ لَا نُؤْمِنُ بِهِ.

"We do not differentiate between any of His messengers. *Just as the people did – i.e. Banū Isrāīl – (when) they said: 'So-and-so is a prophet*

141

and so-and-so is not a prophet. And we believe in so-and-so, but we do not believe in so-and-so.'" (Tafsīr At-Tabarī)

And Jābir ibn 'Abdullāh (*radiAllāhu 'anhu*) narrated:

أنَّ عُمَرَ بنَ الْخَطَّابِ أَتَى النَّبِيَّ صلى الله عليه وسلم بِكِتَابٍ أَصَابَهُ مِنْ بَعْضِ أَهْلِ الْكُتُبِ، فَقَرَأَهُ عَلَى النَّبِيِّ صلى الله عليه وسلم فَغَضِبَ وَقَالَ: أَمُتَهَوِّكُونَ فِيهَا يَا ابْنَ الْخَطَّابِ؟! وَالَّذِي نَفْسِي بِيَدِهِ لَقَدْ جِئْتُكُمْ بِهَا بَيْضَاءَ نَقِيَّةً، لَا تَسْأَلُوهُمْ عَنْ شَيْءٍ فَيُخْبِرُوكُمْ بِحَقٍّ فَتُكَذِّبُوا بِهِ، أَوْ بِبَاطِلٍ فَتُصَدِّقُوا بِهِ، وَالَّذِي نَفْسِي بِيَدِهِ، لَوْ أَنَّ مُوسَى كَانَ حَيًّا، مَا وَسِعَهُ إِلَّا أَنْ يَتَّبِعَنِي

"That 'Umar ibn Al-Khattāb came to the Prophet (sallAllāhu 'alayhi wa sallam) with a writing which he came upon from some of the people of the books, and he read it for the Prophet (sallAllāhu 'alayhi wa sallam). So he became angry and said: 'Are you confused regarding it, O son of Al-Khattāb?! By the One in Whose Hand my soul is in, I have verily come to you with it (i.e. the Straight Path) white and pure. Do not ask them about anything, because they (might) inform you about some truth which you then will reject, or some falsehood which you then will believe. By the One in Whose Hand my soul is in, if Mūsā was living then he would have no other option but to follow me." (Musnad Imām Ahmad)

And among the books revealed by Allāh which were mentioned in the Qurān and *Sunnah* are the *Suhuf* (scrolls) which were revealed to Ibrāhīm (*'alayhi as-salām*), the Zabūr which was revealed to Dāwūd (*'alayhi as-salām*), the Tawrāh which was revealed to Mūsā (*'alayhi as-salām*), the Injīl which was revealed to 'Isa (*'alayhi as-salām*) and finally the Qurān which was revealed to Muhammad (*sallAllāhu 'alayhi wa sallam*).

As for the prophets and messengers sent by Allāh which it is obligatory to believe in, then many of them (*'alayhim as-salām*) are mentioned in the following.

Allāh – the Exalted – said:

﴿ إِنَّا أَوْحَيْنَا إِلَيْكَ كَمَا أَوْحَيْنَا إِلَى نُوحٍ وَالنَّبِيِّينَ مِنْ بَعْدِهِ وَأَوْحَيْنَا إِلَى إِبْرَاهِيمَ وَإِسْمَاعِيلَ
وَإِسْحَاقَ وَيَعْقُوبَ وَالْأَسْبَاطِ وَعِيسَى وَأَيُّوبَ وَيُونُسَ وَهَارُونَ وَسُلَيْمَانَ وَآتَيْنَا دَاوُودَ زَبُورًا ﴾

"We verily revealed to you (O Muhammad), just like we revealed
to Nūh and the prophets after him. And we revealed to Ibrāhīm,
Ismā'īl, Ishāq, Ya'qūb, Al-Asbāt, 'Īsā, Ayyūb, Yūnus, Hārūn and
Sulaymān. And we gave the Zabūr to Dāwūd." (An-Nisā 4:163)

And He – the Exalted – said:

﴿ وَوَهَبْنَا لَهُ إِسْحَاقَ وَيَعْقُوبَ كُلًّا هَدَيْنَا وَنُوحًا هَدَيْنَا مِنْ قَبْلُ وَمِنْ ذُرِّيَّتِهِ دَاوُودَ وَسُلَيْمَانَ
وَأَيُّوبَ وَيُوسُفَ وَمُوسَى وَهَارُونَ وَكَذَلِكَ نَجْزِى الْمُحْسِنِينَ ٨٤ وَزَكَرِيَّا وَيَحْيَى وَعِيسَى
وَإِلْيَاسَ كُلٌّ مِنَ الصَّالِحِينَ ٨٥ وَإِسْمَاعِيلَ وَالْيَسَعَ وَيُونُسَ وَلُوطًا وَكُلًّا فَضَّلْنَا عَلَى الْعَالَمِينَ ﴾

"And We bestowed upon him (i.e. Ibrāhīm) Ishāq and Ya'qūb, and
all of them We guided. And Nūh we guided before (them). And
from his offspring Dāwūd, Sulaymān, Ayyūb, Yūsuf, Mūsā and
Hārūn. And such we reward those who do good. And Zakariyyā,
Yahyā, 'Īsā and Ilyās, all of them among the righteous. And
Ismā'īl, Al-Yasa'a, Yūnus and Lūt, and all of them we preferred
over *Al-'Ālamīn* (all that exists)." (Al-An'ām 6: 84-86)

All of them called to Tawhīd, while their legislations and rulings
would differ according to what Allāh revealed to the messengers
and prophets of their time and people.

Allah – the Exalted – said:

﴿ وَلَقَدْ بَعَثْنَا فِي كُلِّ أُمَّةٍ رَسُولًا أَنِ اعْبُدُوا اللَّهَ وَاجْتَنِبُوا الطَّاغُوتَ ﴾

"And verily, We have sent among every *Ummah* (nation) a
Messenger (proclaiming): 'Worship Allāh (Alone), and avoid (or
keep away from) *tāghūt* (everything worshipped besides Allāh).'"
(An-Nahl 16:36)

And the Prophet (sallAllāhu 'alayhi wa sallam) said:

أَنَا أَوْلَى النَّاسِ بِعِيسَى ابْنِ مَرْيَمَ فِي الدُّنْيَا وَالْآخِرَةِ، وَالْأَنْبِيَاءُ إِخْوَةٌ لِعَلَّاتٍ، أُمَّهَاتُهُمْ شَتَّى، وَدِينُهُمْ وَاحِدٌ

"I am more entitled (i.e. nearest) to 'Īsā ibn Maryam in the dunyā and ākhirah, and the prophets are paternal brother; their mothers are different and their religion is the same." (Saḥīḥ Al-Bukhārī)

And Allah – the Exalted – said:

﴿ لِكُلٍّ جَعَلْنَا مِنْكُمْ شِرْعَةً وَمِنْهَاجًا ﴾

"For everyone We have made a law and and a path."
(Al-Māidah 5:48)

Qatādah (d. 118h) said in the *tafsīr* of the verse:

يقول: سبيلا وسُنّة. والسنن مختلفة: للتوراة شريعة، وللإنجيل شريعة، وللقرآن شريعة، يحلُّ الله فيها ما يشاء، ويحرِّم ما يشاء بلاءً، ليعلم من يطيعه ممن يعصيه. ولكن الدين الواحد الذي لا يقبل غيره: التوحيدُ والإخلاصُ لله، الذي جاءت به الرسل.

"He says: A way and a Sunnah. And the Sunan are different. The Tawrāh has a sharī'ah (legislation), the Injīl has a sharī'ah and the Qurān has a sharī'ah. In it Allāh allows what He wants and He prohibits what He wants as a test, in order to know who will obey Him and those who will disobey Him. But the religion is one (and the same) which is the only one that will be accepted: The Tawḥīd and Ikhlāṣ (sincerity) for Allāh, which (all) the messengers came with." (Tafsīr At-Tabarī)

144

Belief in the Angels

The angels are a creation from the creations of Allāh. They are created from light, they are obedient to Allāh, and they do what they are ordered. Furthermore the angels are not female. Allāh – the Exalted – said:

﴿ الْحَمْدُ لِلَّهِ فَاطِرِ السَّمَاوَاتِ وَالْأَرْضِ جَاعِلِ الْمَلَائِكَةِ رُسُلًا أُولِي أَجْنِحَةٍ مَثْنَى وَثُلَاثَ وَرُبَاعَ ﴾

"All praise is due Allāh the Creator of the heavens and the earth, and the One who made the angels messengers having wings (either) two, three or four." (Fātir 35:1)

And He – the Exalted – said:

﴿ عَلَيْهَا مَلَائِكَةٌ غِلَاظٌ شِدَادٌ لَا يَعْصُونَ اللَّهَ مَا أَمَرَهُمْ وَيَفْعَلُونَ مَا يُؤْمَرُونَ ﴾

"Over it (i.e. Hellfire) are (appointed) angels who are harsh and severe. They do not disobey Allāh in what He orders them, and they do what they are ordered." (At-Tahrīm 66:6)

And He – the Exalted – said:

﴿ إِنَّ الَّذِينَ لَا يُؤْمِنُونَ بِالْآخِرَةِ لَيُسَمُّونَ الْمَلَائِكَةَ تَسْمِيَةَ الْأُنْثَى ﴾

"Verily those who do not believe the Hereafter, they verily give the angels female names."(An-Najm 53:27)

And the Prophet (*sallAllāhu 'alayhi wa sallam*) said:

خُلِقَتِ الْمَلَائِكَةُ مِنْ نُورٍ وَخُلِقَ الْجَانُّ مِنْ مَارِجٍ مِنْ نَارٍ وَخُلِقَ آدَمُ مِمَّا وُصِفَ لَكُمْ

"The angels were created from light, the jinns were created from a smokeless flame of fire and Ādam was created from what has been described for you." (Sahīh Muslim)

Among the angels which have been described in the Qurān and *Sunnah* are: Jibrīl who is responsible for delivering the revelation,

Mikāīl who is responsible for rain and vegetation, Isrāfīl who is responsible for blowing the Horn, Malak Al-Mawt who is responsible for taking the souls, *Hamalah Al-'Arsh* (the Bearers of the Throne), *Al-Hafadhah* (those who protect the slaves), the Guardians of Paradise, the Guardians of Hellfire and others. And it was verily narrated in the Sahīh Al-Bukhārī and Sahīh Muslim that two angels were fighting alongside the Prophet (*sallAllāhu 'alayhi wa sallam*) in the battle of Badr, defending him.

'Abdullāh ibn 'Abbās (*radiAllāhu 'anhu*) narrated that the Prophet (*sallAllāhu 'alayhi wa sallam*) said on the day of Badr:

هَذَا جِبْرِيلُ آخِذٌ بِرَأْسِ فَرَسِهِ . عَلَيْهِ أَدَاةُ الْحَرْبِ

"Here is Jibrīl, holding on to the head of his horse. He is wearing armor for war." (Sahih Al-Bukhārī).

'Adhāb Al-Qabr (the punishment in the grave)

Ahlus-Sunnah believes in what have been correctly narrated from the Messenger of Allāh (*sallAllāhu 'alayhi wa sallam*) regarding the punishment in the grave and its pleasures. Among these correct narrations are:

The Prophet (*sallAllāhu 'alayhi wa sallam*) said:

إِذَا أُقْعِدَ المُؤْمِنُ فِي قَبْرِهِ أُتِيَ، ثُمَّ شَهِدَ أَنْ لَا إِلَهَ إِلَّا اللَّهُ وَأَنَّ مُحَمَّدًا رَسُولُ اللَّهِ، فَذلِكَ قَوْلُهُ: {يُثَبِّتُ اللَّهُ الَّذِينَ آمَنُوا بِالقَوْلِ الثَّابِتِ}

"When the believer is made to dwell in his grave then (the angels) come to him. Then he testifies to Lā ilāha illa Allāh and that Muhammad is Rasūl-Allāh. And that is (the meaning of) His words: **"Allāh makes those who believe firm, with the firm word."** (Ibrāhīm 14:27)*"* (Sahīh Al-Bukhārī)

And 'Āishah (*radiAllāhu 'anhā*) narrated:

أَنَّ يَهُودِيَّةً دَخَلَتْ عَلَيْهَا، فَذَكَرَتْ عَذَابَ القَبْرِ، فَقَالَتْ لَهَا: أَعَاذَكِ اللَّهُ مِنْ عَذَابِ القَبْرِ، فَسَأَلَتْ عَائِشَةُ رَسُولَ اللَّهِ صَلَّى اللَّهُ عليه وسلَّمَ عن عَذَابِ القَبْرِ، فَقَالَ: نَعَمْ، عَذَابُ القَبْرِ قَالَتْ عَائِشَةُ رَضِيَ اللَّهُ عَنْهَا: فَما رَأَيْتُ رَسُولَ اللَّهِ صَلَّى اللَّهُ عليه وسلَّمَ بَعْدُ صَلَّى صَلَاةً إِلَّا تَعَوَّذَ مِن عَذَابِ القَبْرِ.

"That a Jewish woman entered upon her and mentioned the punishment in the grave. She said to her: 'May Allāh give you refuge from the punishment in the grave.' So 'Āishah asked the Messenger of Allāh (sallAllāhu 'alayhi wa sallam) about the punishment in the grave (i.e. whether or not people will be punished in their grave).' So he said: 'Yes, the punishmet of the grave' 'Āishah (radiAllāhu 'anha) said: 'After that I never saw the Messenger of Allāh (sallAllāhu 'alayhi wa sallam) pray any prayer, except that he sought refuge from the punishment of the grave (in it)." (Sahīh Al-Bukhārī)

And Asmā bint Abū Bakr (*radiAllāhu 'anhumā*) said:

قام رسولُ اللهِ صلَّى اللهُ عليه وسلَّم ، خطيبًا فذكر فِتْنَةَ القبرِ التي يُفْتَنُ فيها المرْءُ ، فلما ذكر ذلك ؛
ضَجَّ المسلمونَ ضَجَّةً

"*The Messenger of Allāh (sallAllāhu 'alayhi wa sallam) got up and gave a speech. And he mentioned in it the fitnah of the grave which the person will be put through. So when he mentioned this the Muslims made a loud noise.*" (Sahīh Al-Bukhārī)

Most of the **Khawārij** rejected the punishment of the grave without looking at the evidence which had been narrated that establishes its truth. Others among the other sects also rejected it.

Belief in what has been narrated about Al-Ākhirah

From the principles of *Sunnah* is the belief in the aspects of *ākhirah*[13] which have been narrated in the Qurān and the *Sunnah* without rejecting any of it. Among these things is that a Horn will be blown and then the slave will be resurrected from his dwelling in the grave, to the standing and reckoning on the Day of Judgment. The *kuffār* will be ordered to follow whatever they have worshipped in *dunyā* to Hellfire and Allāh will not speak to them. Allāh will speak to the remaining slaves about what they used to do in *dunyā*; some He will cover over and others He will expose.

Allāh – the Exalted – said:

﴿ وَنُفِخَ فِي الصُّورِ فَصَعِقَ مَنْ فِي السَّمَاوَاتِ وَمَنْ فِي الْأَرْضِ إِلَّا مَنْ شَاءَ اللَّهُ ثُمَّ نُفِخَ فِيهِ أُخْرَى فَإِذَا هُمْ قِيَامٌ يَنْظُرُونَ ﴾

"And the Horn will be blown, and whoever is in the heavens and whoever is on the earth will fall dead except whom Allah wills. Then it will be blown again, and at once they will be standing (on the Day of Judgment), **looking on."** (Az-Zumar 39:68)

And the Prophet (*sallAllāhu 'alayhi wa sallam*) said in a longer *hadīth*:

يُحْشَرُ النَّاسُ يَوَمَ القِيَامَةِ، فَيَقُولُ: مَن كَانَ يَعْبُدُ شيئًا فَلْيَتَّبِعْ، فَمِنْهُمْ مَن يَتَّبِعُ الشَّمْسَ، وَمِنْهُمْ مَن يَتَّبِعُ القَمَرَ، وَمِنْهُمْ مَن يَتَّبِعُ الطَّوَاغِيتَ، وَتَبْقَى هَذِهِ الأُمَّةُ فِيهَا مُنَافِقُوهَا،

"The people will be gathered on the Day of Resurrection, then He will say: 'Whoever used to worship something (in dunyā) then let him follow it.' So some of them will follow the sun, some of them will follow the moon and some of the will follow the tawāghīt (pl. tāghūt). And left will be this Ummah and its hypocrites." (Sahīh Al-Bukhārī)

---

[13] Some of these issues have been described in next sections.

And the Prophet (*sallAllāhu 'alayhi wa sallam*) also said:

يُدْنَى الْمُؤْمِنُ يَوْمَ الْقِيَامَةِ مِنْ رَبِّهِ عَزَّ وَجَلَّ حَتَّى يَضَعَ عَلَيْهِ كَنَفَهُ فَيُقَرِّرَهُ بِذُنُوبِهِ فَيَقُولُ: هَلْ تَعْرِفُ؟ فَيَقُولُ: رَبِّ أَعْرِفُ، قَالَ: فَيَقُولُ إِنِّي سَتَرْتُهَا عَلَيْكَ فِي الدُّنْيَا وَإِنِّي أَغْفِرُهَا لَكَ الْيَوْمَ، فَيُعْطَى صَحِيفَةَ حَسَنَاتِهِ، وَأَمَّا الْكَافِرُونَ وَالْمُنَافِقُونَ فَيُنَادَى بِهِمْ عَلَى رُءُوسِ الْأَشْهَادِ هَؤُلَاءِ الَّذِينَ كَذَبُوا عَلَى اللهِ

"The believer will be brought close on the Day of Judgment to his Lord – 'azza wa jalla – until He will put His Side upon him and He will make him admit to his sins, so He will say: 'Do you acknowledge (your sins)?' So he will say: 'My Lord, I acknowledge.' So He will say: 'I verily covered over them for you in dunyā and I verily forgive them for you today.' Then he will be given the book of his good deeds. But as for the disbelievers and the hypocrites, then they will be called openly in front of the witnesses. These are the ones who lied against Allah." (Ṣaḥīḥ Muslim)

And 'Āishah (*radiAllāhu 'anha*) narrated that the Prophet (*sallAllāhu 'alayhi wa sallam*) said:

مَن حُوسِبَ يَوْمَ القِيَامَةِ، عُذِّبَ فَقُلْتُ: أَلَيْسَ قَدْ قَالَ اللهُ عَزَّ وَجَلَّ: {فَسَوْفَ يُحَاسَبُ حِسَابًا يَسِيرًا} [الانشقاق: 8]؟ فَقَالَ: لَيْسَ ذَاكِ الْحِسَابُ، إِنَّمَا ذَاكِ الْعَرْضُ، مَن نُوقِشَ الحِسَابَ يَوْمَ القِيَامَةِ عُذِّبَ .

"Whoever is called to reckoning on the Day of Resurrection will be punished. So I ('Āishah) said: 'Did Allāh – 'azza wa jalla – not say: "Then he will verily have an easy reckoning?" (Al-Inshiqāq 84:8)' *So he said: 'That is not the reckoning. Verily that is the review (or presentation)[14]. Whoever is argued against in the reckoning on the Day of Resurrection will be punished."* (Saḥīḥ Muslim)

So the *kuffār* will stay in Hellfire forever, the Muslims who were not forgiven for their sins will stay there temporarily and some Muslims will enter into Paradise without being punished and they will stay there forever. Paradise and Hellfire have already been

---

[14] This is the easy account which is described in the previous *hadīth* where Allāh will mention the sins of the slave and make him acknowledge them.

created and prepared for its inhabitants, and they will both exist forever and never cease to exist.

Allāh – the Exalted – said:

﴿ وَسَارِعُوا إِلَى مَغْفِرَةٍ مِنْ رَبِّكُمْ وَجَنَّةٍ عَرْضُهَا السَّمَاوَاتُ وَالْأَرْضُ أُعِدَّتْ لِلْمُتَّقِينَ ﴾

"And hurry to a forgiveness from your Lord and a Paradise whose width is like the heavens and the earth, prepared for the God-fearing." (Āli 'Imrān 3:133)

And He – the Exalted – said:

﴿ وَالَّذِينَ آمَنُوا وَعَمِلُوا الصَّالِحَاتِ سَنُدْخِلُهُمْ جَنَّاتٍ تَجْرِي مِنْ تَحْتِهَا الْأَنْهَارُ خَالِدِينَ فِيهَا أَبَدًا وَعْدَ اللَّهِ حَقًّا وَمَنْ أَصْدَقُ مِنَ اللَّهِ قِيلًا ﴾

"And those who believe and do good deeds, We will verily enter them into gardens under which rivers flow. They will remain therein forever. A promise of truth from Allah. And who is more truthful in speech than Allah?" (An-Nisā 4:122)

And He – the Exalted – said:

﴿ وَاتَّقُوا النَّارَ الَّتِي أُعِدَّتْ لِلْكَافِرِينَ ﴾

"And fear Hellfire which have been prepared for the disbelievers." (Ālu 'Imrān 3:131)

And He – the Exalted – said:

﴿ إِنَّ اللَّهَ لَعَنَ الْكَافِرِينَ وَأَعَدَّ لَهُمْ سَعِيرًا ٠٠ خَالِدِينَ فِيهَا أَبَدًا لَا يَجِدُونَ وَلِيًّا وَلَا نَصِيرًا ﴾

"Verily Allah has cursed the the disbelievers and prepared for them a blazing fire. They will remain therein forever. They will not find any protector nor any helper." (Al-Ahzāb 33:64-65)

And the Prophet (*sallAllāhu 'alayhi wa sallam*) said:

اطَّلَعْتُ فِي الْجَنَّةِ فَرَأَيْتُ أَكْثَرَ أَهْلِهَا الْفُقَرَاءَ، واطَّلَعْتُ فِي النَّارِ فَرَأَيْتُ أَكْثَرَ أَهْلِهَا النِّسَاءَ

"I looked into Paradise and I saw that most of its inhabitants were poor people. And I looked into Hellfire and I saw that most of its inhabitants were women." (Saḥīḥ Al-Bukhārī)

Al-Barbahārī (d. 329h) said:

وكل شيء مما أوجب الله عليه الفناء يفنى إلا الجنة والنار والعرش والكرسي والصور والقلم واللوح ليس يفنى شيء من هذا أبدا ثم يبعث الله الخلق على ما أماتهم عليه يوم القيامة ويحاسبهم بما شاء فريق في الجنة وفريق في السعير ويقول لسائر الخلق ممن لم يخلق للبقاء كونوا ترابا.

"And everything from that which Allāh has enjoined upon it to disappear then it will disappear, except Paradise, Hellfire, the Throne, The Footstool, the Horn, the Pen and the Tablet. None of these things will ever disappear. Then Allāh will resurrect the creation on the Day of Resurrection upon that (i.e. religion and state) which He made them die upon, and He will hold them accountable for whatever He wants. A group will be in Paradise and a group will be in the blazing fire. And He will say to the rest of the creation which has not been created to remain: 'Be dust'." (Sharh As-Sunnah by Al-Barbahārī)

Ash-Shafā'ah (the intercession)

The *shafā'ah* (intercession) of the Prophet (*sallAllāhu 'alayhi wa sallam*) has correctly been narrated in the *Sunnah* with *tawātur*[15]. And this is the belief that the Prophet (*sallAllāhu 'alayhi wa sallam*) will intercede on the Day of Resurrection, by the permission of Allāh, for his *Ummah* to enter faster into Paradise, for some people from his (*sallAllāhu 'alayhi wa sallam*) *Ummah* who were thrown in the fire due to their sins that they will be taken out of it, and that some sinners from his (*sallAllāhu 'alayhi wa sallam*) *Ummah* will avoid entering into Hellfire even though they deserved it due to their sins.

In a longer *hadīth* narrated by Anas ibn Mālik (*radiAllāhu 'anhu*) the Prophet (*sallAllāhu 'alayhi wa sallam*) said:

فَيَأْتُونِي فَأَسْتَأْذِنُ عَلَى رَبِّي، فَيُؤْذَنُ لِي، فَإِذَا أَنَا رَأَيْتُهُ وَقَعْتُ سَاجِدًا، فَيَدَعُنِي مَا شَاءَ اللَّهُ، فَيُقَالُ: يَا مُحَمَّدُ، ارْفَعْ رَأْسَكَ، قُلْ تُسْمَعْ، سَلْ تُعْطَهْ، اشْفَعْ تُشَفَّعْ، فَأَرْفَعُ رَأْسِي، فَأَحْمَدُ رَبِّي بِتَحْمِيدٍ يُعَلِّمُنِيهِ رَبِّي، ثُمَّ أَشْفَعُ فَيَحُدُّ لِي حَدًّا، فَأُخْرِجُهُمْ مِنَ النَّارِ، وَأُدْخِلُهُمُ الْجَنَّةَ،

"Then they will come to me (i.e. the people, after having asked the other prophets to intercede for them) and I will ask permission from My Lord. Then when I see Him I will fall down in sujūd. Then He will let me (stay there), as much as Allāh wills. So it will be said: 'O Muhammad, raise your head. Speak, and you will be listened to. Ask, and you will be given, and intercede, and your intercession will be accepted.' So I will raise my head and praise my Lord with a praise which my Lord will teach me. Then I will intercede, and He gives me a number (of people) and I bring them out of Hellfire and enter them into Paradise." (Al-Bukhārī, Muslim, Ibn Hibbān and others – *sahīh*)

---

[15] A subject which has been narrated with *tawātur* (continuous recurrence) – or a *mutawātir hadīth* – is a *hadīth* or a subject that has been narrated from so many people that it practically is impossible for them to agree upon lying or that they should all make the same mistake without intending it.

And the Prophet (sallAllāhu 'alayhi wa sallam) said:

لِكُلِّ نَبِيٍّ دَعْوَةٌ دَعاها لِأُمَّتِهِ، وإِنِّي اخْتَبَأْتُ دَعْوَتِي شَفاعَةً لِأُمَّتِي يَوْمَ القِيامَةِ. وفي رواية: أُعْطِيَ.

"Every prophet has an invocation which he has made for his ummah. And I have verily saved my invocation as an intercession for my Ummah of the Day of Resurrection." (Al-Bukhārī and Muslim – *sahīh*)

The **Mu'tazilah** rejected that the Prophet (sallAllāhu 'alayhi wa sallam) will make intercession for those who have entered into the fire, due to their belief that whoever dies while he has not repented from a major sin he has committed, then he will enter the fire and Allāh will not forgive him, nor show him mercy.

The **Khawārij** rejected that the Prophet (sallAllāhu 'alayhi wa sallam) will make intercession for those who have entered into the fire, due to their belief that whoever commits a major sin, then he is *kāfir* and will enter Hellfire forever.

And these beliefs are a continuance and expanding of their original innovation which they believed in.

Hanbal (d. 273h) said:

قُلْتُ لِأَبِي عَبْدِ اللهِ يَعْنِي أَحْمَدَ بْنَ حَنْبَلٍ: مَا يُرْوَى عَنِ النَّبِيِّ صَلَّى اللهُ عَلَيْهِ وَسَلَّمَ فِي الشَّفَاعَةِ؟ فَقَالَ: " هَذِهِ أَحَادِيثُ صِحَاحٌ نُؤْمِنُ بِهَا وَنُقِرُّ، وَكُلُّ مَا رُوِيَ عَنِ النَّبِيِّ صَلَّى اللهُ عَلَيْهِ وَسَلَّمَ بِأَسَانِيدَ جَيِّدَةٍ نُؤْمِنُ بِهَا وَنُقِرُّ، قُلْتُ لَهُ: وَقَوْمٌ يَخْرُجُونَ مِنَ النَّارِ؟ فَقَالَ: نَعَمْ، إِذَا لَمْ نُقِرَّ بِمَا جَاءَ بِهِ الرَّسُولُ وَدَفَعْنَاهُ رَدَدْنَا عَلَى اللهِ أَمْرَهُ قَالَ اللهُ عَزَّ وَجَلَّ: {وَمَا آتَاكُمُ الرَّسُولُ فَخُذُوهُ وَمَا نَهَاكُمْ عَنْهُ فَانْتَهُوا} [الحشر: 7] قُلْتُ: وَالشَّفَاعَةُ؟ قَالَ: كَمْ حَدِيثٍ يُرْوَى عَنِ النَّبِيِّ صَلَّى اللهُ عَلَيْهِ وَسَلَّمَ فِي الشَّفَاعَةِ وَالْحَوْضِ، فَهَؤُلَاءِ يُكَذِّبُونَ بِهَا وَيَتَكَلَّمُونَ، وَهُوَ قَوْلُ صِنْفٍ مِنَ الْخَوَارِجِ، وَإِنَّ اللهَ تَعَالَى لَا يُخْرِجُ مِنَ النَّارِ أَحَدًا بَعْدَ إِذْ أَدْخَلَهُ، وَالْحَمْدُ لِلّهِ الَّذِي عَدَلَ عَنَّا مَا ابْتَلَاهُمْ بِهِ"

"I said to Abū 'Abdullāh – i.e. Ahmad ibn Hanbal: 'What was narrated from the Prophet (sallAllāhu 'alayhi wa sallam) regarding the shafā'ah (intercession)?' So he said: 'These are correct ahādīth. We believe in them

and consent to them. And everything which was narrated from the Prophet (sallAllāhu 'alayhi wa sallam) with good chains of narration, then we believe in it and consent to it.' I said to him: 'Will some people exit the fire (after having entered it)?' He said: 'Yes. If we don't consent to what the Messenger came with and we repel it, then we are rejecting the order of Allāh. Allāh – 'azza wa jalla – said: **"And whatever the Messenger gives you, then take it. And what he prohibits you from then refrain from it."** *(Al-Hashr 59:7) I said: 'And the shafā'ah?' He said: 'How many (narrations) are narrated from the Prophet (sallAllāhu 'alayhi wa sallam) regarding the shafā'ah and the hawd (basin). These people reject it and they speak (from their desires), and it (i.e. rejecting it) is the opinion of a group from the Khawārij; that Allāh verily do not bring out from Hellfire anyone after He entered him into it. And all praise is due to Allāh who turned away from us what He has tested them with."* (Sharh Usūl I'tiqād Ahlus-Sunnah by Al-Lālakāī)

Ar-Ruyah (seeing Allāh in ākhirah) – and a mention of Al-'Uluw (the aboveness)

Seeing Allāh in the next life is an issue which has been proved by the Qurān and the *mutawātir Sunnah*. Allāh – the Exalted – said:

$$ ﴿ وُجُوهٌ يَوْمَئِذٍ نَاضِرَةٌ ، إِلَى رَبِّهَا نَاظِرَةٌ ﴾ $$

"Some faces that day will be radiant, looking at their Lord."
(Al-Qiyāmah 75:22-23)

And the Prophet (*sallAllāhu 'alayhi wa sallam*) said:

إذا دخلَ أهلُ الجنَّةِ الجنَّةَ نادى منادٍ: يا أهلَ الجنَّةِ إنَّ لَكُم عندَ اللَّهِ موعِدًا يريدُ أن يُنجزَكموه فيقولون:
ما هو؟ ألم يبيِّضْ وجوهَنا ويثقِّل موازينَنا ويُدخِلْنا الجنَّةَ ويُجِرْنا من النَّارِ؛ قال فيَكشفُ الحجابَ فينظرونَ
إليْهِ فما أعطاهم شيئًا أحبَّ إليْهم من النَّظرِ إليْهِ وهيَ الزِّيادةُ

"When the people of Paradise enter Paradise, a caller will call out: 'O people of Paradise, you verily have a meeting with your Lord, (in which) He wants to fulfill (His covenant) with you.' So they will say: 'What is it? Did He not whiten our faces, make our scales heavy, enter us into Paradise and protect us from the fire?' He said: Then He will remove the cover and they will look at Him. And He did not give them anything more beloved to them, than looking at Him. And this is the extra (mentioned in Sūrah Yūnus)." (Ahmad, Ibn Mājah and An-Nasāī with a slight difference - *sahīh*)

And the Prophet (*sallAllāhu 'alayhi wa sallam*) regarding the words of Allāh – *jalla dhikruhu* (in the translation): **"For those who do good is the best (reward) and extra."** (Yūnus 10:26):

الحُسْنَى الجنَّةُ والزِّيادةُ النَّظرُ إلى وجهِ اللَّهِ لا يَرهَقُ وجوهُهُم قَتَرٌ ولا ذِلَّةٌ بعدَ نظرِهِم إليهِ

"The best (reward) is Paradise, and the extra is looking at the Face of Allāh. No darkness will cover their faces, nor humiliation after they have looked at Him." (Al-Kāmil fī Ad-Du'afā by Ibn 'Adī – *hasan* or *sahīh*)

And Jarīr ibn 'Abdullāh (radiAllāhu 'anhu) said:

كُنَّا جُلُوسًا عِنْدَ النَّبِيِّ صَلَّى اللَّهُ عَلَيْهِ وَسَلَّمَ فَنَظَرَ إِلَى الْقَمَرِ لَيْلَةَ الْبَدْرِ فَقَالَ: " أَمَا إِنَّكُمْ سَتُعْرَضُونَ عَلَى رَبِّكُمْ عَزَّ وَجَلَّ فَتَرَوْنَهُ كَمَا تَرَوْنَ هَذَا الْقَمَرَ لَا تُضَامُونَ فِي رُؤْيَتِهِ فَإِنِ اسْتَطَعْتُمْ أَنْ لَا تُغْلَبُوا عَلَى صَلَاةٍ قَبْلَ طُلُوعِ الشَّمْسِ وَقَبْلَ غُرُوبِهَا فَافْعَلُوا قَالَ: ثُمَّ قَرَأَ {وَسَبِّحْ بِحَمْدِ رَبِّكَ قَبْلَ طُلُوعِ الشَّمْسِ وَقَبْلَ غُرُوبِهَا} [طه: 130] "

"We were sitting with the Messenger of Allāh (sallAllāhu 'alayhi wa sallam) when he looked at the moon on the night of full-moon. Then he said: 'Verily you will be presented to your Lord – 'azza wa jalla – and you will see Him, just as you see this moon, you have no difficulty in seeing it. So if you are capable of avoiding to miss a prayer before the rising of the sun and before its setting, then do so.' He said: Then he recited: **"And exalt your Lord by praising Him before the rising of the sun and before its setting."** *(Tā-hā 20:130)"* (Sahīh Ibn Mājah)

The **Mu'tazilah**, the **Jahmiyyah** and the **'Ashā'irah** rejected seeing Allāh in the *ākhirah* based upon philosophy and their lust and desires.

This philosophy and so-called logic, also drove the Jahmiyyah, the Mu'tazilah and the Ashā'irah to reject the *'Uluw* (aboveness) of Allāh, which is Him being above the heavens separated from His creation with a border. Some of the Mu'tazilah said that Allāh is everywhere, while other said that Allāh is nowhere. The 'Ashā'irah accepted the *'Uluw* (aboveness) of Allāh in His Power and Arrangement, but rejected *'Uluw Adh-Dhāt* (aboveness of the Being of Allāh), while *Ahlus-Sunnah* believe in it all. The Jahmiyyah said that Allāh is everywhere, which includes Him being on earth. And all those who reject *'Uluw Ad-Dhāt* (the aboveness of the Being of Allāh) are *kuffār*.

'Abdullāh ibn Al-Mubārak (d. 181h) said:

نَعْرِفُ رَبَّنَا عَزَّ وَجَلَّ فَوْقَ سَبْعِ سَمَاوَاتٍ عَلَى الْعَرْشِ بَائِنٌ مِنْ خَلْقِهِ بِحَدٍّ وَلَا نَقُولُ كَمَا قَالَتِ الْجُهْمِيَّةُ
هَاهُنَا وَأَشَارَ بِيَدِهِ إِلَى الْأَرْضِ

"We know our Lord – the Mighty and Majestic – above the seven heavens upon the Throne separated from His creation by a border. And we do not say like the Jahmiyyah (that He is) right here. (And he pointed with his hand towards the ground)." (As-Sunnah by 'Abdullāh – thābit 'anhu)

And Imām Ahmad acknowledged these words from 'Abdullāh ibn Al-Mubārak. Abū Bakr Al-Khallāl (d. 311h) narrated:

وأنبئنا محمد بن علي الوراق حدثنا أبو بكر الأثرم حدثني محمد بن إبراهيم القيسي قال: قلت لأحمد
بن حنبل يحكى عن ابن المبارك , وقيل له : كيف نعرف ربنا ؟ قال: في السماء السابعة على عرشه
بحد . فقال أحمد : هكذا هو عندنا

"And Muhammad ibn 'Alī Al-Warrāq informed us (and said): Abū Bakr Al-Athram narrated to us (and said): Muhammad ibn Ibrāhīm Al-Qaysī narrated to me and said: 'I said to Ahmad ibn Hanbal: It is said about Ibn Al-Mubārak when it was said to him: 'How do we know our Lord?' Then he said: 'In the seventh heaven upon His Throne with a border (i.e. separated from His creation).' So Ahmad said: 'It is (also) like that with us.'" (Ithbāt Al-Hadd by Ad-Dashtī)

And Abū Hātim Ar-Rāzī (d. 277h) said:

أدركنا العلماء في جميع الأمصار حجازًا وعراقًا وشامًا ويمنًا؛ فكان من مذهبهم: أن الله عز وجل على
عرشه، بائنٌ من خلقه كما وصف نفسه في كتابه، وعلى لسان رسوله صلى الله عليه وسلم بلا كيف

"We have met the scholars from all of the lands; Hijāz, 'Irāq, Shām and Yaman. And their madhhab was: that Allāh – 'azza wa jalla – is upon His Throne, separated from His creation, just as He has described Himself in His Book and upon the tongue of the Messenger of Allāh (sallAllāhu 'alayhi wa sallam) without (describing) how." (Sharh Usūl I'tiqād Ahlus-Sunnah by Al-Lālakāī 1/197)

The scholars have described the issue of *'Uluw* as an issue known from *fitrah*. It is a necessity which the slave feels within him; that his Lord is above him in the heaven and therefore when he turns to Him in repentance and supplication, he turns towards the heaven. So there is no excuse in rejecting the *'Uluw*, rather some of the dirtiest of *kuffār* and *zanādiqah* who ascribed to Islām were those who claimed the opposite of *'Uluw*; that Allāh is everywhere or nowhere. And from this claim came many abhorrent sayings which cannot even be mentioned.

Allāh – the Exalted – said:

$$﴿ وَهُوَ الْقَاهِرُ فَوْقَ عِبَادِهِ ﴾$$

"And He is the Subduer, above His slaves." (Al-An'ām 6:18)

And He – the Exalted – said:

$$﴿ أَأَمِنْتُمْ مَنْ فِي السَّمَاءِ أَنْ يَخْسِفَ بِكُمُ الْأَرْضَ فَإِذَا هِيَ تَمُورُ ﴾$$

"Do you feel secure that He, Who is in the heaven[16], will not cause the earth to sink with you?"' (Al-Mulk 67:16)

And the Prophet (*sallAllāhu 'alayhi wa sallam*) said in a longer *hadīth*:

$$فقال لها :أين اللهُ؟ قالَتْ :اللهُ في السماءِ، قال: مَن أنا؟ قالَتْ :أنتَ رسولُ اللهِ، قال: إنَّها مُؤمنةٌ$$

"So he said to her (i.e. a slavegirl): 'Where is Allāh?' She said: 'In the heaven.' He said: 'And who am I?' She said: 'You are the Messenger of Allāh.' He said: 'She is verily a believer.'" (Muslim, Abū Dāwūd, An-Nasāī and Ahmad – *sahīh* according to the conditions of Muslim)

---

[16] When Allāh is described as being in 'the heaven' in verses, *ahādīth* and in the sayings of the *Salaf*, then what is meant is according to the description of 'Abdullāh ibn Al-Mubārak when he said: "*Above the seven heavens upon the Throne separated from His creation by a border.*" This is in accordance how the Arabs would understand and use this term in this context.

Ad-Dārimī (d. 280h) said:

ففي حديث رسول الله ﷺ هذا دليل على أن الرجل إذا لم يعلم أن الله عز وجل في السماء دون الأرض فليس بمؤمن، ولو كان عبدا فأعتق لم يجز في رقبة مؤمنة إذ لا يعلم أن الله في السماء؛ ألا ترى أن رسول الله ﷺ جعل أمارة إيمانها معرفتها أن الله في السماء.

"So in this hadīth of the Messenger of Allāh (sallAllāhu 'alayhi wa sallam) there is an evidence for that a person, if he does not know that Allāh – 'azza wa jalla – is in the heaven and not on earth, then he is not a believer. And if he (i.e. this person) was a slave and then he was freed, then it is not allowed to count him as (freeing) a believing slave because he does not know that Allāh is in the heaven (i.e. in aboveness). Is it not seen that the Messenger of Allāh (sallAllāhu 'alayhi wa sallam) made the sign of her īmān her knowledge of Allāh being in the heaven." (Ar-Radd 'alā Al-Jahmiyyah by Ad-Dārimī)

And 'Abdur-Rahmān ibn Muhammad Al-Handhalī (d. 327h) said:

أَخْبَرَنِي حَرْب بن إِسْمَاعِيل الْكَرْمَانِي فِيمَا كتب إِلَيَّ أَن الْجُهَمِية أَعداء الله وهم الَّذين يَزْعمُونَ أَن الْقُرْآن مَخْلُوق وَأَن الله لم يكلم مُوسَى وَلَا يرى فِي الْآخِرَة وَلَا يعرف لله مَكَان وَلَيْسَ على عرش وَلَا كرْسِي وهم كفار فَاحْذَرُهُمْ

"Harb ibn Ismā'īl Al-Karmānī informed me in that which he wrote to me, that the Jahmiyyah are the enemies of Allāh, and they are the ones who claim that the Qurān is created, that Allāh did not speak to Mūsā, that He is not seen in the ākhirah, that no place is known for Allāh and that He is not upon a Throne, nor a Footstool. And they are kuffār, so be aware of them." ('Uluw lil-'Alī Al-Ghaffār by Adh-Dhahabī)

Al-Hawd (the Basin)

The *ahādīth* which have been narrated about the *hawd* (basin) of the Messenger of Allāh (*sallAllāhu 'alayhi wa sallam*) are also on the level of *tawātur*. Among these *ahādīth* are:

The Prophet (*sallAllāhu 'alayhi wa sallam*) said:

إِنَّ قَدْرَ حَوْضِي كَمَا بَيْنَ أَيْلَةَ وَصَنْعَاءَ مِنَ الْيَمَنِ، وَإِنَّ فِيهِ مِنَ الْأَبَارِيقِ كَعَدَدِ نُجُومِ السَّمَاءِ

"Verily the size of my basin is like (the distance) between Aylah and San'ā in Yemen. And in it there are vessels as the numbers of the stars." (Sahīh Muslim)

And he (*sallAllāhu 'alayhi wa sallam*) said:

لَيَرِدَنَّ عَلَيَّ نَاسٌ مِنْ أَصْحَابِي الْحَوْضَ، حَتَّى عَرَفْتُهُمُ اخْتُلِجُوا دُونِي، فَأَقُولُ أَصْحَابِي. فَيُقُولُ لَا تَدْرِي مَا أَحْدَثُوا بَعْدَكَ

"Verily some people of my companions will come to me at the basin, and when I recognize them they will be taken away from me. So I will say: 'My companions.' Then it will be said: 'You do not know what they have innovated after you.[17]'" (Sahīh Al-Bukhārī)

And Abū Dharr Al-Ghifārī (*radiAllāhu 'anhu*) said:

قُلْتُ: يَا رَسُولَ اللهِ مَا آنِيَةُ الْحَوْضِ قَالَ: وَالَّذِي نَفْسُ مُحَمَّدٍ بِيَدِهِ لَآنِيَتُهُ أَكْثَرُ مِنْ عَدَدِ نُجُومِ السَّمَاءِ وَكَوَاكِبِهَا، أَلَا فِي اللَّيْلَةِ الْمُظْلِمَةِ الْمُصْحِيَةِ، آنِيَةُ الْجَنَّةِ مَنْ شَرِبَ مِنْهَا لَمْ يَظْمَأْ آخِرَ مَا عَلَيْهِ، يَشْخَبُ فِيهِ مِيزَابَانِ مِنَ الْجَنَّةِ، مَنْ شَرِبَ مِنْهُ لَمْ يَظْمَأْ، عَرْضُهُ مِثْلُ طُولِهِ، مَا بَيْنَ عَمَّانَ إِلَى أَيْلَةَ، مَاؤُهُ أَشَدُّ بَيَاضًا مِنَ اللَّبَنِ، وَأَحْلَى مِنَ الْعَسَلِ

---

[17] This means: the hypocrites, those who returned to *kufr* after their Islām, and it even includes those after him (*sallAllāhu 'alayhi wa sallam*) who were Muslims but fell in innovations. This *hadīth* cannot be used to accuse the *Sahābah* (*radiAllāhu 'anhum*) for deviating, since Allāh informed that He was pleased with them.

*"I said: 'O Messenger of Allāh. What are the vessels of the basin?'
He said: 'By Him in Whose Hand the soul of Muhammad is, it's
vessels are more than the number of the stars in the sky and its
planets, verily (shining) on a dark clear night. These would be the
vessels of Paradise. He who drinks out of it (i.e. the basin) would
never feel thirsty after that. In it runs two spouts from Paradise.
Whoever drinks from it will not feel thirsty (ever again). It width
is like its length; the distance between 'Ammān and Aylah. Its
water is whiter than milk, and sweeter than honey."* (Sahīh
Muslim)

Some of the **Mu'tazilah** and **Khāwarij** rejected the *hawd* (basin)
based upon innovative beliefs. Some claimed inconsistency in the
narrations, while others refused to accept the location of the basin
which was narrated, and thus rejecting it in totality.

Al-Mīzān (the Scale)

Ahlus-Sunnah believe that the *mīzān* (scale) mentioned in the Qurān and *Sunnah*, which will be brought on the Day of Resurrection, is a real scale upon which the deeds of the slaves will be weighed according to the Qurān and *Sunnah*.

Allāh – the Exalted – said:

﴿ فَمَنْ ثَقُلَتْ مَوَازِينُهُ فَأُولَئِكَ هُمُ الْمُفْلِحُونَ ۞ وَمَنْ خَفَّتْ مَوَازِينُهُ فَأُولَئِكَ الَّذِينَ خَسِرُوا أَنْفُسَهُمْ فِي جَهَنَّمَ خَالِدُونَ ﴾

"Whoevers scale becomes heavy, then these are the successful. And whoevers scale becomes light, then these are those who have lost themselves. In Hellfire they will remain." (Al-Muminūn 23:102-103)

And the Prophet (*sallAllāhu 'alayhi wa sallam*) said:

كَلِمَتَانِ خَفِيفَتَانِ عَلَى اللِّسَانِ، ثَقِيلَتَانِ فِي المِيزَانِ، حَبِيبَتَانِ إِلى الرَّحْمَنِ :سُبْحَانَ اللَّهِ العَظِيمِ، سُبْحَانَ اللَّهِ وبِحَمْدِهِ

"Two words that are light upon the tongue, but heavy on the scale and beloved to Ar-Rahmān: SubhānAllāh Al-'Adhīm, SubhānAllāh wa bihamdihi." (Sahīh Al-Bukhārī)

And 'Abdullāh ibn Mas'ūd (*radiAllāhu 'anhu*) narrated:

أَنَّهُ كَانَ يَجْتَنِي سِوَاكًا مِنَ الأَرَاكِ وَكَانَ دَقِيقَ السَّاقَيْنِ، فَجَعَلَتِ الرِّيحُ تَكْفَؤُهُ، فَضَحِكَ القَومُ مِنه، فقال رسولُ اللهِ صلَّى اللهُ عليه وسلَّمَ: مِمَّنْ تَضْحَكُونَ؟ قالوا: يا نبيَّ اللهِ، مِن دِقَّةِ ساقَيْه، فقال: والَّذي نَفْسي بيدِهِ، لَهُمَا أَثْقَلُ فِي المِيزَانِ مِن أُحُدٍ .

"That he was harvesting siwāk from an Arāk tree and he had thin shins. The wind blew and made him fall over, so people laughed at him. So the Messenger of Allāh (sallAllāhu 'alayhi wa sallam) said: 'Who are you laughing at?' They said: 'O Prophet of Allāh, at the thinness of his shins.' So he said: 'By the one in Whose Hand

163

my soul is, they will both be heavier on the Scale than the mountain of Uhud." (Ahmad, At-Tayālisī and Al-Bazzār – *sahīh li-ghayrihi*)

The **Mu'tazilah** rejected the *mīzān* under the claim that the deeds of the slaves are not masses that have a weight, and therefore it cannot be weighed. This is because they did not believe in the unseen, and they compared the issues of *dunyā* with issues of *ākhirah* leading them to reject things that they could not understand.

As-Sam'u wat-Tā'ah (Listening and obeying) the Islamic rulers

Ahlus-Sunnah believes that as long as the Islamic ruler does not show apparent *kufr* from himself, as long as he rules with the *Sharī'ah* – unlike the situation of the countries today – and as long as he establishes the prayer in the land, then it is obligatory to listen to him and obey him, and it is forbidden to rebel against him or fight against him, and thereby splitting the unity of the Muslims. And this is applicable even if he should sin or perform injustice to those who are under his authority.

The Prophet (*sallAllāhu 'alayhi wa sallam*) said:

خِيَارُ أَئِمَّتِكُمُ الَّذِينَ تُحِبُّونَهُمْ وَيُحِبُّونَكُمْ، وَتُصَلُّونَ عليهم وَيُصَلُّونَ عَلَيْكُم، وشِرارُ أَئِمَّتِكُمُ الَّذِينَ تُبْغِضُونَهُمْ وَيُبْغِضُونَكُمْ، وَتَلْعَنُونَهُمْ وَيَلْعَنُونَكُمْ، قالوا: قُلْنا: يا رَسولَ اللهِ، أَفَلَا نُنابِذُهُمْ عِنْدَ ذلكَ؟ قالَ: لا، ما أقامُوا فِيكُمُ الصَّلاةَ، لا، ما أقامُوا فِيكُمُ الصَّلاةَ، أَلا مَن وَلِيَ عليه والٍ، فَرَآهُ يَأْتِي شيئًا مِن مَعْصِيَةِ اللهِ، فَلْيَكْرَهْ ما يَأْتِي مِن مَعْصِيَةِ اللهِ، ولا يَنْزِعَنَّ يَدًا مِن طاعَةٍ.

"The best of your leaders are those whom you love and they love you. And you pray for them and they pray for you. And the worst of your leaders are those whom you hate and they hate you. And you curse them and they curse you. They said: 'We said: O Messenger of Allāh, should we not oppose them (or separate from them) in this case?' He said: 'No, as long as they establish the prayer among you. No, as long as they establish the prayer among you. Verily, whoever a leader is appointed over and he sees him perform something of disobedience to Allāh, then let him hate what he performs of disobedience of Allāh, but he should verily not pull his hand back from obedience (towards him)." (Sahīh Muslim)

And the Prophet (*sallAllāhu 'alayhi wa sallam*) said:

إنَّه يُسْتَعْمَلُ عَلَيْكُم أُمَراءُ، فَتَعْرِفُونَ وتُنْكِرُونَ، فَمَن كَرِهَ فَقَدْ بَرِئَ، ومَن أَنْكَرَ فَقَدْ سَلِمَ، ولكِنْ مَن رَضِيَ وتابَعَ، قالوا: يا رَسولَ اللهِ، أَلا نُقاتِلُهُمْ؟ قالَ: لا، ما صَلَّوْا.

"Verily leaders will be appointed over you (from which) you will acknowledge (some of their deeds) and reject (others). So whoever

hates (their bad deeds) is innocent. And whoever rejects it is safe. But whoever is pleased and follows it (is destroyed). They said: 'O Messenger of Allāh, should we not fight against them?' He said: 'No, not as long as they pray (the five prayers).'" (Sahīh Muslim)

And the Prophet (sallAllāhu ''alayhi wa sallam) said:

مَن رَأَى مِن أَمِيرِهِ شيئًا يَكْرَهُهُ عليه فَلْيَصْبِرْ عليه فإنّه مَن فارَقَ الجَماعَةَ شِبْرًا فَماتَ، إلّا ماتَ مِيتَةً جاهليّةً.

"Whoever sees something from his leader which he hates (or dislikes), then let him have patience in it. Because there is no-one who separates from them Jamā'ah (even a) hands span and then dies, except that he dies the death of jāhiliyyah." (Sahīh Al-Bukhārī)

And Hudhayfah ibn Al-Yamān (radiAllāhu 'anhu) said:

قُلتُ: يا رَسولَ اللهِ، إنَّا كُنَّا بشَرٍّ، فَجاءَ اللهُ بخَيْرٍ، فَنَحْنُ فيهِ، فَهلْ مِن وَرَاءِ هذا الخَيْرِ شَرٌّ؟ قالَ: نَعَمْ، قُلتُ: هلْ وَرَاءَ ذلكَ الشَّرِّ خَيْرٌ؟ قالَ: نَعَمْ، قُلتُ: فَهلْ وَرَاءَ ذلكَ الخَيْرِ شَرٌّ؟ قالَ: نَعَمْ، قُلتُ: كيفَ؟ قالَ: يَكونُ بَعْدِي أَئِمَّةٌ لا يَهْتَدُونَ بُهَدَايَ، وَلا يَسْتَنُّونَ بسُنَّتِي، وَسَيَقُومُ فيهم رِجالٌ قُلُوبُهُمْ قُلُوبُ الشَّيَاطِينِ في جُثْمانِ إِنْسٍ، قالَ: قُلتُ: كيفَ أَصْنَعُ يا رَسولَ اللهِ، إنْ أَدْرَكْتُ ذلكَ؟ قالَ: تَسْمَعُ وتُطِيعُ لِلأَمِيرِ، وإنْ ضُرِبَ ظَهْرُكَ، وَأُخِذَ مالُكَ، فَاسْمَعْ وَأَطِعْ.

"I said: 'O Messenger of Allāh, we were verily in an evil state and then Allāh sent us the good which we are in now. So is there any evil after this good?' He said: 'Yes.' I said: 'Is there any good after this evil?' He said: 'Yes.' I said: 'So is there any evil after this good?' He said: 'Yes.' I said: 'How?' He said: 'After me there will be leaders who do not follow my guidance, nor do they adhere to my Sunnah. And among them there will be men whose hearts are the hearts of shayātīn (devils) in the bodies of a human.' He (Hudyafah) said: 'I said: How should I act, O Messenger of Allāh, if I live to see this?' He said: 'You listen and obey the leaders. Even if your back is beaten and your wealth is taken, then listen and obey.'" (Sahīh Muslim)

And 'Ubādah Ibn As-Sāmit (radiAllāhu 'anhu) said:

دَعَانَا النبيُّ صَلَّى اللهُ عليه وسلَّمَ فَبَايَعْنَاهُ، فقالَ فِيما أَخَذَ عَلَيْنَا :أَنْ بَايَعَنَا عَلَى السَّمْعِ
والطَّاعَةِ، في مَنْشَطِنَا ومَكْرَهِنَا، وعُسْرِنَا ويُسْرِنَا وأَثَرَةً عَلَيْنَا، وأَنْ
لا نُنَازِعَ الأَمْرَ أَهْلَهُ، إِلَّا أَنْ تَرَوْا كُفْرًا بَوَاحًا، عِنْدَكُمْ مِنَ اللهِ فيهِ بُرْهَانٌ.

"The Prophet (sallAllāhu 'alayhi wa sallam) called us and we pledged allegiance to him. And among that which held us accountable for was: That we pledged allegiance to listen and obey in what we were able to perform and what we disliked, in our difficult times and at our times of ease, to give precedence (to the leader) over ourselves, and not do dispute the issue (of leadership) with its people except if you see clear kufr regarding which you have a clear proof from Allāh." (Sahīh Al-Bukhārī)

The **Khawārij**, **Mu'tazilah** and **Ahl Ar-Raī** (people of opinion) considered the rebellion against the sinning Muslim leaders as allowed and obligatory, and they included this in *al-amr bil-ma'rūf wan-nahī 'anil-munkar* (ordering good and forbidding evil).

Imām Ahmad (d. 241h) said:

وَمَنْ خَرَجَ عَلَى إِمَامٍ مِنْ أَئِمَّةِ الْمُسْلِمِينَ وَقَدْ كَانَ النَّاسُ اِجْتَمَعُوا عَلَيْهِ وَأَقَرُّوا لَهُ بِالْخِلَافَةِ، بِأَيِّ وَجْهٍ
كَانَ، بِالرِّضَا أَوْ بِالْغَلَبَةِ – فَقَدْ شَقَّ هَذَا الْخَارِجُ عَصَا الْمُسْلِمِينَ، وَخَالَفَ الْآثَارَ عَنْ رَسُولِ اللهِ ﷺ:
فَإِنْ مَاتَ الْخَارِجُ عَلَيْهِ مَاتَ مِيتَةً جَاهِلِيَّةً. وَلَا يَحِلُّ قِتَالُ السُّلْطَانِ وَلَا الْخُرُوجُ عَلَيْهِ لِأَحَدٍ مِنَ النَّاسِ،
فَمَنْ فَعَلَ ذَلِكَ فَهُوَ مُبْتَدِعٌ عَلَى غَيْرِ السُّنَّةِ وَالطَّرِيقِ.

"And whoever rebels against a leader among the leaders of the Muslim, while the people have united behind him and they have acknowledged the Khilāfah for him – no matter in what way, either being pleased with him or by force – then this rebel has divided the unity of the Muslims, and he has opposed the narrations from the Messenger of Allāh (sallAllāhu 'alayhi wa sallam). So if the one who rebels against him (i.e. the leader) dies, then he dies the death of jāhiliyyah. And it is not allowed for anyone among the people to fight against the leader, nor to rebel against him. So whoever does

this, then he is an innovator who is not upon the Sunnah and the (straight) path." (Usūl As-Sunnah by Imām Ahmad – the *riwāyah* of 'Abdūs)

Al-Barbahārī (d. 329h) said:

ولا يحل قتال السلطان ولا الخروج عليه وإن جار وذلك لقول رسول الله صلى الله عليه و سلم لأبي ذر الغفاري اصبر وإن كان عبدا حبشيا وقوله للأنصار اصبروا حتى تلقوني على الحوض وليس من السنة قتال السلطان فإن فيه فساد الدنيا والدين

"And it is not allowed to fight against the leader, nor to rebel against him, even if he is unjust. And this is due to the words of the Messenger of Allāh (sallAllāhu 'alayhi wa sallam) to Abū Dhar Al-Ghifārī: 'Have patience, even if he is an Ethiopic slave', and his words to the Ansār: 'Have patience until you meet me at the hawd (basin)'. And it is not from the Sunnah to fight the leaders, because verily in it is the destruction of the dunyā and the religion." (Sharh As-Sunnah by Al-Barbahārī)

And Al-Ājurrī (d. 320h) said:

من أُمِّر عليك من عربي أو غيره، أسود أو أبيض،أو أعجمي، فأطعه فيما ليس لله عَزَّ وَجَلَّ فيه معصية، وإن ظلمك حقًّا لك، وإن ضربك ظلمًا، وانتهك عرضك وأخذ مالك، فلا يَحملك ذَلِكَ عَلَى أنه يَخرج عليه سيفك حتَّى تقاتله، ولا تَخرج مع خارجي حتَّى تقاتله، ولاتُحرِّض غيرك عَلَى الخروج عليه، ولكن اصبر عليه

"Whoever is appointed over you as a leader, whether he is an Arab or a non-Arab, or he is black or white or a foreigner, then obey him in that which is not a sin towards Allāh 'azza wa jalla. (This), even if he is unjust to you in a right which you have (over him). And even if he unjustly hits you and violates your honor and takes your wealth. Then this should not lead you to bring out your sword against him to fight him. And do not rebel along with a khārijī (rebeller) in order to fight against him (i.e. the leader). And do not encourage others to rebel against him, rather you should have patience with him." (As-Sharī'ah by Al-Ājurrī)

168

Judgments in *dunyā* are according to the outwardly

Ahlus-Sunnah believes that in *dunyā* the judgments upon persons are according to the outwardly. So whoever utters, performs or shows *shirk* and *kufr*, or the signs of *shirk* and *kufr*, then he is judged as a *kāfir*. And whoever shows Islām and the signs of Islām, such as saying the *Shahādah*, establishing the prayer along with the other rituals of Islām, then he is judged as a Muslim in this life, and his internal affairs are between him and Allāh. The Qurān and *Sunnah* have established this fact in a very clear way.

Allāh – the Exalted – said:

﴿ فَإِن تَابُوا وَأَقَامُوا الصَّلَاةَ وَآتَوُا الزَّكَاةَ فَإِخْوَانُكُمْ فِي الدِّينِ وَنُفَصِّلُ الْآيَاتِ لِقَوْمٍ يَعْلَمُونَ ﴾

"But if they repent (from *shirk*) **and establish the prayer and pay the *zakāh*, then they are your brothers in religion. And We explain the verses in details for people who have knowledge."**
(At-Tawbah 9:11)

The Prophet (*sallAllāhu 'alayhi wa sallam*) said:

أُمِرْتُ أَنْ أُقَاتِلَ النَّاسَ حَتَّى يَشْهَدُوا أَنْ لَا إِلَهَ إِلَّا اللَّهُ ، وَأَنَّ مُحَمَّدًا رَسُولُ اللَّهِ ، وَيُقِيمُوا الصَّلَاةَ ، وَيُؤْتُوا الزَّكَاةَ ، فَإِذَا فَعَلُوا ذَلِكَ ، عَصَمُوا مِنِّي دِمَاءَهُمْ وَأَمْوَالَهُمْ ، إِلَّا بِحَقِّ الْإِسْلَامِ ، وَحِسَابُهُمْ عَلَى اللَّهِ تَعَالَى

"I have ordered to fight the people until they testify to Lā ilāha illa Allāh and that Muhammad is the Messenger of Allāh, and they establish the prayer and they pay the zakāh. And if they do this, then they have protected their blood and wealth from me, except by the right of Islām, and their account is with Allāh the Exalted."
(Sahīh Al-Bukhārī)

And the Prophet (*sallAllāhu 'alayhi wa sallam*) said:

مَنْ صَلَّى صَلَاتَنَا وَاسْتَقْبَلَ قِبْلَتَنَا وَأَكَلَ ذَبِيحَتَنَا فَذَلِكَ الْمُسْلِمُ الَّذِي لَهُ ذِمَّةُ اللَّهِ وَذِمَّةُ رَسُولِهِ فَلَا تُخْفِرُوا اللَّهَ فِي ذِمَّتِهِ

169

"Whoever prays our prayer, faces our Qiblah and eats from what we have slaughtered, then this is the Muslim who has the protection of Allāh and the protection of His Messenger. So do not betray Allāh in His protection (by violating it)." (Sahīh Al-Bukhari)

And 'Ubayd-Allāh ibn 'Adī ibn Al-Khiyār[18] (d. 95h) narrated:

بَيْنَا رَسُولُ اللَّهِ – صَلَّى اللَّهُ عَلَيْهِ وَسَلَّمَ – جَالِسٌ بَيْنَ ظَهْرَانَيْ أَصْحَابِهِ ، إِذْ جَاءَهُ رَجُلٌ فَسَارَّهُ ، فَلَمْ يَدْرِ مَا سَارَّهُ بِهِ حَتَّى جَهَرَ رَسُولُ اللَّهِ – صَلَّى اللَّهُ عَلَيْهِ وَسَلَّمَ – فَإِذَا هُوَ يَسْتَأْذِنُ فِي قَتْلِ رَجُلٍ مِنَ الْمُنَافِقِينَ ، فَقَالَ رَسُولُ اللَّهِ – صَلَّى اللَّهُ عَلَيْهِ وَسَلَّمَ – حِينَ جَهَرَ : " أَلَيْسَ يَشْهَدُ أَنْ لَا إِلَهَ إِلَّا اللَّهُ وَأَنَّ مُحَمَّدًا رَسُولُ اللَّهِ ؟ فَقَالَ الرَّجُلُ : بَلَى وَلَا شَهَادَةَ لَهُ . قَالَ : أَلَيْسَ يُصَلِّي ؟ قَالَ : بَلَى وَلَا صَلَاةَ لَهُ ، فَقَالَ رَسُولُ اللَّهِ – صَلَّى اللَّهُ عَلَيْهِ وَسَلَّمَ – " أُولَئِكَ الَّذِينَ نَهَانِي اللَّهُ عَنْهُمْ."

"While the Messenger of Allāh (sallAllāhu 'alayhi wa sallam) was sitting amongst his companions a man came to him and informed him about a secret. And it was not known what he said to him in secret until the Messenger of Allāh (sallAllāhu 'alayhi wa sallam) spoke out loud, and he (i.e. the man) was asking for permission to kill a man from the hypocrites. So the Messenger of Allāh (sallAllāhu 'alayhi wa sallam) said when he spoke out loud: 'Does he not bear witness to Lā ilāha illa Allāh and that Muhammmad is Allāhs Messenger?' So the man said: 'Yes, but he has no shahādah (i.e. it is not valid).' He said: 'Does he not pray?' He said: 'Yes, but he has no prayer (i.e. it is not valid).' So the Messenger of Allāh (sallAllāhu 'alayhi wa sallam) said: 'These are the ones whom Allāh has prohibited me from.'" (Muwatta by Imām Mālik and Al-Musnad by Imām Ahmad)

Humayd ibn Abī Humayd At-Tawīl (d. 142h) said:

---

[18] There is a difference of opinion whether or not he was a companion of the Messenger of Allāh (sallAllāhu 'alayhi wa sallam) or he was among the *tābi'ūn*.

سَأَلَ مَيمُونُ بنُ سِياهٍ أنسَ بنَ مالِكٍ، قال: يا أبا حَمزَةَ، ما يُحَرِّمُ دمَ المُسْلِمِ ومالَهُ؟ فقال: مَن شَهِدَ أنْ لا إلهَ إلَّا اللهُ، وأنَّ محمَّدًا رسولُ اللهِ، واستَقْبَلَ قِبْلَتَنا، وصَلَّى صلاتَنا، وأَكَلَ ذَبِيحتَنا، فهو مُسْلِمٌ، له ما للمُسْلِمِينَ، وعليه ما على المُسْلِمِينَ.

"*Maymun ibn Siyāh asked Anas ibn Mālik (radiAllāhu 'anhu) and said: 'O Abū Hamzah, what prohibits the blood of a Muslim and his wealth?' So he said: 'If he testifies to Lā ilāha illa Allāh and that Muhammad is Rasūl-Allāh, he faces our Qiblah, he prays our prayer and he eats our slaughter, then he is a Muslim. He has what the Muslims have (of rights), and upon him is what is upon the Muslims (of obligations)."* (Al-Bukhārī and An-Nasāī – sahīh)

The **Khawārij** that occurred after the death of the Messenger of Allāh (*sallAllāhu 'alayhi wa sallam*) deviated from this principle by declaring *takfīr* upon a Muslim who committed a major sin, which is lesser than major *shirk* and major *kufr*. The Khawārij of today uprooted this principle from the *Sunnah* and claim that a person is not judged according to what he shows in the apparent; rather he is judged upon assumption and the situation of the majority of the people. So when the majority of the people in reality do not know the truth, then the unknown person is assumed to be equal to them in their *hāl* (situation) and therefore given the same judgment as them, without taking the apparent signs into consideration.

This obviously contradicts the Qurān and the Sunnah, and it necessitates for them that they declare *takfīr* based upon their own assumptions and feelings regarding his inner situation. The *Sunnah* from the Prophet (*sallAllāhu 'alayhi wa sallam*) clearly forbids this and commands us to judge upon the apparent.

The Prophet (*sallAllāhu 'alayhi wa sallam*) said:

إِنِّي لم أُومَرْ أنْ أُنَقِّبَ عن قُلوبِ الناسِ، ولا أَشُقَّ بُطونَهم.

"*I was verily not ordered to search in the hearts of the people, nor to split open their bellies.*" (Sahīh Al-Bukhārī)

And 'Umar ibn Al-Khattāb – *radiAllāhu 'anhu* – said:

إِنَّ أُنَاسًا كَانُوا يُؤْخَذُونَ بِالْوَحْيِ فِي عَهْدِ رَسُولِ اللهِ صَلَّى اللهُ عَلَيْهِ وَسَلَّمَ وَإِنَّ الْوَحْيَ قَدْ انْقَطَعَ وَإِنَّمَا نَأْخُذُكُمُ الْآنَ بِمَا ظَهَرَ لَنَا مِنْ أَعْمَالِكُمْ فَمَنْ أَظْهَرَ لَنَا خَيْرًا أَمِنَّاهُ وَقَرَّبْنَاهُ وَلَيْسَ إِلَيْنَا مِنْ سَرِيرَتِهِ شَيْءٌ اللهُ يُحَاسِبُهُ فِي سَرِيرَتِهِ وَمَنْ أَظْهَرَ لَنَا سُوءًا لَمْ نَأْمَنْهُ وَلَمْ نُصَدِّقْهُ وَإِنْ قَالَ إِنَّ سَرِيرَتَهُ حَسَنَةٌ

"Verily the people were judged according to the revelation in the time of the Messenger of Allāh (sallAllāhu 'alayhi wa sallam), and verily has the revelation stopped. And verily do we (now) judge you now from what appears to us from your deeds. So whoever shows us good we consider trustworthy and we bring him close and as for his inner self then we have nothing to do with that, Allāh will hold him accountable for his inner self. And whoever shows us evilness then we don't trust him, and we don't believe him even if he says that his inner self is good." (Sahīh Al-Bukhari)

Ash-Shāfi'ī (d. 204h) said:

وَأَنَّ حُكْمَ اللهِ تَعَالَى فِي الدُّنْيَا قَبُولُ ظَاهِرِ الْآدَمِيِّينَ وَأَنَّهُ تَوَلَّى سَرَائِرُهُمْ وَلَمْ يَجْعَلْ لِنَبِيٍّ مُرْسَلٍ وَلَا لِأَحَدٍ مِنْ خَلْقِهِ أَنْ يَحْكُمَ إِلَّا عَلَى الظَّاهِرِ وَتَوَلَّى دُونَهُمُ السَّرَائِرَ لِانْفِرَادِهِ بِعِلْمِهَا

"And that the judgment of Allāh – the Exalted – in dunyā is accepting the dhāhir (apparent) of the people and that He took responsibility for their inner selves. And He did not allow for a sent prophet nor for anyone else from the creation that they should judge except according to the apparent, and He besides them took the responsibility for the inner selves due to Him being the only One who has knowledge about that." (Al-Umm 6/178)

And Al-Khallāl (d. 311h) narrated:

أخبرني محمد بن أبي هارون، قال: حدثنا محمد بن أبي هاشم، قال: دفع إليّ فوران شيئًا من مسائل أبي عبد الله قال: سألته قال: قلت: اليهود يقول بعضهم: أشهد أن لا إله إلَّا الله وأشهد أن محمدًا رسول الله. فقال: إذا لم يرد الإسلام، أما إذا جاء ليسلم فشهد أن لا إله إلَّا الله وأن محمدًا عبده ورسوله وصلَّى، فأي إسلام أتمّ من هذا؟! أليس يروى عن النبي –صلى الله عليه وسلم- قال: "أُمِرْتُ أَنْ أُقَاتِلَ النَّاسَ حَتَّى يَقُولُوا: لَا إله إِلَّا اللهُ فَإِذَا قَالُوا مَنَعُوا مِنِّي دِمَاءَهُمْ وَأَمْوَالَهُمْ.

"Muhammad ibn Abī Hārūn narrated to me and said: Muhammad ibn Abī Hashīm narrated to us and said: Fawrān passed some of the masāil (issues) of Abū 'Abdullāh to me and said: I asked him. He said: I said: 'Some of the Jews say: I bear witness to Lā ilāha illa Allāh and that Muhammad is the Messenger of Allāh.' So he (i.e. Imām Ahmad) said: 'If he doesn't want Islām (then it is not accepted as his entrance into Islām), but if he came to accept Islām and testifies to Lā ilāha illa Allāh and that Muhammad is His slave and messenger, and he prays, then what Islām is more complete than that? Is it not narrated from the Prophet (sallAllāhu 'alayhi wa sallam) that he said: **'I have been ordered to fight the people until they say Lā ilāha illa Allāh. Then if they say that, then they have prevented me from their blood and wealth.'"** (Al-Jāmi' li-'Ulūm Al-Imām Ahmad 4/172)

Harb ibn Ismā'īl Al-Karmānī (d. 280h) said:

والكف عن أهل القبلة لا نكفر أحدًا منهم بذنب، ولا نخرجه من الإسلام بعمل، إلا أن يكون في ذلك حديث، فيروى الحديث كما جاء وكما روي، ويصدق به ويقبله

"And withholding the hand (i.e. not harming) Ahlul-Qiblah (those who pray), and we do not declare takfīr upon any of them due to a sin (they performed), and we do not exit them from Islām due to any deed, except if there is a hadīth regarding it. Then the hadīth is narrated just as it has been reported, and it is believed in and accepted." (As-Sunnah by Harb Al-Karmānī)

Imām Al-Barbahārī (d. 329h) said:

ولا يخرج أحد من أهل القبلة من الإسلام حتى يرد آية من كتاب الله تعالى أو يرد شيئا من آثار رسول الله ﷺ أو يصلي لغير الله أو يذبح لغير الله وإذا فعل شيئا من ذلك فقد وجب عليك أن تخرجه من الإسلام فإذا لم يفعل شيئا من ذلك فهو مؤمن ومسلم بالإسم لا بالحقيقة.

"And no-one from the people of the Qiblah (i.e. those who pray) are exited from Islām (i.e. declared takfīr upon) before he rejects a verse from the Book of Allāh – the Exalted – or he rejects something of the narrations of the Messenger of Allāh (sallAllāhu 'alayhi wa sallam), or he prays to other

173

than Allāh, or he slaughters for others than Allāh. But if he does any of these things, then it is obligatory upon you to exit him from Islām (i.e. to declare takfir upon him). But if he does not perform any of these things, then he is a believer and a Muslim in name, not in reality" (Sharh As-Sunnah by Al-Barbahārī)

And this is because it is only Allāh who knows the reality. And this innovation is not new, rather can it be found in the books of the scholars when they mentioned the Khawārij.

Al-Lālakāī (d. 418h) narrated:

عن حميد بن هلال عن عبادة بن قرط الليثي، أنه قال للخوارج حين أخذوه بالأهواز : ارضوا مني بما رضي رسول الله صلى الله عليه وسلم حين أسلمت. قالوا: وما رضي به منك رسول الله صلى الله عليه وسلم ؟ قال: أتيته فشهدت أن لا إله إلا الله، وأن محمدا رسول الله، فقبل ذلك مني .قال: فأبوا، فقتلوه

"From Humayd ibn Hilāl, from (i.e. about) 'Ubādah ibn Qurt Al-Laythī that he said to the Khawārij when they took him in Al-Ahwāz: 'Be content with from me what the Messenger of Allāh (sallAllāhu 'alayhi wa sallam) was content with when I accepted Islām. They said: 'And what was the Messenger of Allāh (sallAllāhu 'alayhi wa sallam) content with from you?' He said: 'I came to him and testified to Lā ilāha illa Allāh and Muhammadu Rasul-Allāh, and he accepted that from me.' He (i.e. Humayd) said: 'But they rejected (to accept that) and killed him.'" (Sharh Usul I'tiqād Ahlus-Sunnah wal-Jamā'ah)

And this is a spot-on description of the modern day Khāwarij who under no circumstances will give the *hukm* (judgment) of Islām to anyone except if they have heard the meaning of Tawhīd and its issues from him. But since this is a practice which does not have any basis in the *Sunnah*, it is an innovation which renders the one who believes in it an innovator. Furthermore, the most extreme of these people will declare *takfir* upon those who follow the belief described in the *ahādīth* and the scholars in this issue. So they describe the *manhaj* of the Muslims – all the way from the Prophet (*sallAllāhu 'alayhi wa sallam*), to the *Sahābah* (*radiAllāhu 'anhum*), their followers and whoever came after them of scholars – as *kufr*, and that the one who believes in it have not rejected *tāghūt*. This opinion without a doubt is *kufr* and *zandaqah* due them rejecting the clear evidences and the agreement of the Muslims.

Adhering to the *Sunnah* and leaving the innovator

It is very important to understand that in order to be upon the way of the *Sahābah* (*radiAllāhu 'anhum*) and those who followed them in goodness, a person must hold a correct belief and firmly adhere to that which has its foundation in the sources that has been described in this book. There is no exception or excuse when it comes to not following or believing in the *Sunnah*.

Al-Barbahārī (d. 329h) said:

وليس لأحد رخصة في شيء أخذ به مما لم يكن عليه أصحاب رسول الله ﷺ أو يكون رجل يدعو إلى شيء أحدثه من قبله من أهل البدع فهو كمن أحدثه فمن زعم ذلك أو قال به فقد رد السنة وخالف الحق والجماعة وأباح الهوى وهو أشر على هذه الأمة من إبليس ومن عرف ما ترك أهل البدع من السنة وما فارقوا منها فتمسك به فهو صاحب سنة وصاحب جماعة وحقيق أن يتبع وأن يعاون وأن يحفظ وهو ممن أوصى به رسول الله ﷺ.

"And there is no permission for anyone to take (i.e. believe in) something which the Companions of the Messenger of Allāh (sallAllāhu 'alayhi wa sallam) were not upon, or that a man invites to something which was innovated by someone before him by the people of innovation, then (in that case) he is like the one who innovated it. So whoever claims this, or holds this opinion, then he has verily rejected the Sunnah and opposed the truth and the Jamā'ah, and he has allowed the desires (i.e. innovation) and he is worse for this Ummah than Iblīs. And whoever knows what the people of innovation left of the Sunnah and that which they separated themselves from, and he then adheres to it, then he is a follower of the Sunnah and a follower of the Jamā'ah. This person is deserving of being followed, aided and protected, and he is among those towards whom the Messenger of Allāh (sallAllāhu 'alayhi wa sallam) advised." (Sharh As-Sunnah by Al-Barbahārī)

So the person, who is a *Sunnī* in reality, must not mix his beliefs with innovation, and he must completely cut off the people of innovation in any way.

Ibn 'Umar (*radiAllāhu 'anhu*) said regarding the people who did not believe in the *Qadar* (Divine Decree):

إِذَا لَقِيتَ أُولَئِكَ فَأَخْبِرْهُمْ أَنِّي بَرِيءٌ مِنْهُمْ وَأَنَّهُمْ بُرَآءُ مِنِّي

"If you met those people then inform them that I am free from them and they are free from me." (Sahīh Muslim)

'Abdullāh ibn Imām Ahmad (d. 290h) said:

وَدَخَلَ رَجُلَانِ مِنْ أَصْحَابِ الْأَهْوَاءِ عَلَى مُحَمَّدِ بْنِ سِيرِينَ فَقَالَا: يَا أَبَا بَكْرٍ نُحَدِّثُكَ بِحَدِيثٍ قَالَ: لَا، قَالَ: فَنَقْرَأُ عَلَيْكَ آيَةً مِنْ كِتَابِ اللَّهِ عَزَّ وَجَلَّ، قَالَ: «لَا، لَتَقُومَانِ عَنِّي أَوْ لَأَقُومَنَّ»، قَالَ: فَقَامَ الرَّجُلَانِ فَخَرَجَا، فَقَالَ بَعْضُ الْقَوْمِ: يَا أَبَا بَكْرٍ مَا كَانَ عَلَيْكَ أَنْ يَقْرَأَ آيَةً مِنْ كِتَابِ اللَّهِ عَزَّ وَجَلَّ، فَقَالَ مُحَمَّدُ بْنُ سِيرِينَ: «إِنِّي خَشِيتُ أَنْ يَقْرَآ عَلَيَّ آيَةً فَيُحَرِّفَاهَا فَيَقِرُّ ذَلِكَ فِي قَلْبِي»

"And two men from the people of hawā (desires) entered upon Muhammad ibn Sīrīn and said: 'O Abū Bakr, we will narrate a hadith to you.' He said: 'No'. They said: 'Then we will recite a verse from the Book of Allāh – the Mighty and Majestic – for you.' He said: 'No. Either you will get up away from me, or I will get up (away from you).' He said: So the two men got up and went out. So some of the people said: 'O Abū Bakr, what would it harm you if they recited a verse from the Book of Allāh the Mighty and Majestic.' So Muhammad ibn Sīrīn said: 'I verily fear that they would recite a verse for me, and they would distort it and that would be established in my heart.'" (As-Sunnah by 'Abdullāh)

And the *āthār* (narrations) from the *Salaf* are filled with the disassociation from the people of innovation. Because in the disassociation of the people of innovation lies the preservation of the religion and the protection of one's self. Al-Barbahārī – *rahimahullāh* – gathered the meaning of cutting off and boycotting the people of innovation when he said:

فالله الله في نفسك وعليك بالآثار وأصحاب الأثر والتقليد فإن الدين إنما هو التقليد يعني للنبي ﷺ وأصحابه رضوان الله عليهم أجمعين ومن قبلنا ممن لم يدعونا في لبس فقلدوهم واسترح ولا تجاوز الأثر وأهل الأثر وقف عند متشابه القرآن والحديث ولا تقس شيئا ولا تطلب من عندك حيلة ترد بما على أهل

177

البدع فإنك امرت بالسكوت عنهم فلا تمكنهم من نفسك أما علمت أن محمد بن سيرين مع فضله لم

يجب رجلا من أهل البدع في مسألة واحدة ولا سمع منه آية من كتاب الله تعالى فقيل له فقال أخاف

أن يحرفها فيقع في قلبي شيء .

"So (be aware of) Allāh, (be aware of) Allāh regarding yourself. And obligatory upon you is the āthār (narrations) and the companions of the athar, and following (these). Because verily is the religion (only) following; that is (following) the Prophet (sallAllāhu 'alayhi wa sallam) and his Companions – may the Pleasure of Allāh be upon all of them. And those who came before us did not invite us in ambiguity, so follow them and relax. And do not exceed the athar and the people of athar, and stop at the ambiguous of the Qurān and the hadīth, and do not make analogy with anything nor seek a plot from yourself with which you answer the people of innovation. Because you are verily ordered not to speak with them and not to make yourself possible for them (to manipulate). Do you not know that Muhammad ibn Sīrīn – along with his virtues – did not answer a man from the people of innovation in a single issue, nor did he listen to one verse from the Book of Allāh from him? So it was said to him: ('Why?') So he said: 'I fear that they would distort it (i.e. the verse) so that something (of innovation) would befall my heart.'" (Sharh As-Sunnah by Al-Barbahārī)

A mistake that many people fall in today – perhaps with good intention – is that they gladly enter into discussion or debate with the people of innovation. Or they seek to correct the people of innovation and refute them in conversation with them. This is not from the way of the *Salaf* at all. Rather this is an unwise boldness and lack of fear of being infected with the poison of the innovators. Because there is no doubt that many of the people of innovation have been given eloquence, and they all bring some sort of distorted argument for their innovation. So the *Sunnah* in this issue is the refrain from every form of conversation with them.

Al-Barbahārī (d. 329h) said:

وإذا جاءك يناظرك فاحذره فإن في المناظرة المراء والجدال والمغالبة والخصومة والغضب وقد نهيت عن
جميع هذا وهو يزيل عن طريق الحق ولم يبلغنا عن أحد من فقهائنا وعلمائنا أنه جادل أو ناظر أو
خاصم قال الحسن الحكيم لا يماري ولا يداري حكمته ينشرها إن قبلت حمد الله وإن ردت حمد الله
وجاء رجل إلى الحسن فقال أنا أناظرك في الدين فقال الحسن أنا قد عرفت ديني فإن كان دينك قد
ضل منك فاذهب فاطلبه وسمع رسول الله ﷺ قوما على باب حجرته يقول أحدهم ألم يقل الله كذا
ويقول الآخر ألم يقل الله كذا فخرج مغضبا فقال أبهذا أمرتكم أم بهذا بعثت إليكم أن تضربوا كتاب
الله بعضه ببعض فنهاهم عن الجدال

*"And if he (i.e. the innovator) comes to debate, then be aware of him.
Because verily in debating there is arguing, discussing, fighting,
disputing and the anger, and you have verily been prohibited from all of
it, and it removes a person from the Path of the Truth. And it has not
reached us from anyone among our fuqahā and 'ulamā that he would
discuss, debate or dispute. Al-Hasan said: 'The wise person does not argue
nor does he flatter. He spreads his wisdom, then if it is accepted then he
praises Allāh, and if it rejected then he praises Allāh.' And a man came to
Al-Hasan and said: 'I want to debate with you in the religion.' So Al-
Hasan said: 'As for me, then I already know my religion. So if your religion
has strayed from you, then go and search for it.' And the Messenger of
Allāh (sallAllāhu 'alayhi wa sallam) heard a people outside the door of his
room, when one of them said: 'Did Allāh not say this?' And the other one
saying: 'Did Allāh not say that?' So he went out very angry and said: 'Is
this what you have been ordered to do? Or is it with this I have been sent
to you; that you use something from the Book of Allāh as argument against
something else (from the Book of Allāh)?' So he prohibited them from
debating."* (Sharh As-Sunnah by Al-Barbahārī)

So whoever indulges in debate and discussion with the people of
innovation and then goes astray, he should blame nobody but
himself if his heart becomes afflicted with their poison, and he no
longer is able to remove it again.

The place of *takfīr* in the religion

The issue of *takfīr* is also an easy issue for the one who knows the place of the issue of *takfīr* in the religion. Every saying or deed has its category in the religion and must therefore be treated accordingly. So whoever is able to recognize the category of the saying or deed, then by that he will know whether or not declaring *takfīr* is obligatory upon him or not. Some saying and deeds might be clear cut in their indication of *kufr*, while other might be ambiguous, in which case the Muslim can ask his brother what he has intended by it, and then judge based upon the given explanation.

As for the categories where a saying or a deed of *kufr* can occur, then these are three:

The first: Issues of the fundamentals of Tawhīd and *shirk akbar* (major *shirk*). These are issues which are related to the knowledge of Allāh which is known through *fitrah*, such as the description of Allāh with Attributes of perfection that negates faults and deficiencies for Allāh, such as that Allāh is Living, Seeing, Hearing, All-Powerful, All-Knowing, the Creator, the Sustainer, the Arranger of affairs, the *'Uluw* (Aboveness) of Allāh and that He Speaks. These are the things that if a person rejects them or doubts regarding them, then he has rejected perfection for Allāh or doubted regarding it, which is *kufr* before and after the establishment of the argument. Furthermore the types of worship are also included in this category. So if the slave dedicates a type of worship for others than Allāh with his deeds or beliefs, then this also are from the things which are *kufr* before and after the establishment of the argument.

Thus, if the Muslim sees any mistakes from another Muslim in this category – whether this is in words or deed – then it is obligatory to exit him from the religion and consider him a non-Muslim until he repents from what he has committed of *kufr*.

'Abdullāh ibn Ahmad (d. 290h) narrated:

سَمِعْتُ أَبِي رَحِمَهُ اللَّهُ، وَسَأَلَهُ عَلِيُّ بْنُ الْجَهْمِ عَنْ مَنْ قَالَ: بِالْقَدَرِ يَكُونُ كَافِرًا؟ قَالَ: " إِذَا جَحَدَ الْعِلْمَ، إِذَا قَالَ: إِنَّ اللَّهَ عَزَّ وَجَلَّ لَمْ يَكُنْ عَالِمًا حَتَّى خَلَقَ عِلْمًا فَعَلِمَ فَجَحَدَ عِلْمَ اللَّهِ عَزَّ وَجَلَّ فَهُوَ كَافِرٌ "

"I heard my father – rahimahullāh – when 'Alī ibn Al-Jahm asked him regarding the one who holds the opinion of the Qadar, is he a kāfir? He said: 'If he rejects the knowledge[19] (he is kāfir). If he says: 'Verily Allāh – 'azza wa jalla – did not have knowledge until He created knowledge, (first) then He knew.' So he rejects the knowledge of Allāh – 'azza wa jalla – then he is kāfir." (As-Sunnah by 'Abdullāh)

Muhammad ibn Ismā'īl At-Tirmidhī (d. 280h) said:

سَمِعْتُ الْمُزَنِيَّ يَقُولُ: لَا يَصِحُّ لِأَحَدٍ تَوْحِيدٌ حَتَّى يَعْلَمَ أَنَّ اللهَ عَلَى الْعَرْشِ أَنْ يَعْلَمَ اللهَ عَلَى الْعَرْشِ بِصِفَاتِهِ. قُلْتُ لَهُ: مِثْلُ أَيِّ شَيْءٍ؟ قَالَ: سَمِيعٌ، بَصِيرٌ، عَلِيمٌ قَدِيرٌ.

"I heard Al-Muzanī say: 'Tawhīd is not valid for anyone before he knows that Allah is upon the Throne with His Attributes (i.e. and he establishes the Attributes of Allah).' I said to him: 'Such as what?' He said: 'Hearing, Seeing, Knowing, Omnipotent." ('Uluw lil-'Alī Al-Ghaffār by Adh-Dhahabī, Siyar Al-A'lām An-Nubalā and others)

Al-Bukhārī (d. 256h) said:

بَابُ الْمَعَاصِي مِنْ أَمْرِ الْجَاهِلِيَّةِ وَلَا يُكَفَّرُ صَاحِبُهَا بِارْتِكَابِهَا إِلَّا بِالشِّرْكِ

"Chapter: The sins are from the affairs of jāhiliyyah, and takfīr is not declared upon the one performing them, except if it is shirk." (Sahīh Al-Bukhārī)

---

[19] This means: If he rejects that Allāh has pre-existing knowledge about everything which will happen before it happens.

Ad-Dārimī (d. 280h) said:

فَمَنْ لَمْ يَسْتَيْقِنْ أَنَّ الْقُرْآنَ غَيْرُ مَخْلُوقٍ؛ لَمْ يُؤْمِنْ بَعْدُ بِأَنَّهُ نَفْسُ كَلَامِ اللَّهِ، لِأَنَّهُ لَوْ آمَنَ بِأَنَّهُ نَفْسُ كَلَامِ

اللَّهِ لَعَلِمَ يَقِينًا أَنَّ الْكَلَامَ صِفَةُ الْمُتَكَلِّمِ، وَاللَّهُ بِجَمِيعِ صِفَاتِهِ وَكَلَامِهِ غَيْرُ مَخْلُوقٍ .

"So whoever is not certain that the Qurān is not created he has not yet believed that it (i.e. the Qurān) is the kalām (speech) of Allāh itself. Because if he believed in that it is the kalām of Allāh itself, then he would have known with full certainty that the speech is an attribute of the one who can speak (or the one who speaks). And Allāh with all of His Attributes and His Speech is not created." (Al-Naqd by Ad-Dārimī)

And whoever dives into the books of the *Salaf* will find that they are filled with similar words of *takfīr* upon whoever rejects or denies anything from this category of knowledge or that he should dedicate an act of worship to others than Allāh the Exalted.

The second: The well-known issues, or issues which are known from the religion by necessity. And the difference between these two are, that the well-known issues might be well-known in some places and not others, while that which is known from the religion with necessity is something that both scholars and normal people among the Muslims know, and even the non-Muslims know this about Islām and therefore the Muslim cannot be excused in it. So when an issue becomes well-known in one place it is dealt with in that place as if it was known from the religion by necessity. And whatever falls in this category then there is no excuse in the mistake in it, except for the one who has just entered into Islām – under the condition that the issue is not known even amongst the *kuffār* – and the one who lives far away in the desert and did not have access to knowledge.

Among these issues are: The five prayers, the pilgrimage, the fast, the alms, the prohibition of pork and alcohol and interests and immoral deeds. So whoever rejects any of these then he is not excused due to the status of these issues, and *takfīr* is declared upon him immediately due to the argument already being established in such issues, unless he is among the two mentioned types of people. So if a person says: 'There are only 3 prayers in Islām', or 'Zinā (fornication) is allowed' or 'The fast is not obligatory' then takfīr is declared upon him directly due to the issues being either well-known or known from the religion with necessity.

The third: The hidden issues. And these are the issues that the normal Muslims do not have knowledge about, and where the scholars are those who have knowledge about these things. If a person among the normal Muslims should have a mistake in some of these issues, then takfīr is not declared upon him before the establishment of the argument which if he denies it he becomes a kāfir.

And among these issues could be: the details of inheritance, the judgment of the child born from zinā, the kaffārah (expiation) for the one who wore pants in his pilgrimage etc. So whoever holds a wrong belief in these issues then takfīr is not declared upon him until the argument – which is sufficient for declaring takfīr upon the one who rejects it – with certainty has been established upon him, and he thereafter still rejects the clear evidences after they came to him.

Ash-Shāfi'ī (d. 204h) explained the second and the third category when he said:

فقال لي قائل: ما العلم؟ وما يجب على الناس في العلم؟ فقلت له: العلم علمان: علم عامة، لا يسع بالغا غير مغلوب على عقله جهله .قال: ومثل ماذا؟ قلت: مثل الصلوات الخمس، وأن لله على الناس صوم شهر رمضان، وحج البيت إذا استطاعوه، وزكاة في أموالهم، وأنه حرم عليهم الزنا والقتل والسرقة والخمر، وما كان في معنى هذا، مما كلف العباد أن يعقلوه ويعملوه ويعطوه من أنفسهم وأموالهم، وأن يكفوا عنه ما حرم عليهم منه.وهذا الصنف كله من العلم موجود نصا في كتاب الله، وموجودا عاما عند أهل الإسلام، ينقله عوامهم عن من مضى من عوامهم، يحكونه عن رسول الله، ولا يتنازعون في حكايته ولا وجوبه عليهم .وهذا العلم العام الذي لا يمكن فيه الغلط من الخبر، ولا التأويل، ولا يجوز فيه التنازع.

"If someone would say to me: 'What is the knowledge? And what is obligatory for the people regarding knowledge?' Then I would say to him: 'The knowledge is of two types. (The first is) the general knowledge. No-one who is of age and not insane is allowed to be ignorant regarding this.' He says: 'Such as what?' I say: 'Such as the five prayers, that the people owe to Allāh to fast in Ramadān and perform the pilgrimage if they are capable and (paying the) zakāh from the wealth, and that He has forbidden fornication, killing, stealing and alcohol. And whatever has the same meaning of that which the slaves are obliged to understand, perform and give from themselves and their wealth. And that they avoid that which He has forbidden for them. And this category all of it is from the knowledge which is present in text of the Book of Allāh, and it is generally present among the people of Islām; the normal people among them (i.e. not scholars) convey it from those of their normal ones who passed away. They narrated it from the Messenger of Allāh and they do not disagree in the narration of it or in its obligation upon them. This is the general knowledge in which it is not possible to make a mistake in the information or the interpretation, and it is not allowed to dipute regarding it.'*

قال: فما الوجه الثاني؟ قلت له: ما ينوب العباد من فروع الفرائض، وما يخص به من الأحكام وغيرها، مما ليس فيه نص كتاب، ولا في أكثره نص سنة، وإن كانت في شيء منه سنة فإنما هي من أخبار الخاصة، لا أخبار العامة، وما كان منه يحتمل التأويل ويستدرك قياسا.

He says: 'Then what is the second type?' I say to him: 'That which comes close to the slaves from the branches of the obligatory deeds, and that which is related to it of judgments and other things, among that which there is no text from the Book, nor is their in the most of it a text from the Sunnah. And if there in any of it exists some Sunnah, then it is verily among the informations of the specific people (i.e. scholars) and not the information of the normal people. And in some of it, it is possible to interpret it (in different ways) and to achieve understanding of it through qiyās (analogy).'" (Ar-Risālah by Ash-Shāfi'ī)

A last detail to mention here is the difference between two types of persons which must be taken into consideration. One person may not believe in an Attribute of Allāh – which can only be known

184

through the textual evidence – due to the knowledge about it not having reached him yet. In this case he is informed and the argument is established upon him, and if he insists on his rejection then *takfīr* is declared upon him. But another person who rejects the same attribute, but does this due to his *jahmī* principles of *kufr* (i.e. to reject the Names and Attributes of Allāh in general) then he is not excused, due to his *kufr* is that he has fundamental principles of *kufr* in his beliefs. So this type of person would not be excused even if the knowledge has not yet reached him, because he has already fallen in *kufr* before that. And like this every situation is looked into in detail when it comes to *takfīr*.

The predecessors vs. the latecomers

There is no doubt whatsoever, that the one who leaves the books of the *Salaf* (predecessors) and solely studies the religion from the books of the latecomers, he will remain in doubt and confusion. The reason for this is that the books of the *Salaf* contain the truth which they heard from the *Sahābah* (*radiAllāhu 'anhum*) and they were very strict on not accepting the opinions of the innovators and those who were accused in their religion, either of lying or of believing in an innovation. Thus you have chapters and even books from the *Salaf* that dealt with the leaders of misguidance, discrediting them and warning against them.

But as for the latecomers then these principles were and are not maintained with the same vigor as the *Salaf* did. And the result of this is, that people who held beliefs that for the *Salaf* were considered innovation – and in some cases *kufr* – are referred to as *Imām* or *Shaykh* or *Hāfidh*, while this is giving their name and their words a status in the religion which is not befitting for them. This then results in the people accepting their words, or at least considering it a valid opinion in the religion, while in reality it is not. Furthermore many of the latecomers would describe the innovators as being from *Ahlus-Sunnah* while they in reality are not. And like this confusion arises, because how can an innovator be an Imām? And why are people referring to such and such person as *Shaykh*, when he in reality is a *kāfir*? And why does a presumably acknowledged and accepted scholar speak in favor of *kufr* and *innovation*?

The solution to this problem lies in studying in the books of the *Salaf* to get to know their *'aqīdah*. With this a person acquires a scale with which he can measure the words of those who came after them. Because the lesson is not in the name or status of a person, rather the lesson lies in that which agrees with the Qurān and the *Sunnah* according to the understanding of the *Salaf*. And what is besides this is misguidance, even if most of the people are gathered upon it.

Hudhayfah ibn Al-Yamān (radiAllāhu 'anhu) said:

اتَّقُوا اللَّهَ يَا مَعْشَرَ الْقُرَّاءِ ، وَخُذُوا طَرِيقَ مَنْ كَانَ قَبْلَكُمْ ، فَوَاللَّهِ لَئِنِ اسْتَقَمْتُمْ لَقَدْ سَبَقْتُمْ سَبْقًا بَعِيدًا ، وَلَئِنْ تَرَكْتُمُوهُ يَمِينًا وَشِمَالا لَقَدْ ضَلَلْتُمْ ضَلَالا بَعِيدًا

"Fear Allāh O you readers (of the Qurān)! And take the path of those who came before you. Because by Allāh, if you remain steadfast upon that, you have verily went ahead with a great advantage. But if you leave it (in order to go) right or left, then you have verily went far astray." (Az-Zuhd war-Raqāiq by Ibn Al-Mubārak)

And Imām Mālik (d. 179h) said:

لن يَصْلُحَ آخِرُ هذه الأمة إلا بما صَلَح به أولها؛ فما لم يكن يومئذٍ دينًا، لا يكون اليوم دينًا

"The last of this Ummah will not be correct except through that which the first of it was correct by. So whatever was not from the religion at that time will never be from the religion today." (Kitāb Al-I'tisām by Ash-Shātibī)

And Imām Ash-Shāfi'ī (d. 204h) said:

كل من تكلم بِكَلَامٍ في الدّين أو في شَيْءٍ من هَذِهِ الأَهْوَاء لَيْسَ لَهُ فِيهِ إِمَام مُتَقَدم من النَّبِي صلى الله عَلَيْهِ وَسلم وَأَصْحَابه فقد أحدث في الْإِسْلَام حَدثا

"Whoever speaks some words regarding the religion, or regarding something of these desires (i.e. bida') and he does not have an imām (leader) who said this before him from the Prophet (sallAllāhu 'alayhi wa sallam) and his Companions, then he has verily invented something new in Islām." (Al-Intisār li-Ashāb Al-Hadīth by Abū Al-Mudhaffar As-Sam'ānī)

And Ishāq ibn Abdir-Rahmān ibn Hasan (d. 1319h) from the *da'wah* of Najd said:

ومن تغذى بكلام المتأخرين ، من غير إشراف ، على كتب أهل السنة المشتهرين ، ككتاب ((السنة)) لعبد الله بن الإمام أحمد ، وكتاب ((السنة)) للخلال ، وكتاب ((السنة)) للالكائي ، والدارمي ، وغيرهم ، بقي في حيرة ، وضلال

"And whoever nurtures himself by the words of the latecomers, without staying within the scope of view of the famous books of the people of Sunnah, such as Kitāb As-Sunnah by 'Abdullāh ibn Al-Imām Ahmad, and Kitāb As-Sunnah by Al-Khallāl, and Kitab As-Sunnah by Al-Lālakāī, and Ad-Dārimī and others than them, he will remain in confusion and misguidance." (Ad-Durar As-Saniyyah 4/336)

Thus, acquiring ones *'aqīdah* and fundamental principles from the books of the *Salaf* is not an issue which under any circumstances may be underestimated. Rather, whoever does not establish his fundament, his *manhaj*, his method and his beliefs upon what he finds in the books of the *Salaf*, then he is not safe from falling into misguidance without even noticing it.

Seeking knowledge, adhering to the _Jamā'ah_ and maintaining _īmān_

Seeking the knowledge which is sufficient to have the correct _'aqīdah_ is an obligation upon every single individual, no matter who he is or where he comes from, and verily does the correct knowledge and _'aqīdah_ come before speech and deeds. Allāh – the Exalted – said:

$$ \text{﴿ فَاعْلَمْ أَنَّهُ لَا إِلَهَ إِلَّا اللَّهُ وَاسْتَغْفِرْ لِذَنْبِكَ وَلِلْمُؤْمِنِينَ وَالْمُؤْمِنَاتِ ﴾} $$

"So know, that _Lā ilāha illa Allāh_ (no-one is worthy of worship besides Allāh) and ask for forgiveness for your sin, and for the believing men and women." (Muhammad 47:19)

What testifies to this fact – as it has previously been explained – is that Allāh does not accept anything except if it is performed with Tawhīd, nor does He – the Exalted – accept anything except if it is performed according to the _Sunnah_.

Add to this, that if a person performs _shirk_ while worshipping Allāh then all of his deeds will be in vain, and on the Day of Judgement Allāh will turn it into scattered dust. Allāh – the – Exalted – said:

$$ \text{﴿ ذَلِكَ هُدَى اللَّهِ يَهْدِي بِهِ مَنْ يَشَاءُ مِنْ عِبَادِهِ وَلَوْ أَشْرَكُوا لَحَبِطَ عَنْهُمْ مَا كَانُوا يَعْمَلُونَ ﴾} $$

"That is the guidance of Allāh with which He guides whomever He wills of His slaves. And if they had committed _shirk_, then everything which they used to do would be in vain (or come to nothing)." (Al-An'ām 6:88)

And as for the innovator – whose innovation has not reached the level of _kufr_ which takes him out of the fold of Islām – then Allāh will not accept anything of his good deeds, not the obligatory nor the voluntary.

Al-Awzā'ī (d. 158h) said:

كَانَ بَعْضُ أَهْلِ الْعِلْمِ يَقُولُونَ : لَا يَقْبَلُ اللَّهُ مِنْ ذِي بِدْعَةٍ صَلَاةً وَلَا صِيَامًا وَلَا صَدَقَةً وَلَا جِهَادًا وَلَا حَجًّا وَلَا عُمْرَةً وَلَا صَرْفًا وَلَا عَدْلًا

"Some of the people of knowledge used to say: Allāh does not accept from the innovator any prayer, nor fast, nor sadaqah, nor jihād, nor hajj, nor 'umrah, nor any obligatory or voluntary acts.'" (Kitāb Al-I'tisām by Ash-Shāṭibī 1/142)

And Al-Hasan Al-Basrī (d. 110h) said:

لا يقبل الله لصاحب بدعة صوماً ولا صلاة ولا حجاً ولا عمرة حتى يدعها

"Allāh does not accept for an innovator any fast, or prayer, or hajj, or 'umrah until he leaves it (i.e. his innovation)." (Sharh Usūl I'tiqād Ahlus-Sunnah by Al-Lālakāī 1/138-139)

So the first step on the road to salvation is seeking knowledge and correcting the beliefs. And a prerequisite for seeking knowledge in reality is learning the Arabic language. Al-Islām is a religion which was revealed in Arabic to an Arab people, thus whoever wants to fully understand its sources and evidences must learn the Arabic language to be able to do so.

Another aspect of seeking knowledge is surrounding ones-self with circumstances that enables and encourages the person to seek knowledge. Included in this is:

- Befriending the righteous, scholars, and students of knowledge.
- Keeping away from sinners, sin and places where sins are committed.
- Adhering to the *Jamā'ah* and spending time with Muslim brothers.
- Acknowledging your defiency in fulfilling the rights of Allāh.

- Acknowledging your need for Islamic knowledge, and good deeds.
- Acknowledging and realizing that Allāh is with the *Jamā'ah* and not those who separate from it, or seeks to divide it with debate and discussion.

There is no doubt that these things help in reviving the heart and increasing the desire for seeking knowledge.

Many people today make the grave mistake that when they learn issues about Tawhīd and its pillars and conditions, they think they have learned enough and they stop in their tracks without improving. Thus you find them ten years after having learned these issues, completely in the same condition, or even worse. No memorization of the Qurān, no new issues learned in the religion and no increased amount of worship. And this is the trap of Shaytān which he – may the curse of Allāh be upon him – wants the Muslim to fall in. Because whoever does not improve in the religion, then he is more than likely to end up in a worse state than when he started, which the honest person easily can testify to.

Other people learn a few issues in the religion and immediately run out to debate everybody and everyone, causing them to fall in many mistakes without realizing; especially speaking about the religion without knowledge which is among the biggest of sins that a person can perform.

So the slave must acknowledge his lowly state in front of Allāh, attain *ikhlās* (sincerity) and then humbleness, humbleness, humbleness.

Recommended books

As for the books which it is recommended for the students of knowledge to read, then these are:

Sharh As-Sunnah by Al-Barbahārī

As-Sunnah by Al-Karmānī

Al-Ibānah As-Sughrā by Ibn Battah (*tahqīq* 'Ādil Ālu Hamdān)

Al-Ibānah Al-Kubrā by Ibn Battah (*tahqīq* 'Adil Ālu Hamdān)

Al-Jāmi' fi 'Aqāid wa Rasāil Ahlus-Sunnah wal-Athar by 'Ādil Ālu Hamdān (except one narration ascribed to Ash-Shāfi'i narrated from Al-Hakkārī, which it not correct neither in chain of narration, nor in its text)

Al-Ihtijāj bil-Athar As-Salafiyyah by 'Ādil Ālu Hamdān

As-Sunnah by 'Abdullāh ibn Al-Imām Ahmad (*tahqīq* 'Adil Ālu Hamdān)

As-Sunnah by Al-Khallāl (*tahqīq* 'Adil Ālu Hamdān)

Ash-Sharī'ah by Al-Ājurrī (*tahqīq* 'Adil Ālu Hamdān)

Kitāb At-Tawhīd by Ibn Khuzaymah (*tahqīq* Samīr Az-Zuhayrī, while being aware of the mistake which Ibn Khuzaymah fell in regarding the *hadīth* of the *Surah*, so one must skip that part)

Ar-Rad 'alā Al-Jahmiyyah by Ad-Dārimī

Naqd 'Uthmān ibn Sa'īd 'alā Al-Marīsī Al-Jahmī Al-'Anīd fīma Iftarā 'alā Allāh fit-Tawhīd (*tahqīq* Mansūr As-Samārī)

Tanbīh Al-Atqiyā by Abū Al-Muhannad At-Tūnisī

Kitāb At-Tawhīd by Muhammad ibn 'Abdul-Wahhāb

Usūl Ath-Thalāthah by Muhammad ibn 'Abdul-Wahhāb

Usūl As-Sittah by Muhammad ibn 'Abdul-Wahhāb

Qawā'id Al-Arba'ah by Muhammad ibn 'Abdul-Wahhāb

Sharh Sittah Mawādi' min As-Sīrah by Muhammad ibn 'Abdul-Wahhāb

Risālah Aslud-Dīn by Muhammad ibn 'Abdul-Wahhāb

Ma'nā At-Tāghūt by Muhammad ibn 'Abdul-Wahhāb

The seeker of knowledge must always abide by the principles and the limits of the *Salaf*. So if he reads from the latecomers then he should not rely solely upon their words without referring the issues back the *Salaf* and their *manhaj*. So he should not accept any disagreement or opinion that exceeds the words of the *Salaf*. Nor should he consider from *Ahlus-Sunnah* those who have innovations in their religion, he should not ask for mercy for them, or consider their opinions to be valid.

Conclusion

So whoever belives in what has been stated in this book, and he adheres to the pricinples of the *Salaf* in the religion, then Allāh has verily guided him to much good. The reader is advised to submit himself, both his soul and his body, to what came from Allāh and His Messenger (*sallAllāhu 'alayhi wa sallam*) and not to be pleased with anything that opposes any of this, no matter who it might come from. We are obliged to worship Allāh following the Qurān and the *Sunnah* according to the understanding of the *Salaf*. Upon this the Muslims will achieve unity in *dunyā*, and based upon this – without the slightest doubt – they will be judged in the *ākhirah*. So glad tidings to the one who rectifies his *'aqīdah* before death approaches him and his deeds will be cut off. We ask Allāh for a beautiful ending.

Glorifed is Allāh and all praise is due to Him. We bear witness that no-one is worthy except Allāh Alone Who has no partner, we ask Him for forgiveness and we turn to Him in repentance.

And may the peace and abundant blessings of Allāh be upon our Prophet Muhammad, his family, his companions and whoever followed them in goodness until the Day of Judgment. *Allāhumma āmīn.*

~ Completed ~

Written by: Abū Hājar

Printed in Great Britain
by Amazon

45193361R00111